DREAMERS & DEALERS

DREAMERS & DEALERS

AN INTIMATE APPRAISAL OF

THE WOMEN'S MOVEMENT

LEAH FRITZ

BEACON PRESS   BOSTON

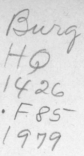
Grateful acknowledgment is made to the following: Karen Lindsey, for permission to quote from her poem "Women Who Love Men," which appears in her book *Falling off the Roof* (Cambridge, Mass.: Alice James Books, 1975); Fran Winant, for permission to quote from her poem "Looking at Women," which appears in her book *Looking at Women* (New York: Violet Press, 1971); and Alfred A. Knopf, Inc., for permission to quote from *History: A Novel* by Elsa Morante, translation copyright © 1977 by Alfred A. Knopf, Inc.

Library of Congress Cataloging in Publication Data

Fritz, Leah, 1931-
   Dreamers & dealers.
   Includes bibliographical references and index.
   1.   Feminism—United States. I. Title.
HQ1426.F85   1979   301.41'2'0973   78-73852
ISBN 0-8070-3792-3

To my mother,
Esther B. Hurwit,
"with all my heart
and all my soul
and all my might"

ACKNOWLEDGMENTS

There are so many people I am indebted to for encouragement and aid in preparing this book. Perhaps most important of all is Emily Jane Goodman, whose belief in my writing and willingness to act as my agent gave me the sense of self-worth necessary to push aside other obligations and undertake this project. And then a series of charming coincidences led me to Boston and MaryAnn Lash, director and editor-in-chief of Beacon Press, whose feminist and literary sensibilities provided a rare editorial empathy. For their hospitality and support in the environs of that city, I want also to thank Allison Platt, editor of *Sojourner*, and the poet-journalist Karen Lindsey; and to remember, too, Deborah, who, in spite of some profound political differences, befriended me there.

I truly owe several pages of gratitude to Andrea Dworkin for listening to me read from various manuscript drafts over long hours on the telephone. In no way responsible for the content, upon which she never offered judgment, Andrea simply lent me a respectful and patient ear, the greatest gift a writer can provide. There have been other friendly listeners as I worked out various ideas: Minda Bikman, Diana Bloom, Phyllis Chillingworth, Barbara Deming, Ellen Frankfort,

Jane Gapen, Ruth Gerchick, Karla Jay, and Pamela Kearon. Especially helpful was June Rook, editor of *The Thirteenth Moon*, who typed the manuscript and provided valuable criticism. Thanks, too, to Florence Rush and Barbara Mehrhof for making certain documents available to me.

In many ways, the whole community of feminist writers can take credit (or blame) for the inception of this work. Colleagues who have encouraged me over the years include Susan Brownmiller, Phyllis Chesler, Erika Duncan, Joanne Edgar, Karen Malpede, Robin Morgan, Grace Paley, Kenneth Pitchford, Adrienne Rich, Gloria Steinem, and John Stoltenberg.

Finally, I want to thank Amy and Monica Fritz, who sacrificed privacy to give me "a room of one's own," and Howard Fritz, whose endurance and generosity are fundamental to my life.

CONTENTS

Acknowledgments   vii

Introduction   xi

PART I. CONCEPTS AND CONTROVERSIES OF
   MODERN FEMINISM   1

1. Ms. Allgood, Me, and Some Basic Concepts of Feminism   3
2. The Early Years of the Women's Liberation Movement and the Start of Some Schisms   22
3. Problems of Structure and Leadership   37
4. The Lesbian Revolution: Lilith and Eve   83
5. Feminism and the Left   112

PART II.   WOMEN AND CLASS   169

6. Slavery, Inequity, Disunity   171
7. Three Classes of Poor Women   191
8. Rich Women   218
9. The Middlewomen   227

PART III.   EPILOGUE   249

10. Deals & Dreams   251

Notes   273

Index   283

INTRODUCTION

Roughly speaking, the first decade of modern feminism is behind us. In terms of practical accomplishment, very little has happened, but this should not come as a shock to people who have been in subjugation as long as women have.

The word has gone out and, as words do these days, it has traveled very far—across the whole world, in fact. It has been spread by the media, because news of a woman's uprising is sensational, and sensationalism moves products. Through selective exposure, the media hope, also, to confuse the issues by channeling (literally!) essentially revolutionary content into the controllable lines of upward mobility. Upward mobility is, indeed, one of the short-range aims of feminism and, lest one think this is a shoddy capitalistic goal, it is important to remember that ruling classes (those empowered to make decisions, whether they are moneyed or not) exist everywhere—in China no less than in the United States—and nowhere do women figure in sizable numbers among them. But getting into the patriarchal power structure—anywhere—does not begin to answer the question, "What do women want?"

In any case, since time is needed to organize a people so isolated and scattered as women, the media's light regard for a movement with such devastating implications has made it possible for considerable work to take place behind the smoke screen of liberal verbiage. Many books have been written and published and translated which speak of a profound dissatisfaction with all the ways of mankind and an urgent need to deliver the earth out of predatory hands. In a courageous and beautiful essay, Jane Alpert issued a call to women to "save the planet."[1]

Because the established media reach more women than analytical books or even feminist magazines, much confusion still exists, both within the amorphous women's movement and outside it, regarding the multiplicity of means and goals envisioned by feminist theory. Feminist books cover a bewildering variety of subjects, all stemming from a rapidly awakening consciousness. Peremptory actions have been taken and attitudes adopted which add to the confusion. In declaring the personal to be political, feminists were thinking of universals and may have failed to take into account the diversity of female experience—a diversity which has come home in the form of painful and apparently destructive conflict. Even the essential concept of sisterhood turns out to be unmanageably complex when tested against real life. (Most of us were brought up in nuclear families where sisterly antagonisms are more often the rule than sisterly solidarity.)

But the many contradictions feminism presents are not only expressive of conflict; they have positive implications, too. We have begun to rediscover a conspiracy so vast that we are simply staggered by the number of problems which need to be addressed. Throughout the world and in every area of our lives we have begun to strike out for at least equality, at least justice. And some of us have imagined more: a thorough and complete change in values, feelings, behavior—the very terms of our social existence. Some of us have dreamed of a dramatic upheaval which would sweep away all ills at once, but it has become clear through consciousness-raising that the complexity of our problems required a different approach, one more sophisticated and sensitive.

Not all, however, is diversity and conflict. A universal *has* been discovered in the colonialization and exploitation of women's bodies. The popularity of such books as *Our Bodies, Ourselves; Against Our Will; The Hite Report;* and *Of Woman Born* attests to the gut awareness of women everywhere that our bodies and their fruit have been appropriated.[2] Our most potent pressure has been exerted for rape prevention, the right to abortion, the lesbian option, changes in gynecological practice, and an end to our service as objects of sexual gratification to men. Deeper analysis reveals that our sexual subjugation is the archetype of all colonization and that all the many ways women are oppressed derive from this. Hence the insistence of radical feminists that we deal with our bodies—the sexual and reproductive systems—first. Hence the insistence that we leave the "left" behind with its stubborn refusal to look beyond economic causality, even after so much evidence of predatoriness and oppression in socialist countries.

It is true that we are still hammering away at patriarchal causality and have changed few threads in the fabric of our lives. But it is early yet, early as people who have been enslaved for thousands of years measure time. It is not early, however, for the billions of women now alive who will not benefit from such slow, evolutionary changes. For us, living now, the root problem is but one of the problems we face in our daily existence. Clearly it *is* the root, and clearly it brutalizes every breath we take, when we lie down and when we rise up, but its offshoots oppress us also, and we must address these as well—and immediately. Our bellies are also housed in the temples of our souls; our bellies are also oppressed.

Here I must tread very carefully (as I have learned to do as a feminist) because the patriarchy is always out there waiting to trivialize our insights about sexual causality, to return to its rapes and degradations in the name of the *greater good*. Radical feminists are aware of economic inequities. They have pointed out that women have no real control over money; we are the possessions of men, whether we are owned by the state or by private enterprise.[3]

And yet, and yet—there *are* economic differences *among women*. There are also social, racial, cultural, ethnic, religious, ideological, intellectual, and temperamental differences. Involved as we have been in diagnosis and patchwork activism, we have scarcely had a chance to take adequate account of these differences, to deal with them in any but a rough-and-ready fashion which often leads us into harsh clashes. The "slave mentality" is a catch-phrase sometimes used to explain away this strife within the movement. While it's true that we are slaves, even among slaves there are differences in treatment by masters, differences in needs, differences in temperament.

For slaves, survival and freedom can turn out to be mutually exclusive goals. Survival depends on the will of the master, which means such freedoms as we obtain must be wheedled out of him. While freedom abhors demeaning manipulation, dignified rebellion can be fatal. Caught in such a dilemma, women naturally behave in ways which seem contradictory.

But the infighting we have seen does not arise from ignorance or orneriness; it is the result of a realistic despair. Unorganized slaves have no recourse except to fend for themselves, and even when we join together in small, isolated groups, the interests we promote are the interests of those groups—not necessarily the interests of all women. The means we choose reflect our greater or lesser powerlessness. Inevitable frustrations lead to fury at all those other women who have been giving their energy to other interests—their own. Even feminist theorists, those who have been struggling to understand and explain the fundamental nature of the malady, succumb to parochialism. Inundated by troubles of our own, we hear a roar in our heads that drowns out isolated, distant anguish.

And so the poor ones, the ones victimized by racism, turn to the left with its randy promises or withdraw altogether from struggle. So the middle-aged matron, returning to school for a law degree, shuts out feminist insights because she depends on a man's income to get her through. So the lonely, underpaid secretary makes the bar scene in hopes of finding a husband to rescue her from the typing pool. So the topless dancer turns the other breast for a buck. So the welfare mother who can barely take care of herself and her kids shelters a drunken lover for warmth. So the suburban housewife endures a beating—and keeps quiet about it—to send her children to school properly dressed. So a lesbian becomes the madam of a whorehouse. And so the feminist spokeswoman accepts a kiss and a blank look from a television emcee to sell her book.

We are all involved in the slave mentality. It cannot be used as an epithet by one group or one individual against another. It is the condition of our existence and must be understood piece by piece. All the voices of our differences must be heard.

We have had enough of guilt-tripping, name-calling,

and internecine squabbling—although these will probably go on for some time to come and may not always be
unwelcome as reminders of our primitive state and as
goads to advance us onward. (Gossip is a way of expressing criticism when unequal power blocks direct speech. It
derives from fear, of course—fear of the object's male
protector—and so it has a devious quality, often disguis-
ing the real reason for anger under the cover of some
violated conventionality. The married woman isn't really
angry at the fact that a prostitute moved into an apartment down the hall; she's just afraid her husband will
visit the prostitute and she'll lose what small amount of
control she has over him. She is angry at anticipated betrayal, not the "immorality" of the prostitute.)

We must, I think, move onward, beyond the small
group struggling alone. Our theory must mature to comprehend a computer's worth of parameters and deal with
them through a feminism united around one all-encompassing truth: *the problems of women include all the
problems of the world; the patriarchy is everywhere.* We
must develop a feminist means suitable, as they say in
the clothing ads, "for any occasion." We must continue to
support each woman around her individual needs and
make connections between these needs and those of the
rest of us. We must ask for the time, energy, and money
of every woman who would have her freedom—and her
survival, too.

It is to this enormous task that this book is addressed. I
will try to discern in the following pages what some of the
conflicts are which have arisen amongst us, to move from
the antagonisms to the different needs they reveal, and
to imagine, if possible, a workable approach for meeting
these needs.

In other words, from the shape and density of the trees, I hope to map out the forest. And do not ask me, please, to burn it down. Men have burned too many forests in the name of "humanity." In fact, where we are standing may not be a forest at all—but a wasteland waiting for women to reclaim it.

DREAMERS & DEALERS

PART I CONCEPTS AND CONTROVERSIES OF MODERN FEMINISM

CHAPTER ONE

Ms. Allgood, Me, and Some Basic Concepts of Feminism

Let me begin with Ms. Allgood.

Soon after attending the National Women's Conference in Houston, Texas,[1] I went to a meeting of a women's organization in New York to hear an informal talk on the conference. The club was the kind men generally approve of for their wives and mothers (and make fun of behind their backs). Although men complain about being excluded from feminist meetings, women's civic and charitable organizations rate only their derision. Like the kitchen, these clubs are regarded as places where women go primarily to serve men and their institutions—not to threaten them. And so the warm, homelike room where coffee and cake were served to women seated in easy chairs and on couches lacked the subliminally conspiratorial tension of many feminist gatherings. The women there were, most of them, over forty and dressed according to middle-class standards of good taste.

Seated comfortably among cushions with her stockinged legs crossed, the main speaker, a journalist I'll call Ms. Allgood, told her story in colorful detail. She described the clothes worn by the delegates and observers ("It was pretty much a blue-jeans affair"), the bright costumes of some women from island territories, the great variety of wheelchairs brought by handicapped delegates, and a few quaint touches on banners identifying the states ("One banner sported a bra!"). She gave some attention to fashions worn by the three First Ladies who attended ("well coifed"), and commented that Rosalynn Carter didn't know how to use a microphone, that Betty Ford had a bad speech writer. Lady Bird Johnson, she said, spoke most "to the point."

Getting into the meat of the conference, she noted how much like men's conventions it was, with its wheeling and dealing and decisions made in smoke-filled rooms. She seemed to revel at this display of women's adroitness in practical politics and at how clever the chair and the delegates must have appeared in men's eyes. From time to time, particularly when she noted how "utopian" the conference's resolutions were, she would cast a nervous glance around the room and remark that all these far-reaching recommendations would be "good for men, too." She concluded, with obvious delight, that "middle-class" women could now begin to run the movement because, while all the other groups have special interests—black women, lesbians, and so on—"middle-class women could comprehend the whole."

I felt a fury rise in me: *this*—in 1977! Was I experiencing déjà vu? Certainly I was dizzy with rage and despair.

Ms. Allgood's liberal sentiments thrust me back in time to the end of the black civil rights movement—the death of it. They brought me back to the agonies of people in black ghettoes suffering under the weight of government studies and programs, all of them ineffectual or withdrawn as soon as they began to show progress, leaving the people feeling even more powerless than before; as if they, themselves, were now *proved* to be responsible for the government's many failures, as if these failures hadn't been cynically built into those programs! They brought me back to the assassinations of black leaders, to the co-optation of do-gooder whites and of blacks who had foolishly accepted a specious identification with the middle class and walked into the arms of Big Brother.

Her words brought me, most significantly, back to my-self—that self which had existed before the women's liberation movement and which was so hard to unlearn and outgrow that I must forever be alert to its vestigial presence. For Ms. Allgood and I have more in common than the simple fact of our womanhood.

I am also past forty, live in moderately comfortable circumstances, have been married for half my life, and have raised two daughters to adulthood. This is how most of the world views me, as a middle-class housewife and mother. Like Ms. Allgood, I'm a writer, deeply interested in public affairs, and I want very much to do good. I am also vocally aggressive, a colorful and sometimes long-winded talker. And, confused by my appurtenances (which my dictionary aptly defines as "rights and privileges belonging to a property"), I used to identify *myself* as middle class. My tendency, like Ms. Allgood's, is to be good-naturedly managerial. I, too, think I can see the gestalt! Although we wear different clothes and espouse different politics, there is a Ms. Allgood in me.

Thinking about these similarities, I realized that my rage at her conclusion had been heated up several degrees by this unwanted recognition of kinship. As a matter of fact, both Ms. Allgood's superficial political assessment and my precipitate overreaction revealed where we both were, respectively, in terms of feminist consciousness.

She had, as it were, discovered a full-blown political movement of historical proportions which lacked only the right sort of leadership to bring it solidly into the mainstream—for surely those scraggly, braless wonders cannot lead all the mainstream women they've attracted! In the first blush of enthusiasm and pride, she didn't question her imperialistic maternalism—hadn't yet come to question any of her traditional behavior or attitudes.

Over the past decade and more, I have learned to question all of my habits of thinking and doing in the light of the new knowledge feminism has given me about my own oppression, the way that oppression has distorted my view of the world and my place in it. I have lived and suffered and grown with the women's movement, observing its strengths, its wisdom, its weaknesses, its absurdities; absorbing its character into my own and giving my creativity to it. But apparently I have not yet fully assimilated the most valuable quality feminism has to impart: that appreciation of the self in others which is the mark of sisterhood.

Beyond my emotional response to Ms. Allgood's present, and my former, complacency, however, there were implications in what Ms. Allgood said that deserve more objective analysis. Because the event she described is of historic importance to feminism, and because it may have marked a turning point for the women's movement,[2] I will use her remarks as a jumping-off point to discuss some basic concepts and controversies of contemporary feminism.

Here are the places where she came into conflict with feminist theory: Her *pride in women being capable of acting like men* where male behavior would be questionable touches on a dilemma which has been with us since the beginning of the women's liberation movement. Ms. Allgood's *satisfaction with our having been granted a national convention under patriarchal government auspices*—and my dismay that women had sought such a "favor"—touch on another. Her *anxiety about the possible effects of women's achievements on men* raises more political questions. Her notion that the *reforms agreed upon by the delegates were utopian* betrays confusion about what the truly utopian aims of feminism are (an understandable confusion, since there is no firm agreement among feminists). And, of course, her *remarks about movement leadership* reach into what might be called the preamble of the unwritten feminist constitution.

REFORMS AND UTOPIANISM

Fundamentally, feminists make a distinction between the reformism necessary to obtain "women's rights"—that is, equality under patriarchal law—and the truly utopian aspiration of ending the primacy of man: his entrenched habits of sadomasochistic thinking and behavior (whether expressed by men or internalized by women) as well as his dominion over this planet. (This is about as far as I can go in expressing feminists' vision of the future without running into conflict with the ideologies of different groups whose views run from readjusting the male psyche to eliminating men altogether, including everything—and I mean everything—in between.)

The delegates at the Houston conference presented a plea for women's rights, and, progressive as their proposals were in relation to the barbaric conditions under which women live in the United States today, they were hardly utopian. The American dream is not a feminist dream, nor is the Marxist: neither is far-reaching enough. Legislation, important as it is, will not change the basic relationship between women and men upon which *all* present societies rest. To call any appeal for changes in patriarchal law "utopian" is to trivialize the thinking of such brilliant theorists as Mary Daly, Andrea Dworkin, Shulamith Firestone, and Kate Millett, to name a few (not to mention Virginia Woolf and others of earlier generations). Even socialist-feminists like Evelyn Reed regard Marxism as only a step toward what women want[3]—so how can a few remedial acts of Congress or even an amendment to the United States Constitution be considered utopian?

PATRIARCHAL PROCEDURES VS. FEMINIST PROCESSES

Attending a conference under the auspices of a patriarchal government meant a real compromise of values to feminists. Because the conference was to be held whether we wanted it or not, many feminists participated in the state meetings which led up to it and in the conference itself only out of *self-defense*. The outcome, without that participation, might have been a total disaster for all our present demands. Although I'm glad we didn't lose the Battle of Houston to those who would send women back to the dark ages of foot binding and witch burning, it neither came as a total surprise nor was it a cause for unmitigated exultation that women acquitted themselves smartly there at men's games of power politics. Anyone who has ever been to a PTA meeting will not be shocked to find women adroit at realpolitik. We understand parliamentary procedure—including how to manipulate it!

But parliamentary procedure is a method devised to make peaceful compromise possible among men whose political goals are in *violent* disharmony. Manipulation—even trickery—is recognized, at least during the time of the meeting, as preferable to coming to blows.

On the other hand, the deepest desire of women is not to compete with, but to understand and support one another. Therefore, parliamentary procedure is an unsuitable process for feminist councils compared to the forms we normally use: consciousness-raising, the speak-out, the *circle* of discussion where decisions are made by consensus.

Ironically, the best thing that happened in Houston from my point of view was that we used the conference as a means of communicating with and supporting each other in spite of the unwieldiness of the patriarchal format. The desires of women from minority groups and of women on welfare were approved as they, themselves, spelled them out, not as the government-appointed planners had estimated them.

In the original "plan," the government-appointed commission had not taken into account the self-knowledge of handicapped women, women from minority groups, and women on welfare. These groups articulated proposals of their own which were much farther reaching than those on the original agenda. Offering their new proposals at the conference as "substitute motions," they received overwhelming support from the majority of the delegates. Feminist self-knowledge and self-leadership were speaking and recognized in the language of the substitute proposals. The fact that the patriarchal press interpreted what happened at the Houston conference as a victory for middle-class liberalism rather than for grassroots radical feminism was but another attempt by the media to trivialize the profundity of change desired by women—to render the mass appeal of feminist radicalism impotent.

DEFERRING AND REFERRING TO MEN

Another source of satisfaction to Ms. Allgood was that women's parliamentary astuteness was broadcast where men might finally observe it, and in a quasi-governmental context. In other words, it had moved out of the elementary school auditorium and gone public. The conference provided evidence, if more were needed, that women are capable of serving as legislators under men's rules.

How women appear in men's eyes, however, is, at the very least, irrelevant in the eyes of feminists. We have learned the hard way that men interpret women's actions (often, even those which *support* men) negatively. Trying to impress men positively, particularly when we are working to benefit *ourselves*, is a predictably losing effort.

Similarly, Ms. Allgood expressed one more concern relating to men: she was anxious to reassure herself that what was good for women would turn out, in the end, to be good for men, too. Part of her concern no doubt involved the realistic fear all women have of threatening men and thus opening ourselves to unimaginable, or all too imaginable, reprisals. But there was also a real caring for the fate of those males with whom our lives have been, are, or might be, intertwined.

Almost all women are attached to men by one or more emotional ties, whether it be as a mother, a lover, a daughter, a sister, or a friend. Although some feminists will deny this, I have known virtually none, even among the most ardent separatists, who doesn't harbor at least a *memory* of some man who occupied a place of affection in her life. Though it is difficult to ignore both fear of reprisals and remembered love, feminists have learned we must harden ourselves against these feelings if we are to accomplish anything at all for women; we must agree, at least temporarily, to shove such considerations aside.

There are a number of reasons for this. In the short run (which is likely to last a very long time!), men undoubtedly will be affected adversely by the rise of women. They will resist losing their dominant positions; they will feel threatened by job competition; their sexual habits will undergo disturbing changes; many of them will be (are being) rejected outright as lovers. Too generous a compassion for this kind of suffering inhibits women from moving for our own freedom. We fear the fate of Lot's wife.

Moreover, concentrating on men's problems is a method women use to avoid concentrating on our own. In the beginning of consciousness-raising, women often try to move the spotlight away from themselves, because speaking of one's own pain is painful![4]

In addition, of course, we have all been carefully trained to feel guilt if we dare to consider ourselves important apart from men. Discussing men's problems becomes a diversion and, at the same time, assuages our guilt feelings and fears. Since the main point of consciousness-raising is to acknowledge the deeply felt pain women have repressed—to regain, in Gloria Steinem's phrase, "the dignity of our own suffering"[5]—feminists deliberately resist the temptation to refer to the problems of men. In any case, we have all been raised on litanies of male suffering, from the Dead Sea Scrolls to Kurt Vonnegut. The compulsion to reiterate them while searching out our own is surely of dubious value.

Very simply, feminism is concerned with women, as the Teamsters Union is supposed to be concerned with truck drivers, and it would be improvident for either to expend energy in guilt-ridden, or even philosophical, compassion for bosses when organizing a strike!

AVOIDING SUPERFICIALITY

Ms. Allgood's expression of anxiety, both about how women appear in the eyes of men and how our advancement may affect them, stemmed from her ignorance of feminist analysis. (Perhaps a feminist etiquette is developing, because what she said in this connection seemed to me like a faux pas.) Much of this theory can now be gleaned from books, but it is still essential, in order to comprehend it on a visceral as well as an intellectual level, to examine one's own oppression in the company of other women. Without such mutual searching, any political attitudes are likely to be superficial. Because traditional education has obscured the truth about ourselves, and because our own perceptions are continually denied *to our faces* by those who have an interest (or *think* they have an interest) in maintaining the status quo, it is essential to receive both challenge and confirmation from other women seeking the truth.[6]

As Fran Winant put it in her poem "Looking at Women":

> But I am suspicious of
> any woman who tells me
> she has seen her own face
> knows what her voice sounds like
> the shape of her body
> or how her hands feel to themselves
> We must all look at each other[7]

AVOIDING BIGOTRY

On the other hand, one can arrive at equally superficial conclusions by looking *too* closely to others for a "correct line," and I think it is valuable here to discuss this symptom of insecurity which can lead to a cruel form of prejudice. I once told a group of women who might be called "feminist bigots" that to be utterly correct, one must be a "lesbian prostitute on welfare who lives in a separatist community and has aborted several male embryos." In this connection, the word "suspicious" in Winant's poem is disturbing. Valid consciousness is, ultimately, self-knowledge. What is truly universal will be felt by each individual woman to be accurate about *her* —after some process of introspection and reality-checking. Those truisms that don't, after honest self-questioning, ring true for *you*, are simply not universal!

The worst despair I know comes when I feel I must explain and defend the way I live to other feminists. It's bad enough when I see derogatory and false images of myself as housewife-and-mother on the television screen. (Shopping for a roll of toilet paper or a bar of soap, I want to boycott every advertised brand because of the personal slander it brings to mind.) It is just too cruel, then, to be categorized in the same patriarchal terms by other feminists! But it does happen.

Because I am compulsive about telling the truth, I am often forced to follow my admission about my "lifestyle" with a complete dossier: my attitude toward social change, my attitude toward lesbianism, what I do or do not do in bed and how I like it, if my husband regards himself as a feminist, how my daughters are sexually oriented, how I would react if one or both "came out" as a lesbian (or got married), how I earn my living, how much money I have, how I relate to poor women, to rich women, to minority women (as a Jew, I *am* a minority woman, but this often goes unheard), to famous women, to "leaders"! Making new acquaintances among feminists is no easy matter.

Women too often approach each other in a spirit of inquisition rather than support. This is an obvious hangover from our rivalry with each other for the favors of men. It is why many feminists insist that consciousness-raising be nonjudgmental; but to carry that injunction out beyond the CR group and into the world is another matter.

Even though all of the above questions have political validity, they should be questions one asks oneself, rather than challenges from others.[8] Expressions of opinion invite challenge, even argument. But nobody, except oneself, has the right to question the terms of one's existence. What, after all, are we struggling for if not the freedom to make our own decisions about our own lives? The choices we make during this transition period are very experimental, very volatile. A housewife today may be a lesbian tomorrow, and vice versa. Must each "transformation," as Robin Morgan termed it,[9] be accompanied by a manifesto? In a memorable conversation, Ellen Frankfort dubbed this syndrome of suspicion the "sorority mentality," and sorority is a far cry from sisterhood![10]

When we put from our minds consideration of how women appear in the eyes of men and how feminist decisions may affect men, it is well to remember that ambivalence toward men is still a reality for most of us. Not referring to this ambivalence is a deliberate choice. Consciousness-raising (the technique, as distinguished from such idiosyncratic personal methods of acquiring awareness as reading and casual conversations) has incorporated certain rules to prevent its leading to "personal solutions."[11] Considering men's reactions obfuscates the issue feminism strives to emphasize: the oppression of women *by* men, mankind, the patriarchy. When we stop agonizing over men's problems, we lift a cloud which has threatened to suffocate us—but we lift it only hypothetically. Concern about men is still with us, in reality; when Ms. Allgood speaks of it, she is speaking to something in each of us. She has not violated any truth, but simply a rule of the game feminists have agreed upon.

A number of feminist theorists who have been through years of consciousness-raising and have helped codify the details of female oppression by men are now beginning to turn some of their attention to the "man question."[12] In addition, such male supporters of feminism as John Stoltenberg, in a number of essays, and Kenneth Pitchford, poet and editor of a magazine called *The Effeminist*, have provided important insights. An anthology of male profeminist essays also adds to our knowledge.[13]

While I do not wish to "legitimize" feminism to men by emphasizing this continuing, if controlled, concern about them, I think it is important not to trivialize Ms. Allgood's anxiety. There will come a time when her expression of it will be of value both for herself and for the development of feminist theory. But right now she still has a good deal to learn about her own condition of slavery so that she can come to understand how it is related to that of all other women.

LEADERSHIP

It is to the conclusion of Ms. Allgood's talk, her notion that one group of women would be particularly effective in leading the whole movement, that I want to address myself now, leaving for a later chapter the question she raised about "class."

At this point it's well for me to state that I have no doubt Ms. Allgood's desire to lead did not come from personal ambition. Her interest was warmhearted and altruistic: she wished to give of herself, her talents, her privileges, her guidance. These are qualities the women's movement needs and should encourage in every woman who exhibits them. The question is: would it be appropriate and/or useful for Ms. Allgood and a group of women she considers her peers, or any woman or group of women, to lead the movement?

In the beginning, the women's liberation movement said, decisively, no. In fact, the women who began the movement were, many of them, quite fanatical about this.[14] (Here I am differentiating the women's liberation movement, the radical arm of the women's movement, from the National Organization for Women, which is structured, more or less, along parliamentary lines.) At first, their horror of leadership came from a visceral sense of its intrinsic immorality; later, from their hatred of male domination which the thought of *female* leadership brought frighteningly to mind.

An earlier, nonfeminist women's political protest group, Women Strike for Peace, had also tried to avoid leadership because they had seen so many leftist leaders jailed and their movements fall apart in their absence. Black civil rights groups suffered when their leaders were assassinated, jailed, exiled, or co-opted. Gandhi, a leader whose assassination dissolved nonviolent protest in India, expressed the thought that leaders often fall behind their followers in understanding changing needs and even in inventing new tactics. Public prominence can sever vital ties between a leader and the people she leads.

But the women's liberation movement had still another reason for avoiding leadership: it was interested in developing strengths in women to lead ourselves, individually. Because so many of our struggles necessarily had to be carried on in isolation, in one-to-one relationships with men, it was imperative for women, as individuals, to gain the confidence to act autonomously, to lead *oneself*. So the moral distaste for leadership *by others* became an intensely practical tactic, completely appropriate to the tasks to be performed.

A lot of confusion, however, emanated from these original insights. Some of that confusion is still a debilitating force in the movement, and it stems, I believe, from an inadequate definition of what leadership is. Ironically, it was the *leaders* of the nascent movement (and leaders did arise almost immediately!) who were most responsible for confounding the aspect of the term "leadership" which means power over others, with the aspect of it which means, simply, individual achievement. As originally stated, the question the women's liberation movement asked itself was, "how can we avoid leadership?" And it looked for enforceable answers. Unfortunately, it did not ask the more fundamental questions: "what is leadership?" nor "why does leadership arise?"

These questions will be dealt with more specifically in Chapter Three, but they should be borne in mind as you read on. I do not, however, want to move ahead without attempting to answer the question Ms. Allgood stirred in me: can one segment of the movement effectively lead others?

We are used to the assertion, often made hypocritically by demagogues, that the people know what's best for them, and ultimately their decisions are wisest. In practice, the "people" are often confused and misled by better-educated opportunists. The "people" usually means men. Women know that men's values are easily distorted by abstractions owing to a lack of contact with their own survival needs, which are usually ministered to by women; by the desire for a dominant image, for which they are willing to sacrifice security and even life itself; and by the foolishness that sets in when one is constantly surrounded by associates (women) chosen not to offer constructive criticism, but simply to admire.

This is not to say that, in contrast, women are all wise. Women are also taken in by glamor and flattery, especially when we are isolated from other women and have no one but the man or the mirror to turn to for advice.

But when we gather together in groups to talk about our lives, when we take our shoes off and let our hair down together—in short, when we strive to become feminists—we come very close to an appreciation of our own needs and find the courage, in mutual support, to state them. Then we are very wise indeed. We become experts on ourselves, and nobody knows better than we what to demand for ourselves. Then leadership by another group, an elite, becomes not only presumptuous, but inefficient as compared to our own ability to articulate our needs, to bargain for ourselves with conviction born of collective self-knowledge.

On the other hand, a liaison group, one that can open channels through which women knowledgeable about their own needs can find an audience with the powers which control their lives, may deserve consideration—as long as the liaison group does not presume to translate those needs into messages they think men in power will find palatable. (People are so often content to remove, a toe at a time, the foot that is standing on *another* person's neck and to urge patience on the sufferer.) In such a group, with carefully delineated duties, an informed Ms. Allgood (and I presume she will now hasten to get herself informed) might play a part worthy of her abilities and her desire to put them to good use.

Chief among the technical equipment needed to play liaison is the knowledge most women have had to learn in early childhood: how to turn a trick to get what one wants. That knowledge doesn't lead to fundamental change (it can lead away from it, in fact) but it can achieve interim reforms. On the way to resuscitating a dying world, we will, I'm afraid, have to turn many tricks.

The arts of prostitution were not invented by women. Men use them every day, with great sophistication, to advance in their hierarchical structures. They are, in fact, only *illegal* for women. We have managed to learn them anyway, for our survival. We cannot afford to give them up just yet. Many, many reforms are essential *right now*, and there is probably no other way to obtain them than by getting in bed (figuratively, if possible) with the government. The important question is, how much will it pay — and what kind of obscenities will we have to perform? Unless we have some power base, we may wind up selling our favors too cheaply, selling ourselves, in fact, back into slavery.

Prostitution, for women, is a dangerous game — whether actually leasing the use of one's body or analogously trading political favors with a patriarchal government. In the latter case (wheeling and dealing for the women's movement), the gravest danger is forgetfulness: forgetting that a mandate from the movement, or the segment of the movement concerned, is necessary to ratify any trading in its name; forgetting that prostitution is still the name of the game and that it can lead to tokenism and the suppression of other women's aspirations as a price for maintaining one's own position of favor in the hierarchy; forgetting that one is not operating, in the government, among friends, but on an essentially hostile turf, and that those in power intend to sustain their dominance over women, wherever the negotiations may lead them temporarily; forgetting, in sum, that one is still a woman and, in the eyes of men who make the laws which control our lives, a woman trafficking illegitimately and by their sufferance among men—that the government has the power to stop negotiating and reverse gears at any time—*and will use that power*. The ultimate interest of any government which wishes to maintain its power is to suppress dissidence by any means whatever. If it feels it can buy the silence of feminists at a price it considers reasonable, it will do so. If not, it will use its power more overtly against us.

The only hope for real, lasting change for women lies in our finding our own collective strength. We are a majority of the people, and so we have potential strength in our numbers. But the effort to reach each other, to cross those chasms which separate us from one another, has just begun. It is in the government's (all governments') interest to prevent us from organizing ourselves—nationally and internationally—to serve the real interests of women everywhere. To this end, they will attempt to co-opt any leadership which arises, to convince women that *their* chosen "feminist" leadership is of *our* own choosing (when it is patently the government selecting whom it wants to represent us), and thus distract us from continuing the organizing process.

It is important to remember that the women who have taken unto themselves the task of negotiating with the government on behalf of the movement have received no legitimate mandate from either the movement nor the greater body of enfranchised women in this country. It is my opinion that the women's movement—the women's *liberation* movement—should observe these women closely, support those demands made in our name which truly answer our needs, and endeavor not to expend all of our energy on governmental programs. The strings attached to those packages can be strangulating. Our major job, organizing *ourselves*, is still very much with us, and should command the better part of our efforts.

CHAPTER TWO

The Early Years of the Women's Liberation Movement and the Start of Some Schisms

I wasn't there at its inception, either. The people I know who were and the books I've read about it make me slightly envious, although I wonder if the tortuous beginnings of the women's liberation movement wouldn't have sent me flying into the arms of the first "personal solution" I met, as they did so many others!

The fact is, I lived a bit uptown for the action. (The "Yippies"-evolving-into-feminists I knew never traveled above Fourteenth Street in Manhattan.)[1] My daughters had recently started elementary school, and I was involved in the struggle for "integrated, quality education" (later, for community control of schools)—both participating in it and writing about it. I was also writing for two pacifist publications, practically commuting to Albany and Washington for peace and civil rights demonstrations. The kids and I were getting a lot of exercise, too, marching around United Nations Plaza and attending be-ins and love-ins and happenings in Central Park. At home, our apartment was always full of young people recuperating from protests (and the beatings which followed) in the South; hitchhikers from Alaska who knew somebody who knew somebody who knew me and crashed for months at a time; the sound of the Beatles and the smell of pot. The late sixties and early seventies were a kind of reprise of adolescence, and most of the time, as in my *first* youth, I quivered on the edge of a nervous breakdown.

I got my first glimpse of the women's liberation movement's existence in 1967 at a peace demonstration in Washington where I joined a "women's caucus," but didn't much understand what it was all about. This caucus—which featured an angry and bewildering speech by poet Denise Levertov, who delivered it while standing on a chair—was sponsored (or should I say "improvised"?) by New York Radical Women, the first New York women's liberation group. Since this Washington peace demonstration was the second I had attended within two months, I wasn't at all sorry to be drawn away from the usual pacifist speeches into the chaos and surrealism of a "women's caucus." It appeared that a great many young women wanted to speak about a great variety of subjects having to do with women. As the emphasis of the peace demonstration had been on ending the war in Vietnam, I had at first supposed that these young women, in drawing people away from the regular program, would be expressing more radical attitudes about ending that war than were Bella Abzug, Coretta King, and Dagmar Wilson. It was a great surprise to me that they wanted to talk about another subject altogether!

It wasn't until the fall of 1968 when, responding to a leaflet I received in the mail, I attended the first protest against the Miss America contest in Atlantic City, that I understood a whole new movement was afoot. And *that* protest was quite an eye opener! The most impressive aspect of the experience was not the demonstration itself, but the expressions of hostility by male bystanders. As I marched around and around in our exhausting picket-cir-

cle, I would hear, alternately, shouts of, "Hey, Good-look-
ing—watcha doing tonight?" and "Boy, get a load of *that*
one. What a dog!" The men acted as if *we* were conduct-
ing a beauty contest! I had been to other demonstrations
where we were heckled—even by Nazis in full, obscene
regalia—but I never before had such a feeling of humiliation, of being *spat* upon. Thus I learned, with a terrifying
immediacy, the meaning of the new term "sex object,"
and how, henceforth, to regard both the physical flattery
and the physical insults of men. From that moment, I
have never smiled back at a flirting construction worker
or truck driver, nor given a damn about the way I appear,
physically, in the eyes of men. The experience was worth
perhaps a hundred CR sessions.

THE BIRTH OF A MOVEMENT

In the mobile, energetic mid-sixties, a group of activists
who had dropped out of S.D.S. (Students for a Democratic Society, a male-dominated New Left protest group
of the sixties) moved to Chicago where they hoped to organize poor people for the left. It wasn't at all unusual at
the time for young idealists to pick up stakes and go
wherever they sensed a calling, whether it was to join the
Peace Corps, to develop a communal farm, or to help
people in distress in urban ghettoes. With a number of
years of struggle behind them, the New Left had developed a common-sense strategy of organizing oppressed people around their own problems. This was a
refinement of methods Marxists had used in the early
part of the century to form unions. The new addition was
a process called "participatory democracy," which
would—theoretically—do away with leadership or, at
least, encourage the development of indigenous leadership. (It was also new to consider university students an

"oppressed" group, and to organize them around the difficulties of dealing with repressive administrators. After the attack on the women's movement by the left for being "bourgeois," it is well to remember this bit of American Marxist history.) Meetings were open and apparently unstructured, with everyone given equal opportunity to express himself (masculine pronoun intentional).

Of course, leaders did emerge in the New Left. At the "agendaless" meetings there were hidden agendas. And there were also, as we know now, FBI and CIA provocateurs organizing men around their bravado.

The women in the Chicago New Left group had been reading, on their own, Simone de Beauvoir and Betty Friedan; they knew about the recent formation of N.O.W. (which they felt was too moderate) and about the militancy of women revolutionaries in China. They became increasingly aware of their own passive position in their political enclave: they were "earth mothers" during the day, knitting and baking bread and making endless pots of coffee while the men talked Marx, Lenin, and Mao; and "sex kittens" at night, providing the free-sex games the men found so liberating. If they attempted any serious participation in the discussions, they were branded "aggressive" or "sexless"—or worse; if they expressed emotional needs (for stability, tenderness), they were called "demanding"—or worse. These women were creative and intelligent, a number of them brilliantly innovative, as we know now, and they grew more and more irritated and restive under the domination of men who, in relation to women, differed little, if at all, from "establishment" men.

Unlike other leftist women at that time, the Chicago women weren't content to form a caucus within the group. They moved out of it entirely to form what is widely believed to be the first autonomous radical women's group of the sixties devoted solely to female concerns. In the beginning, their purpose was to organize women around our own issues *for the left*. A number of women's liberationists still consider this to be their main purpose—to form a "united front" of all oppressed peoples of the world (the other "peoples" understood to be men, with women as a mere constituency among them). But gradually, for some, the emphasis shifted and they decided to organize themselves as women *for women* (for all the oppressed *women* in the world, which meant *all* the women in the world—not just those dubbed "working class" according to the men to whom they were attached). The leftist men *they* were appended to might be middle class, but these women came to recognize themselves as oppressed beyond any categories devised by Marx. If they worked with poor women or with black women, it would be as true equals, because all women are subject to the same sexual abuses by men. And since working-class men were not less sexually abusive than middle- and upper-class men, why look to alliances with working *men*?

In the summer of 1967, two of the Chicago women, Shulamith Firestone and Pamela Allen, decided to move to New York and build a women's liberation movement there.[2]

Firestone called a meeting of about a dozen New York women in the fall of that year and out of this meeting a group called the New York Radical Women emerged. Action-oriented, they were the ones who later organized the women's caucus at the peace demonstration in Washington mentioned earlier. Out of this group a number of others evolved, including the Redstockings. Some time later, Firestone and others attended a Redstockings meeting. They arrived in the midst of a consciousness-raising session. The Redstockings were discussing sex and Firestone recognized their CR to be a valuable organizing tool. Shortly thereafter, Minda Bikman, Diane Crowthers, Anne Koedt, Cellestine Ware, and Firestone started the New York Radical Feminists. (The originally proud title of the new movement had been abbreviated—and trivialized—by the media into "women's lib." The term "radical women" was too vague: radical for what? in what way? "Feminism" was definitive, and it had a tradition.)

The Redstockings, at that time primarily a consciousness-raising group, were not preprared to do mass organizing, so the New York Radical Feminists took it upon themselves to help set up CR groups throughout the city. They worked out guidelines for discussions and connected interested women who telephoned them for information with other interested women in their own neighborhoods. (When I had tea with Minda Bikman recently to discuss the "early days," she told me NYRF had arranged hundreds of CR groups throughout the city: "everywhere," she said, "but on the Upper East Side. There wasn't enough interest there." I smiled knowingly. "That's where *I* live," I said. There was one of those awkward little silences, until we both laughed.)

NYRF had monthly meetings which any woman could attend, but when the group began, a woman was required to participate in at least three months of consciousness-raising and three months of group study prior to voting. The study groups acquainted themselves with feminist history and literature. (This was, presumably, to prevent a Ms. Allgood from jumping in and assuming leadership.) Bikman told me that not all of the women who passed through this initiation continued to be active in NYRF, but certainly it must have affected the quality of their personal lives.

NYRF also organized mass "speak-outs," assemblies where women would bear witness to the crimes against them. The one on rape was particularly effective: it inspired women to set up rape crisis centers and to pressure law enforcement agencies to give fairer and more sympathetic attention to rape victims. Perhaps just as important, it inspired Susan Brownmiller to begin work on her exhaustive study, *Against Our Will: Men, Women, and Rape*, which helped to bring rape, as a political issue, to worldwide attention.[3]

During the early seventies, feminist groups proliferated everywhere in the United States. Many were working collectives, producing periodicals, building archives, arranging cooperative child care, setting up women's centers and gynecological clinics. Others concentrated solely on consciousness-raising, some with specific angles such as race, religion, age.

CONGENITAL PROBLEMS

Originally there had been some disputes between women who favored direct action and women who preferred to work purely on analyzing their problems through CR. At an early meeting I attended, one woman remarked, "We've been slaves for thousands of years. We can afford to take a few years off to figure out what that means." (This was in answer to a common complaint against "navel-gazing.")

Actually, CR and activism are complementary. It seems more a matter of temperament than of "correct politics" which discipline a woman chooses to emphasize. The CR groups felt unhurried about making decisions, and when they did take on an activity, it often had a solidity about it that more impetuous actions lacked. They tried to arrive at decisions "organically," out of thoroughly analyzed and emotionally felt needs. This was the theory, and it frequently worked.

The problem of activism versus CR was more easily resolved among radical feminists than three other "congenital" problems: (1) differences between those women who still emphasized Marxism (that is, they identified capitalism as the source of sexism and continued to support male-dominated leftist issues) and radical feminists (those who saw sexism as the origin of all evil, including both capitalism and socialism-as-it-exists); (2) differences between lesbians and heterosexual women; and (3) problems of structure.

THE MARXIST-RADICAL FEMINIST DISPUTE

In general, the Marxist groups emphasized the economic and racial oppression of women, and did not support those issues which affected white women with access to money. For instance, they readily supported (as did radical feminists) Joan Little, a black prisoner who killed the Southern white jailer who had raped her in her cell. The Marxists were, however, less interested in the plight of Patricia Hearst, the heiress who was kidnapped, raped, and terrorized by a group of "revolutionary" men and women. (One Marxist woman even applauded the murder of Sharon Tate by Charles Manson.)

The priorities of leftists were strictly codified. They were based on the "enemy" theory, and the only enemy they could see was capitalism, from which they assumed both sexism and racism derived. Any sexist or racist assaults which came from sources other than capitalism were ignored or excused. (The racism against Jews in socialist countries is condoned by many Marxists.)

Some radical feminists went equally far with *their* "enemy" theory. They purged women who consorted with men for *any reason*—even women who bore and nurtured male children. In an unpublished essay, Andrea Dworkin identified this attitude with Nazism.

Both the loyalty to orthodox Marxism and the absolutism of certain radical feminists arose from a continuing attachment to patriarchally approved abstractions and generalizations—the conversion of people into symbols, by which men justify war, rape, and other atrocities. Women are essentially refugees. We are the victims of all wars, all rapes, all atrocities. We are the people you see in the newsreels, fleeing with our children from the conquering army, begging for handouts of chocolates and cigarettes and nylon stockings—"apolitical" for our survival. All armies look alike to us. The army of liberation is as vicious to women as the army of repression. Women who look to absolutes do not consider the reality of women's lives, the reason why tenderness is so important to us.

The Marxist women who were later to show such a passionate loyalty to male leftist "heroes" were expressing a preference for the brother over the sister—a desire to be accepted on the boys' team, not to be identified with those who "play with dolls." They derived their sense of importance from the priorities of men. They accepted the male revolutionary notion that the problems of "bourgeois" women are trivial—that somehow Patricia Hearst was not a real woman being raped and tortured but a "Shirley Temple doll," all dressed up in lace dainties, the plaything of the rich.

There is, underlying the rape of the "Shirley Temple

doll" woman, of nuns in Africa, a ferocious obscenity which has nothing to do with the righteous hatred of oppressors. The revolutionary man wants to get into the pants of the pampered, pure woman—to rape the innocent virgin. (Innocence is often the product of the overprotection, the sheltering, which rich men give their daughters to fulfill their own obscene fantasies.) The revolutionary man wants what the rich man has, wants to defile it—and to him, the ultimate possession of the rich man is his daughter, his wife; the ultimate possession of the oppressive church is its nuns. The Marxist woman knows in her heart that revolutionary men are attracted by the scent of expensive perfume, and so she may encourage his viciousness toward the daughters of rich men to elicit the lie she wants to hear: that the revolutionary man really prefers the rough hands of working women.[4] She elicits his admiration by supporting his vice, as Victorian women tolerated bordellos (provided the prostitutes who staffed them were considered "bad") so that their husbands would continue to value the chastity they had so painfully achieved. When men "admire" women for a particular virtue—whether it is chastity or loyalty to the revolution—you can be sure that there is a bordello or a rape victim close by: a woman who caters to their real passion, hatred.

The Marxist-radical feminist split divided women across patriarchal political issues. This split did incalculable damage to many women and to the trust which had been sisterhood. It could not have been more disastrous had it been initiated by FBI and CIA provocateurs.

THE LESBIAN-HETEROSEXUAL DISPUTE

In the beginning, lesbians remained either outside the women's liberation movement or closeted within it; in some cases "secreted in it" would be the better term, because there were groups which from the beginning were discreetly lesbian dominated. As early as the Washington women's caucus in 1967 it was clear that a number of women were interested in meeting other women to express their sisterhood sexually. In N.O.W. and most of the early radical groups, however, lesbianism was a forbidden subject or barely tolerated as an aberration. The *right* of lesbians to exist within some groups was acknowledged, but their *need* for specific recognition and approval was ignored. To N.O.W., lesbians were an embarrassment; to Marxists, they were a "problem" caused by capitalism; to heterosexual radical feminists, they were invisible.

Lesbians began to defect from one women's group after another, to move around in search of a place where they would feel at home, a place which would serve both the totality of their needs as women and their specific needs as lesbians. Rita Mae Brown resigned her position as editor of New York N.O.W.'s newsletter[5] and Karla Jay withdrew from the Redstockings.[6] (Jay described Redstockings to me as a group which had the typical Marxist attitude toward homosexuals: a "personal problem," a "product of capitalism.") Jay at first moved on to become chairperson of the predominantly male Gay Liberation Front, but she and others soon grew uncomfortable with being part of a "ladies auxiliary."

Eventually, a group of women including Rita Mae Brown, Sidney Abbott, Barbara Love, and March Hoffman came together to form an autonomous lesbian feminist movement. About a third of them, Karla Jay told me, had defected from N.O.W. and other feminist groups. A number, like her, came from the Gay Liberation Front, and still others from the Daughters of Bilitis, a lesbian organization antedating the women's liberation movement. A few just wandered in. Together they organized Radicalesbians.

They were very angry at being placed in the position of "stepsisters" in the women's movement. Betty Friedan had referred to lesbians as the "lavender menace,"[7] and Susan Brownmiller countered in a trivializing way, the lesbians felt, by referring to them as the "lavender herring." Responding to this double-barreled attack, the Radicalesbians prepared a psychological offensive of their own, which began with the usual outrageous manifesto. They wrote and published a pamphlet called *The Woman-Identified-Woman*, which along with new information about the clitoral orgasm, had a profound effect on the women's movement throughout the Western world.

One of the Radicalesbians' first actions was a "zap" of the Second Congress to Unite Women. Radicalesbians distributed themselves casually throughout the meeting hall. They were wearing the usual feminist garb—jeans and sweatshirts or sweaters. Suddenly, at a prearranged moment, one of them (who had earlier "cased the joint") switched off the electricity, plunging the meeting into darkness. When the lights came on again, the room was ringed by women wearing T-shirts which read "LAVENDER MENACE"—and, alternately, "LAVENDER HERRING."

The number of empty chairs in the room and the number of women ringing it impressed on the women's movement that it could no longer sweep the lesbianism in its midst under the rug—or the whole rug might rise and walk away!

Minda Bikman told me that by 1973, New York Radical Feminists was a predominantly lesbian organization. The lesbian influence spread rapidly throughout the women's movement; women's centers everywhere reflected this trend. N.O.W. elected Karen de Crow, a lesbian, as its president. (Crudely, clothing designers picked up on this fashion, and women's pants suits with vests and ties became de rigueur for elegant women who barely knew of the movement's existence!)

The success of the lesbian strategy in declaring lesbianism the logical avant-garde of feminism was to produce a new form of tyranny. Although in many ways it was a liberating influence, as a by-product it produced bigotry against heterosexual women, and in its extreme versions, it even had a negative effect on lesbians: Karla Jay left later lesbian groups in part because her editorial collaboration and close friendship with Allen Young, a gay man, rendered her beyond the pale of separatism.

SUMMATION AND OBSERVATIONS

The complexities of the leftist and lesbian influences on the women's liberation movement, and vice versa, deserve more detailed attention than I have given them here; they will be treated further in Chapters Four and Five. Here I just wanted to sketch roughly a picture of the beginnings of modern feminism, in which one can glimpse the origins, not only of that just future toward which women everywhere are hopefully groping, but also the conflicts which obscure the way.

The tendency of patriarchal writers is to ignore feminist history, to treat it (if at all) as trivial. After all, what can we expect? We are a radical movement of *women*, outside the mainstream of what men have chosen to record. Television comedies about family strife and single women interested in careers are calculated to suppress the profoundly philosophical and political nature of emerging feminism, its inner substantiality, and the development of a society-within-the-society which, while it still may be a "subculture," threatens to erupt and subsume the superculture.

With calculated care the media are beginning to pay attention to the phenomenon of homosexuality, willing to make a temporary alliance, if necessary, among men of varied sexual preferences—in order to press women firmly back into oblivion. In San Francisco and New York, where there are large homosexual populations, the police and other establishmentarians have sat down with homosexual men in an attempt to alleviate difficulties between the law and male "deviants."[8] There is also a growing eagerness to support the image of men as good fathers, good custodians of children *apart* from mothers; to emphasize child abuse by mothers, leaving the sexual and sadistic abuse of children by fathers (and of women by men, except where this latter abuse is *encouraged* by violence-as-entertainment) still largely a taboo subject.

Men control the media as they control every other facet of the dominant society. They will allow only the most innocuous and inescapable aspects of feminism to surface. It is exhausting to insist on attention, to fight for it, like a child tugging at an adult's clothing when the adult is engaged in "important" conversation. Feminists, within the limits of our relative poverty, do create our own media, but they reach few of us. Still we are dependent on the television picture, the authority of patriarchal newspapers, the selections of the Book-of-the-Month Club. In our own minds, this heroic struggle we are engaged in, the labor to bring forth a new world, is still relatively insignificant. Our profound and earthshaking conflicts among ourselves about how we will shake off the repugnant oppression of men does not make even the *women's* pages of the dailies!

There is a dignity in our antagonisms, in our feminist dialectic. Somehow we must find the dignity within ourselves, in spite of all instructions to the contrary, to appreciate the nobility of our struggle, the importance of our hostilities—to give them in our own eyes the epic proportions men give their philosophical and political wranglings. For if the struggles among men are primarily to establish the "most dominant" male, the struggles among women are to bring forth our own being, to imagine and live our own destiny.

So it is not in shame, but in celebration, that I call these struggles into prominence.

CHAPTER THREE

Problems of Structure and Leadership

It is difficult to talk about radical feminist attitudes toward structure and leadership without frequent allusions to an early women's liberation group called, simply, The Feminists, and to Ti-Grace Atkinson, an extraordinary woman who dominated this group during its brief existence. This small organization published many position papers on aspects of feminist politics. Atkinson was a persuasive writer and speaker, and early in the movement gained acceptance by the media as a flamboyant personality. The Feminists' attitude toward structure and process was to have a surprisingly strong influence on the movement as a whole.

But perhaps not so surprising, since feminist communication from the beginning has been so extraordinary. In the early years women across the world hungered for feminist theory, and words on mimeographed sheets circled the globe as if on enthusiasm alone.

The patriarchal media, delighted with the novelty of "liberated" women and the jokes they could make at our expense, featured feminist "spokeswomen" on talk shows. But even in such a stupid and hostile environment, feminists were capable of communicating vital information.

Feminist writers traveled back and forth across the country, lecturing at universities and at newborn women's centers. As college students translated themselves overnight from "co-eds" into women, they carried the word home on Christmas vacations, taught it to their mothers and their kid sisters, backpacked it to Europe.

Robin Morgan says in *Going Too Far*, "Since early in 1970 I had been one of a number of American feminists who were in touch with like-minded women organizing all over the globe. Synchronicity, word-of-mouth, books smuggled into countries where the facist, capitalist, socialist, Protestant, Catholic, Jewish, Moslem, Hindu, or atheist male governments did not smile upon such literature—these were the ways our ideas were shared."[1]

Feminists from abroad bring news here, too. In New York, I have met women from Holland, Italy, Sweden, Israel, India, Argentina, and Japan. They come here for many reasons, but always now they want to talk to women—to find out what is happening, to bring news to us. So we learn about battered wives' shelters in London and abortions in Milan and a women's island in Denmark.

Not only feminist advances traveled across the world but our controversies about lesbianism and process and those men-on-the-left echoed from Lisbon to San Francisco. I would not be surprised to drop in on a feminist discussion about hierarchical structure at a women's center in Tokyo. (It *is* surprising, come to think of it, that this dispute didn't *first* arise in Tokyo!)

Women are very quick to *apply* new learning. Too often, perhaps, uncritically. The upbringing of a whole generation of children was revolutionized almost overnight with the publication of one book—by Dr. Benjamin Spock. (This passive acceptance of new ideas is something to bear in mind when examining modern feminism.)

REACTIONS TO HIERARCHICAL STRUCTURE

It was the New Left background of many American radical feminists which led them originally to question traditional structures. Two years prior to the organization of The Feminists, Ti-Grace Atkinson thrust the issue into the mainstream by resigning her presidency of New York N.O.W. over it. In a press release explaining her decision, Atkinson said: "The younger dissenting faction of which I am a part has been trying for a long time to change the unequal power relationships within the organization, i.e., the power hierarchy represented by officers: Executive Committee, Board of Directors, membership." She called for a "N.O.W. Version of Participatory Democracy: Multiple and Cyclical Presidents." She went on to say, "You cannot destroy oppression by filling the position of the oppressor. I don't think you can fight oppression 'from the inside'; you either *are* on the inside or the outside and you fill one of those two ranks with your presence."[2] (Emphasis Atkinson's.)

This was the first of many either-or positions Atkinson would publicly take. She has recorded her flamboyant shifts through the women's movement and out of it in a book called, appropriately, *Amazon Odyssey*. Whether she actually led the movement into some of its wobbly extremes or merely typified them, her influence was of no small consequence.

Atkinson's behavior in 1968 was not unique in terms of male-dominated radical politics (although feminists in general were trying not to expose our own disagreements in the patriarchal press). Like many New Left anarchists, she directed her zeal for radical change at less radical institutions within the movement. If moderate organizations view radicals as an embarrassment, radicals often view moderate organizations as the devil incarnate, out to destroy the purity of their ideal.

For example, in 1968 when I worked for *Liberation*, a left-pacifist magazine edited by Dave Dellinger,[3] I had a passion to end the hierarchical structure there. I believed then that every radical enterprise should be run collectively. At the time I was only one of two women on the staff, the other being Dellinger's secretary.

Looking back on the experience now, I think I was more disturbed by the oppression I suffered as a woman there than by the hierarchical structure. (As a writer, I have come to prefer magazines on which one person is ultimately responsible for editorial policy. Then it isn't so easy for an editor to worm her way out of responsibility for a correction by laying the blame on "others in the collective.") Whether my rebellion against the structure of *Liberation* came from simple ingestion of an S.D.S. cliché or from my not-yet-conscious anger at the way the men there were treating me, I am not sure — but I was full of a zeal not unlike Atkinson's.

Although Atkinson's attack on the young N.O.W. was perhaps premature and the virulence of it ill-considered (she knew *at the time* that attempts at participatory democracy hadn't prevented a ruling clique from forming in S.D.S.[4]), there *is* reason to question the efficacy of traditional structure. Bureaucratic chains of command are notoriously slow to bring news of changing needs to those in power. In 1968, N.O.W. had indeed been slow to respond to the movement's push for repeal of abortion laws; lesbians in N.O.W. were quietly but firmly ignored. Both of these errors in judgment have since been corrected under pressure, but the mechanism of a national organization is likely to be cumbersome.

An example of this inadequacy in N.O.W. is cited in *Nobody Speaks for Me!*, an anthology of verbal "self-portraits" edited by Nancy Seifer. In this book, Bonnie Halascsak, the founder of Steelworkers N.O.W., a chapter made up of union women working for U.S. Steel, reported in 1975 that her group was dropped "like a hot potato" by Chicago N.O.W. (which had helped to organize it) when the steelworkers got into a territorial dispute with another local N.O.W. (nonindustrial) chapter. The tremendous value of having an industrial group within N.O.W.'s network was apparently lost on the parent organization; and it appears to have been lost *in the shuffle*. In all likelihood, national headquarters had not been made aware of the conflict in time to do anything about it, and the steelworkers, exhausted by their battles with both their male-dominated union and male-dominated management, had no energy left for a prolonged struggle with the N.O.W. bureaucracy.

Halascsak's conclusion: "While I'm no longer organizing a community N.O.W. chapter, I'm probably just as much a feminist as ever. . . . Whether we band together in a group or go it alone, we each have something to contribute."[5]

The radical black civil rights movement complained about NAACP conservatism, and the peace movement was often stymied by the businessmen who ran SANE (Committee for a Sane Nuclear Policy). N.O.W., while much more responsive to movement radicals than either of these organizations were, does have bureaucratic drawbacks. Its structure still doesn't sit well with many radical feminists, but no other structure has yet been worked out for a national organization which successfully avoids hierarchy. Even Women Strike for Peace, a non-feminist national women's association opposed to the Vietnam War and organized along the lines of participatory democracy suggested by Atkinson for N.O.W. (W.S.P. had no officers at all), developed a central power clique early in its existence.

Essentially, the problem of domination-submission is a deeply entrenched psychic one, absorbed from the patriarchal modes which surround us. Until we have thoroughly analyzed and exorcised this possession from ourselves as individuals, we will continue to reproduce its symptoms in our groups. Consciousness-raising is helpful because, among other things, it tends to deglamorize would-be leaders and encourage would-be followers to develop a feeling of self-importance. The speak-out, whereby women bear witness to their oppression publicly, helps to foster understanding and empathy, also. But there is some question as to whether national organizations, themselves, are not the central culprit. Is it always necessary to tie the whole country into a neat package, when regional needs are often so different?

In any case, N.O.W.'s avowed purpose is to put pressure on the patriarchy, *as it is*, for women's rights. It is *not* a utopian organization. To quote from the statement of purpose adopted at its organizing conference (which Atkinson attended):

We organize to initiate and support action, nationally, or in any part of this nation, by individuals or organizations, to break through the silken curtain of prejudice and discrimination against women, in government, industry, the professions, the churches, the political parties, the judiciary, the labor unions, in education, science, medicine, law, religion and every other field *of importance to American society*.[6] (Emphasis mine.)

N.O.W. wants equal rights for women *within the present society*. Although its aims are quite comprehensive, structural change of the society as a whole is not included. It does seem quixotic, then, for Atkinson to have joined the organization at its inception, moved up the hierarchical ladder to a position of power, and then kicked over the traces—especially if all along she believed feminists shouldn't work from within.

Bonnie Halascsak's experience reflected the practical limitations of a national organization. She has moved away from the kind of activism which requires such a structure. However, imperfect and frustrating as N.O.W. can be, there is still a need for such an organization in the movement. And, as far as it goes, it is an honest organization, because its means *are* consistent with its ends— those ends being the achievement of civil rights for women within this society. That work is of the utmost importance, although it need not be the central focus for every feminist. After all, our goals today may become anachronisms in the next generation. In a world that changes so fast, can we predict with certainty the dreams of future women? But without freedom, will they be able to dream at all?

Perhaps if radical feminists can develop a workable nonhierarchical structure, N.O.W. will adopt it—or dissolve. But for the present, radical groups have a high mortality rate (possibly suggesting that the constantly shifting focus of radical analysis doesn't require permanence in that segment of the movement) while N.O.W. has existed since 1967. Should a nonhierarchical structure be invented which shows signs of enduring, it may mean we have finally purged ourselves of the last vestiges of our thralldom to men. For this reason, it is vital that radicals continue this search, wherever it leads us. *Robert's Rules of Order* and participatory democracy are both competitive, demeaning, patriarchal institutions; and we should not stop questioning them along with marriage, capitalism, socialism, organized religion, and all other such institutions. But in the process we must also question why our minds are fertile grounds for their perpetuation.

At the time Atkinson withdrew from N.O.W., I also might have exhibited such impatience (had I been drawn to join it in the first place), but these days I am beginning to recognize, like Bonnie Halascsak, that what are political priorities for me are not necessarily such for all feminists. I can see that the fiery temperament which leads one to rage against differences—complete with press releases—may come from the fear, instilled in women by men, that our reasonable complaints will be ignored altogether. Monolithism in the form of the impersonal national organization certainly reinforces this fear. With more and more experience of attention, respect, and support from other women, such destructive flashiness may disappear. I have already seen its diminution in younger women who have grown up in the movement and avoided the kinds of involvement with men which lead to unbearable frustration and loss of ego. I have been the recipient of a warm and calming understanding from them when a fury of associations has suddenly been triggered in me by a slight which might go unnoticed by others. This support is not condescending, but rather sensitively compassionate, as if these younger women are feeling for the sufferings I must have (and *truly* have) gone through in a lifetime of struggles with men. In contrast they have, at least from early adolescence, had the experience of *shared* suffering, of perceptions validated by their peers and by the growing body of feminist literature. In terms of poise and self-management, this experience can make all the difference in the world and is a reason for hope for real change.

Women who pour their energies into national feminist

endeavors have their job to do, and those who work best individually or in smaller groups have theirs, as Halascsak observed. The accomplishments and mutual criticism of moderate and radical feminists can be complementary. This notion of complementary relationships was probably not conceivable in 1968, however, when Atkinson's gesture of resigning a prestigious post in N.O.W. was widely hailed by radical feminists as courageous.

Letting off steam is therapeutic for people under pressure, but the danger of public flamboyancy is that it commands attention from the established news media and, often, the wrong kind of attention from what I will call "manifesto-oriented" feminists as well. It has the riveting effect of a temper tantrum which, in articulate adults, can sound like a call to arms—a call which, accustomed as we are to male revolutionary heroics, we may respond to with habituated acclaim. Such acclaim can be as intoxicating to a woman as to a man, and visions of omnipotence may stir in the mind of the person receiving it, visions which can push anyone over the edge into megalomania—the chronic disease of patriarchal leaders.

ATKINSON AND CLASS

From N.O.W., Ti-Grace went on to form another group in New York, originally called the October 17th Movement, for the day in 1968 when it first got together (October has heavy male-revolutionary associations). Shortly afterwards it was renamed The Feminists, possibly suggesting a hope that this group would set the tone for the whole movement. Atkinson was still concerned with what she would later dub the "equality issue," still determined to develop a structure which would insure the equality of all members in every endeavor. Most of the other feminist groups were also loosely structured, and tried to work out ways to keep one or a few women from hogging the stage, to prevent elites from forming. But Atkinson, a former student of philosophy at the doctorate level, wanted to find a foolproof structure, one which would help the movement reach out beyond the women of upper middle-class origin whom she assumed (with no demonstrable evidence) comprised the majority of radical feminists.

Once again, we run into this strange notion that the women's movement is bourgeois. Even in Marxist terms, most New York radical feminists came from working-class or lower middle-class backgrounds; a few were daughters of middle-income professional men who, themselves, had struggled out of dire poverty. One generation from Ellis Island was the general rule. This includes most of the feminists who later became prominent. In any case, patriarchal class distinctions are hardly applicable to women, and Atkinson must have read Friedrich Engels on that subject in the course of her philosophical studies.

Nevertheless, she divided women across traditional class lines according to something she called "identification"—a derivative classification which carried with it all the stigma involved in male categorizations and few of the benefits. Among the deprived, she went looking for the really, truly deprived—and identified them as the women who gravitated to her. These women said they felt different from some of the more assertive women in the movement, and without any demographic evidence, themselves ascribed this difference to "class." Two members of The Feminists, Pamela Kearon and Barbara Mehrhof, after some dialogs with each other, organized a "class workshop" for women from various feminist groups who felt themselves somehow to be oppressed *within* the movement, no doubt encouraged and influenced by Atkinson.[7] By the end of August 1969, The Feminists' tightly disciplined organizational code had been thoroughly worked out.[8]

In a lecture at Juniata College in February 1970, Atkinson described The Feminists in these words: "With the exception of myself, we are lower- or lower-middle-class and/or black."[9]

The class identification Atkinson made for herself, reinforcing her co-members' feeling that they were somehow lower in class than the *majority* of radical feminists, was, for practical purposes, specious. She came from an "old" Southern upper-class family which, in her native city of New Orleans, may have given her some advantages or the illusion of them. This class distinction was purely social, however: as she explained to The Feminists, it was necessary for her to earn her living by speaking and writing. But in a megalopolis where the social terrain is difficult even for subway-toughened natives to maneuver in, an outsider, particularly one without ethnic credentials, can become hopelessly lost. It is possible she felt strange in these junglelike surroundings and so *comforted* herself with an image of "class" superiority. Like the fictional Ms. Allgood, Atkinson apparently confused the social class of her parents and her education with the benefits *men* usually derive from such advantages, but which do not, in themselves, elevate a *woman's* economic class. Thus her relationship to the other members of The Feminists was one of false noblesse oblige.

Most of The Feminists had either graduated from, or were still attending, college. They were very young and a number of them were shy, but the majority aspired to professional careers at which some might be expected to equal or even exceed Atkinson in accomplishment. The point is that the difference between one social class and another in New York can be one generation or four years in college. Since Atkinson was a few years older than the others in her group and more experienced in public speaking, she might have legitimately assumed what Jean Baker Miller called a "temporary inequality"[10] as a teacher. Had The Feminists accepted her in that role, the imbalance might have had a more honest rationale and many of the structural rigidities which were later adopted apparently to equalize this *felt*, but *inadequately understood*, imbalance might have been obviated.

But Atkinson seems to have had trouble "relating" on a teacher-student basis as well. Wherever she went, she seems to have inferred unbridgeable gaps between herself and others, and so perpetuated her isolation. Hence the condescending tone in which she spoke to her class at Juniata College a year before her lecture on equality:[11]

Feminism is usually not relevant to any woman before she has left college. . . . The college girl, or any woman prior to her early twenties, is money in the bank, and the Man is not about to blow it. Try comparing the young woman's treatment with that of the darling little pickaninnies of the plantation; the whip was rarely applied before the black became serviceable.[12]

Then she spoke of her own unhappiness at age seventeen:

If I had been a boy with my particular spirit for adventure, no doubt I would have left home and wandered about the world. . . . But because I was a woman with the female role obliterating any human possibility I might have, leaving the family or the daughter role left one alternative: wife or prostitute. What I saw as my life and destiny at seventeen intuitively, I see now to be, in popular phraseology, the "correct analysis."[13]

Aside from the unnecessarily limited options she envisioned as her only future (women *did* hold jobs other than wife and prostitute even way back then!), she failed to attribute to her young audience a capability for intuition equal to her own at that age.

Then she confessed her bitterness in remembering:

I feel as if I'm speaking to myself as I was ten years ago, and I don't want to remember how I was tricked. . . . What I feared in coming here was to see myself from before, bewildered and compelled, and to feel again the bitterness and hate for the injustice done to me and my kind, women.[14]

Now, back to condescension:

What I am trying to say is that feminism, thank God for your sake, is not yet quite relevant for you, and that I am not at all convinced that to come here to tell you about it can, first of all, possibly be comprehended, and second, to the degree you do understand feminism, I'm not sure that it is in your present interests to understand its issues.[15]

Here we see her running away from herself, running away from the possibility that her own very common youthful experience might be shared and understood by women who were currently living through it. She created, by means of a ten-year gap, a "class" difference between herself and her audience — and once again *hers* was the (defensively?) superior class. In other words, when she was speaking to peers, she had a habit of elevating herself above them, not acknowledging the equality which may, in fact, have existed and thus creating for herself a chasm to (heroically) cross. We see her inventing differences where they hardly exist, nuances of inequality.

COMPASSION FOR SELF, EMPATHY WITH OTHERS

It is often easier for women of similar backgrounds to converse comfortably with each other than it is for them to communicate cross-culturally, both because of commonality of experiences and a similarity of speech patterns. Understanding this, most feminists either assumed (probably, for the most part, correctly) that whatever group they were in was a peer group, or else they deliberately joined groups comprised of women who, in a general way, shared their interests. This was a time when feminists were relieving themselves, at least temporarily, of women's indoctrinated obligation to work solely for the good of others.

Most of us had been unthinking do-gooders all our lives. Now we were concentrating on our *own* oppression: trying to understand it, how it happened, what it did to us, how we felt about it. In the process, we were learning that aside from, and above and beyond, our oppression by "class" or race, we were all oppressed *as women*. Once we understood how we, ourselves, were oppressed, we might be able to work cross-culturally, relating to other women with a deeply felt empathy, instead of self-righteous sympathy. To bring out one's own long-hidden suffering, to feel it *as* suffering and—for once—not to trivialize it, is a step toward forging a bond with all others who have suffered, whether they can yet speak of it or not.

Women's suffering under sexist tyranny is a common bond among all women, transcending the particulars of the different forms that tyranny takes. *Suffering cannot be measured and compared quantitatively*. Is the enforced idleness and vacuity of a "rich" woman, which leads her to madness and/or suicide, greater or less than the suffering of a poor woman who barely survives on welfare but retains, somehow, her spirit? There is no way to measure such differences, but should these two women survey each other without the screen of patriarchal class, they may find a commonality in the fact that they are both oppressed, both miserable. They might be able to help each other to survive. The urge to do good, then, could reassert itself as a mutual experience.

But this kind of empathy cannot be learned in a group whose members, with a seemingly impenetrable patriarchal screen between them, perceive only their differences. It can best be done in a group of women who immediately recognize each other as peers, who will have no need to fear that the expression of their suffering will be derided as trivial.

There is no doubt in Ti-Grace Atkinson's writings that she was aware, on an intellectual level, of the common suffering of women. But the fact that she chose to work at this time with women whom *she defined* as being of a different class may indicate that she was still trying to avoid coming to terms with her own suffering as a woman, that she preferred to *give sympathy* rather than to *feel empathy*, which can only truly be done when one is convinced of the reality and importance of one's own oppression.

In a lifetime, most of us will be able to achieve such empathy only imperfectly. It may be that within one generation, imbued as we have been since infancy with a need to "quantify" every experience—to assign a degree of goodness or badness to it—we cannot truly empathize even with close friends, much less cross-culturally. Perhaps it will be necessary, for a long time to come, for feminists to remain somewhat parochial in the hope of developing solidarity at least within what we can recognize, with our patriarchally screwed-on heads, as "peer" groups. Better that than to burden others with guilt-inspired "favors," which seldom answer anybody's need.

But this does *not* mean that, conscious of our own limitations as empathizers, we cannot lend a hand cross-culturally when help is requested. It does *not* mean that we must vote in the patriarchy only for those reforms which will help our peer group, blind to the needs of others. It *may* mean that we cannot presume to know, without their informing us, the needs of others, and that we cannot ever again forget our own. We *can* begin to distinguish the privileges that are real from those that are merely disguised forms of oppression. Knowing these distinctions is essential to prevent us from being unthinking do-gooders who, in the end, do more harm than good, both to others and to ourselves.

EQUALITY OF SELF-EXPRESSION

If The Feminists were not all peers, or didn't recognize themselves as peers, this imbalance helped them to develop at least one extremely valuable concept: *equality* of self-expression. This concept goes much deeper than the *freedom* of self-expression "guaranteed" in the Bill of Rights.

Even if there weren't innumerable restrictions placed on the latter according to the whims of those in power (often called the "mood of the country" or "the temper of the times"), for all practical purposes this constitutional freedom is primarily available to those who financially control the media—and to those who are able to *please* those who financially control the media, the bulk of whom are white males.

When I say "media" here, I am referring to all major outlets of self-expression: the airwaves, the press, films, books, symphony halls, art galleries, the stage. While the airwaves show a decided preference for blandness in both form and content (violence, by long custom, having become a form of blandness), some of the other outlets aim for an intellectual market; the form may reach a very high level of artistic competence and even, on occasion, be downright experimental. But even here it must not violate one taboo: never seriously offend white males.

According to the intellectuality (and power) of the audience it is aimed at, there may be a wider or narrower definition of what constitutes a threat to white male power. Exxon, for instance, sponsored a series of silent Russian post-Revolutionary films on public television in 1978. Art museums heavily endowed by the richest men in the United States proudly exhibit works by Picasso and other communist artists. I will not here go into all the vagaries of political challenge men in power will or will not accept (we all have seen exhibits of the range). It should be sufficient to say that those in control determine which works of self-expression are "safe" to show to a popular audience. Either they are so highbrow as to be uninteresting to most people or so old as to have lost their sting.

There is, in addition to having the acceptable biases, another qualification required for one's self-expression to reach an audience: one must have some (slight) recognizable competence in a craft. Since the public education system is a disgrace—particularly for women,[16] minorities, and poor people—it is very difficult for these groups, who might at least *attempt* to break through the communications barrier, to learn the necessary skills. Literacy figures in the United States, particularly among the urban poor, have been in decline for many years, a situation too convenient to the rulers not to be top-level policy.

Finally, the person who does not belong to the "in" group must have an indomitable will to succeed. The slightest hesitancy, the slightest sensitivity, the slightest self-doubt is enough to relegate one to the backwaters. One must go out at all times in impenetrable armor.

The Feminists insisted on not just *freedom* of expression, but *equality* of expression, too. In concept, this was an important step forward.

To achieve this equality within their group, they imposed certain restrictions and disciplines on themselves. In discussions and decision making, they found that some people spoke too often and others too seldom, so The Feminists devised this system: each woman was given a number of chips at the beginning of a meeting, each chip representing a chance to speak. Whenever a woman took a turn, she would discard a chip. (The solution did not quite live up to the analysis. It was a quantitative reform with uneven results. Some women felt it created an oppressive atmosphere; nor did it prevent inequalities from arising.)

Although the analysis of equality of self-expression and freedom of self-expression, in general terms, was brilliant, it didn't quite describe the situation of The Feminists among themselves. For one thing, the only self-expression they were dealing with in this connection was discussion among a small group of people. Second, the solution devised was based on the assumption that women who talk a lot are in somehow better shape than women who are more circumspect. This isn't necessarily true. The ebullient woman may set up a smoke screen of talk to hide her vulnerability; the quieter woman, thinking carefully before she speaks, may speak with great effectiveness. Had they devoted more time to searching out the specific experiences in their lives which determined their speech habits, rather than imposing arbitrary restrictions, they might have produced very valuable information for women working with each other.

It is well to remember that the inequalities which existed among The Feminists were *nuances*. They in no way reproduced, even in microcosm, the major inequalities in our society at large. While the nuances are important for us to understand if we are to educate ourselves and each other, to legislate against them without understanding them is self-defeating.

Most of the women's liberation groups were attempting to build in some method to encourage self-expression among the more timid members. In the patriarchal world women are so often squelched and told we "talk too much" that radical feminists made an early decision to listen to each other with respect. A number of them emulated The Feminists; others just set reasonable time limits and looked at their watches. What has emerged from this early structural experimentation is a tendency in feminist discussions to allow each woman to speak as long as she needs to, and to trust that she will consider others equally.

A similar consideration for individual self-expression exists in black communities. At many political meetings in Harlem, no matter how they are structured, even long-winded bores and people on the edge of insanity are allowed to hold the floor as long as they feel the need to. Despite powerful efforts now being made by the media to liquidate this sense of solidarity, the terms "sister" and "brother" are still used by black women and men. Because they have lived in *acknowledged* servitude, their comprehension of their oppression as a race grew deep. Even black bureaucrats will often give priority to the individual's need to "speak pain," at least with respect to oppression by whites. Unlike women, because they weren't isolated from one another in their oppression, they didn't have to import this understanding from China.

But women suffering *sexist* oppression (and this, of course, includes white and black women), are isolated from one another. Our affectations of passivity go everywhere with us—even to bed. In our isolated oppression, we lose conviction about the validity of our own feelings; we think of them as personal, idiosyncrasies—unverifiable—and so we repress them. When once again, in the company of other women, we find them, we are often slow at unraveling them and impatient at listening to others going through the same process. To connect the two—one's own need for self-expression and that of one's newly found sisters in slavery—involves learning for all concerned. It is not surprising, then, that women, who have so recently rediscovered our connection with one another, should struggle to develop new structures which will allow orderly and satisfying communication without resorting to *Robert's Rules*, which leave so much unsaid.

EQUALITY OF TYPE AND AMOUNT OF LABOR

The Feminists, having assigned themselves the work of developing a radical feminist code of behavior, raised a second egalitarian issue. It was closely connected to the first, equality of self-expression. This second issue had to do with the quality and amount of labor each member would be expected to perform.

The categories they arrived at were "privileged" work—writing position papers and speaking publicly; and "routine" (more informally called "shit") work—mimeographing, collating, mailing, and so on. They very carefully rotated all these jobs so that nobody would be stuck all the time with the "routine" work, and everybody would get a chance at the goodies. A reading from The Feminists' "Organizational Principles and Structure" gives a fair idea of the way work was distributed as well as the tone of The Feminists' thinking:

THE FEMINISTS is an organization without officers which divides work according to the principle of participation by lot. Our goal is a just society all of whose members are equal. Therefore, we aim to develop knowledge and skills in all members and prevent any one member or small group from hoarding information or abilities.

Traditionally official posts such as the chair of the meeting and the secretary are determined by lot and change with each meeting. The treasurer is chosen by lot to function for one month.

Assignments may be menial or beyond the experience of a member. To assign a member work she is not experienced in may involve an initial loss of efficiency but fosters equality and allows all members to acquire the skills necessary for revolutionary work. When a member draws a task beyond her experience, she may call on the knowledge of other members, but her own input and development are of primary importance. The group has the responsibility to support a member's efforts, as long as the group believes that member to be working in good faith. A member has the duty to submit her work for the group—such as articles and speeches—to the group for correction and approval.

In order to make efficient use of all opportunities for writing and speaking, in order to develop members without experience in these areas, members who are experienced in them are urged to withdraw their names from a lot assigning those tasks. Also those members, experienced or inexperienced, who have once drawn a lot to write or speak must withdraw their names until all members have had a turn.[17]

Ti-Grace Atkinson's personal prominence brought her more opportunities to speak publicly, on television and at lectures, than the rest of the group. She explained, according to a former member, that she earned her living from such speaking engagements. Most of the non-televised, "privileged" work emanating from the group, therefore, was rotated among the other members, and Atkinson acted as a resource for them. (She also shared with them her invitations to speak without pay, whenever this was possible.) This practice helped a number of the young women to realize new potentials, and it is still used in some feminist collectives. Shy people overcome their shyness; aggressive people learn to take turns. It can be a way of averting the "spokeswoman" syndrome, always a problem to the movement, but in this case it did not, since Atkinson continued in that public role.

This sharing of "privileged" work and "routine" work provided a sound learning experience for many of the young women in the group. It can be efficient enough so long as the work is, as in the case of The Feminists, of a similar kind. When the work is more varied, however, as on a magazine, where not only writing is involved but also artwork, production, business management and, possibly, advertising, constantly shifting jobs may result in no skill being learned to proficiency. This isn't to say that all persons shouldn't be able to apprentice in all fields and learn, over the course of time, a number of different skills. I am referring here to the egalitarian mode widespread in the movement after The Feminists' example in which *all* jobs were switched every week or every month, so that all work remained amateur. Particularly for women, whom all society expects to remain in the amateur class forever, this is to be avoided.

In the early days of the movement, proficiency was generally regarded as a hoarding of skills, and deeply distrusted, perhaps because of an intuitive understanding that such skills could eventually be put to use in the patriarchy and against the women's movement. (This fear is not entirely without a realistic basis.)

Many small movement magazines followed the job-rotating model of The Feminists, and the results were often appalling. Some went even further, into "artistic collectivism." On these publications, the authors of all the articles were *anonymous*. The groups also demanded the use of special "revolutionary" jargon, the kind of language beloved by the traditional left. This was true of *Rat*, a New Left "underground" paper of the sixties which was taken over by the women members of its staff. In attempting to avoid the "cult of personality," personality was stamped out altogether. Robin Morgan, an irrepressible literary stylist, describes eloquently in *Going Too Far* how she suffered as a writer on *Rat*.[18] In still other groups, every written piece was put together collectively—sentence by sentence. This tedious method led inevitably to tedious results, but many of the participants insisted they were setting new "collective" standards of beauty!

There is often an assumption made by people who are literate that writing, unlike drawing or music, is something less than an art. They see it simply as a propaganda tool, but even if it is used as such, a considerable amount of craft is necessary to persuade. The writer's signature on an article, moreover, is the surest way to encourage criticism and debate. "Collective" writing may satisfy the vanity of those who participate in it but it seldom serves the purpose of persuasion, either through manipulation *or* honest argument. Ultimately, when what is produced is perceived to be incompetent, it depresses those who produced it, too.

Until recently—and still, perhaps, in certain

groups—proficiency was frequently confused with attempts to gain power over others: with leadership, or with what has been called "elitism"—erroneously, as Joreen was to point out in an excellent essay called "The Tyranny of Structurelessness":[19] " 'Elitist' is probably the most abused word in the women's liberation movement. . . . Within the movement it commonly refers to individuals, though the personal characteristics and activities of those to whom it is directed may differ widely. An individual, *as an individual*, can never be an elitist, because the only proper application of the term 'elite' is to groups."[20] (Emphasis Joreen's.)

Women's individual acquisition of proficiency is obviously vital for the movement as a whole. Whether proficient women will use these skills ultimately to benefit the movement or exclusively for their own advancement in the patriarchy is quite a separate question, and a very important one. Since the patriarchy is the repository of all wealth, women who make their way through its hierarchy as a result of the efforts of the women's movement clearly have an obligation to give some of the money and power they obtain back to the movement. Having this money in their personal possession, however, does endow them with the privilege of deciding how to distribute it—and this puts them in a position of power vis-à-vis the women's movement.

This is a conundrum of the capitalistic system, one of the ways it maintains its power. Similarly, rich men control the left in America, perhaps one reason why that political faction of the American scene generally behaves in such self-defeating ways. On the other hand, whether power is measured by wealth, as it is in capitalistic countries, or by political influence, as it is in socialistic countries, the government stands to control any movement which must go to the hierarchy for its ultimate source of power.

One answer, and it is a shaky one at that, is for women to plow their gains in the patriarchy into feminist "alternative" enterprises and put the decision making into collective hands. This, of course, then shifts the burden to the honor, commitment, and vigilance of the rank and file.

THE "CONSISTENCY" ISSUE

Another structural innovation introduced by The Feminists was a "quota system." Although this rather eccentric compromise was not widely imitated in the movement as a whole, the concept behind it was later to be adopted by some lesbian separatist groups. It was neither egalitarian in intent nor in effect. Spelled out in capital letters for emphasis, it appeared in a paper on "Membership Requirements and Benefits": "WE HAVE A MEMBERSHIP QUOTA: THAT NO MORE THAN ONE-THIRD OF OUR MEMBERSHIP CAN BE PARTICIPANTS IN EITHER A FORMAL (WITH LEGAL CONTRACT) OR INFORMAL (E.G., LIVING WITH A MAN) INSTANCE OF THE INSTITUTION OF MARRIAGE."[21]

This rule evolved from one of the "privileged" labors The Feminists performed: a study of marriage. There is no question but that the institution of marriage promotes female subservience and exploits women, nor that the economically dependent married woman is, whether she wishes to be or not, subject to political manipulation by the patriarchy through her husband. But all of the institutions of our society serve, more or less, that same function. No living woman earns her existence without some connection to an institution determined to keep her in subjection. This is what the women's struggle is basically all about. Attacking the *institution* of marriage is therefore one of its important and legitimate obligations, but attacking the woman who depends on it for her livelihood is not.

The Feminists engaged in an "action" to leaflet brides at the New York marriage bureau with information about the inequities of the marriage contract. By the time a woman has stepped up to the altar, she is usually in no condition to change her mind on the spot (what with pressure from relatives and, perhaps, a pregnancy), but the action did receive some publicity which, presumably, reached other women *thinking* about taking a step. Thus it was a meaningful one and not at all absurd, as it was pictured in the press.

The "quota system" adopted by The Feminists, however, betrayed a deep and serious confusion between the *institution* of marriage and the woman caught up in that institution. The implicit concept, that women should be ostracized for their involvement in institutions which oppress them, inevitably led to self-righteous attacks against women with male connections. Women, instead of the institutions which enslave us, became the enemy. Malicious gossip, encouraged as a divisive tactic among women by the patriarchy for centuries, became rampant in the women's movement itself.

In an astonishingly gentle and reasonable essay on "Man-Hating," Pamela Kearon, one of The Feminists who participated in the marriage bureau action, put her finger on the problem:

There is no dearth of hatred in the world, I agree. But the thing is, people keep on hating the wrong people. . . . Oh, I know we ought to hate the sin and love the sinner. But too often we end up loving the sinner and hating his victim (as when one woman seeing another put down, or hearing about her unhappy affair, calls it masochism and that's the end of it).

. . . If it is a choice between woman-hating and man-hating, let it be the latter.[22]

The "quota system," according to a former member of this group, represented a compromise with Ti-Grace Atkinson, who originally wanted The Feminists to be made up entirely of single women, but then had to limit her sights when it turned out that several charter members were already married or (and I think the term is appropriate in this context) "living in sin." The quota was established in August 1969; in February 1970, Atkinson began publicly to declare her own separatism: "I have separated myself off from men more decisively than any woman I know of in the Movement."[23] (This was an amazing statement, considering how many avowed lesbians there were in the movement.) A day later, she was to qualify that from the same lectern: "I, personally, have taken the position that I will not appear with any man *publicly*, where it could possibly be interpreted that we were friends."[24] (Emphasis mine.)

On March 4, 1970, speaking in Kingston, Rhode Island, she got down to cases: "The consistency issue is that there must be some consistency between a person's beliefs and its [sic] actions. Thus, since The Feminists is against marriage, we instituted a quota that no more than one third of our membership could be married. The consistency issue is at the heart of the failures of the last and of the current women's movement. There was and still is enormous resistance to the consistency issue in the Movement. But I believe it will be one of the key issues in the next couple of years."[25]

By December of the same year, her support of the

quota had escalated: "In war, even political warfare, there is no distinction between the political and the personal. (Can you imagine a Frenchman, serving in the French army from 9 A.M. to 5 P.M., then trotting 'home' to Germany for supper and overnight? That's called game-playing, or collaboration, not political commitment.)"[26]

Comments Anne Koedt:

> The original genius of the phrase "the personal is political" was that it opened up the area of women's private lives to political analysis. Before that, the isolation of women from each other had been accomplished by labeling a woman's experience "personal." Women had thus been kept from seeing their common condition as women and their common oppression by men. . . .
> . . . While it is true that there are political implications in everything a woman *qua* woman experiences, it is not therefore true that a woman's life is the political property of the women's movement. And it seems to me to show a disrespect for another woman to presume that it is in any group's (or individual's) prerogative to pass revolutionary judgment on the progress of her life.[27]

Koedt's analysis touches on the problem of female "purity" which has plagued women down through the ages and perhaps could not have been expected to be absent from our struggles for freedom. Atkinson's analogy with battles between Frenchmen and Germans unintentionally throws this form of oppression into relief.

In just about every country in the world which has suffered conquest by another nation, the women of the conquered country have been persecuted for "fraternizing" with the enemy—"fraternizing" being a euphemism for "having sexual relations." It never mattered whether the fraternization came about through a woman's own desires or was forced upon her by threatened starvation or rape.

However she came to the conqueror's bed (men have always accused women of being attracted to conquerors!), the woman was made to suffer for the man's guilt—too often at the hands of other women, "revolutionary" women. In France after World War II, French women who had "fraternized" with German soldiers were forcibly shaved.

The ultimate enactment of the slave mentality—of "sucking up" to the oppressor—is the punishment of one slave by another.

Furthermore, I *can* imagine instances similar to Atkinson's example which were perfectly acceptable to the French underground in World War II. Many Frenchmen worked for the Germans (or the puppet Vichy government) from 9 A.M. to 5 P.M. and then served the Resistance at night, bringing valuable information about the enemy from their daytime jobs. Indeed the word "sabotage" was invented by the French, and this act could not have been accomplished *except* by working for the enemy!

The assumption that a subjugated woman's loyalty to her master comes before her desire for her own freedom is the self-serving assumption of masters; the blindness it instills in those masters can be very useful to feminists. The idea that a woman can be a "spy in the house of love," to use Anaïs Nin's phrase, apparently hasn't yet captured the imagination of the women's movement.

The complexities of women's connections with men do not, however, fall within the scope of a discussion of structure and leadership. It is enough to note here that restrictions on participation by married women were built into the structure of The Feminists and fostered a distressing prejudice against women with heterosexual connections in the whole radical feminist movement for some time thereafter. The effect of such strictures on women struggling within personal relationships with men was to make many of us ashamed of ourselves again, doubt our own perceptions again, and retreat into silence, lies, and smiles. One member of The Feminists felt the need to hide the fact that she had a male lover staying at her house. A former Catholic, she was afraid of being excommunicated by The Feminists!

QUESTIONS OF INDIVIDUAL LEADERSHIP

Underlying all of the above runs a concern with the question of leadership, a question that is of greater importance now that the movement is enlarging more rapidly than it was in the early years when small radical groups were wrestling with nuances of inequality. It is important to ask whether some kind of leadership is indeed becoming necessary, and if it is not inevitable, anyway. At this point, however, I want to survey the leadership picture as it exists in the women's movement right now.

So far, except in some of the more moderate organizations such as N.O.W., the movement has, for better or worse, avoided individual leadership. Although Ti-Grace Atkinson and a number of other individuals have exerted a powerful influence, no one, by herself, has so far commanded the women's movement as, say, Martin Luther King led the black movement. This statement may raise the eyebrows of some feminists, and there is the possibility, events moving as swiftly as they do, that this will no longer be true even at the time of this book's publication! But at the present writing it is a fact, and one important to recognize—a fact, though, only if we agree about what does and what does not constitute leadership.

Many pseudoleaders have been laid on us by the patriarchy. Recently on a television news broadcast, Gloria Steinem, a ubiquitous feminist media figure (but not yet, in the strict sense, a leader), was quoted as objecting to the treatment of Rosalynn Carter in Saudi Arabia, where the First Lady was forced by the customs of that country to walk several steps behind her husband Jimmy. The media cast around for another "leader" to counteract Steinem's protest and came up with Helen Gurley Brown, editor of the reactionary women's magazine, *Cosmopolitan*, who called herself a feminist and then said that the situation in the Middle East was more important than the women's issue. The media might as well have called on Marabel Morgan.[28]

A great many feminist writers appear on television and go on lecture tours to promote their ideas and books. Those writers who are suddenly in the limelight are put there, by and large, by patriarchal publishers—by Book-of-the-Month-Club selection rather than by movement election. Although a good number of celebrated feminist writers have justly earned the respect of large portions of the women's movement, even such respect does not constitute an election to leadership.

The only way a woman can legitimately be called a feminist leader is if she holds office in a feminist political group, and *then* she can only properly be identified as a representative of that particular group. Thus, Gloria Steinem, for example, can only realistically be referred to as an editor of *Ms.* magazine and a member of whatever other organizations she belongs to.

It is clearly in the patriarchy's interest to divert, confuse, and co-opt us. To an alarming extent it has the power to do so by arbitrarily naming feminist leaders. If most feminists disclaim such designations, some "spokeswomen" do like to think of themselves that way and confuse the adulation their writings sometimes engender among feminists with a *mandate* to lead. Not infrequently these women later do, say, or write something which offends a large number of feminists and —plop!—they find themselves dumped and perhaps "trashed" into the bargain.

I hope we are arriving at a point where most feminists have learned to ignore such "media elections" and can enjoy the accomplishments of women in the limelight without giving extra weight to their opinions, either positively, or negatively, because of their celebrity. (Martin Luther King didn't just appear at civil rights benefits. He was the elected head of a bona fide civil rights organization and led vast protest marches. One didn't have to go looking for him at the MacDowell Colony!)

Feminist writers are engaged in the important work of gathering information to inform us about our history, our options, ourselves; developing feminist theory; creating works of art—the culture we so badly need. As people with political views, their work should be questioned and criticized, neither with undue adulation nor with the hope of destroying it, but with a generous appreciation of the truly difficult and, more often than not, underpaid labors they perform; with an understanding, too, of the need both the movement and they have for intelligent evaluation. It should be clearly understood that buying a book or a ticket to a lecture is not an electoral process.

In my small home library there are over one hundred volumes written or edited by feminists over the past ten years—and half as many more by earlier women writers. As I read them, I feel sudden rushes of enthusiasm and empathy, even occasional rage. I am glad, so glad, that they are there. Together these scholars and artists do say something about the movement: they say that it has genius, it is diversified, it is alive, and it is leaderless.

We have seen, then, that feminist leaders cannot be appointed by media fiat unless the movement accepts their designations. The government, also, has ways of trying to bypass our franchise. Feminists have been appointed to prestigious, if essentially powerless, government posts. This is the government's way of trying to please us without actually doing anything for us. It is a strategy to confuse and co-opt the movement. Midge Costanza, for instance, was involved in feminist politics in Rochester, New York, but even more involved in the politics of the Democratic party. She worked very hard for Jimmy Carter's election as President, and was rewarded not with a cabinet post but with a job as his personal trouble-shooter with dissident groups. Rather than acting as an intelligence agent *for the movement*, she was appointed to act as an aide to the President in squelching protest.

When dissidents were invited by her to the White House, they were encouraged to impart their grievances to her. It was all very polite. The dissidents were awed by the White House, they wore their best clothes, they felt powerful—like real citizens, like real lobbyists. Costanza listened to them, "empathized" with them, imparted their grievances to her boss.

He already knew most of those grievances. He had read his mail, witnessed the protests.

He returned a polite message through Costanza that he could or would do nothing or very little (whatever he had already planned to do) about the grievances.

The dissidents thanked Costanza. They toured the

White House, felt that they had been "received." In their fancy clothes, they may have felt too "establishment" to go back and protest out on the streets!

Costanza's job, and most other presidential appointments of women are pure public relations. If she is accepted by feminists as a leader, the President can hope to have input into feminist deliberations: he has, in effect, appointed a leader of the opposition! No wonder we see a great deal of publicity about such appointments in the patriarchal press.

On the other hand, there is no reason to question the sincerity of feminists who accept such appointments. Intent on peaceful change, women must pursue every nonviolent option available. There is always the possibility that one can influence those in power by staying close to them. It is, to be sure, a remote possibility—but nonviolent movements live on faint hopes.

The usual pattern is for a falling-out to occur between the person in power, whose aim is to forestall change, and the appointee, who wants to push for it. An early resignation is predictable, and this, of course, is what happened in the case of Midge Costanza, who resigned in August of 1978.

It would be more useful for feminists to put that energy into electing representatives to patriarchal offices rather than to urge such appointments. Elected representatives respond to blocs of voters who can swing their election. Particularly in state legislatures, where many things which directly affect women's lives are decided, favorable representatives should be backed and unfavorable ones driven from office. The "women's vote" must finally become a reality, but *real* feminist issues, not phony "law-and-order" issues (otherwise known as racism) should be the criteria. Street attackers, of course, must be stopped, but that is the routine job of the police. Politicians who promise to "crack down" usually go after so-called welfare frauds (women who take off-the-books menial jobs to survive) and prostitutes first. Real feminists who have political talent should be sought out, encouraged, and supported.

The important thing to remember is that no woman, however much she is admired and trusted by feminists, is a feminist leader unless she is chosen by feminists for leadership of a feminist organization—and then her leadership is restricted to that organization.

. . . AND OF ELITES

Let's move now from the individual leader to another potential area of domination: the elite.

In Chapter One we saw Ms. Allgood marshaling the forces of "middle-class" women to realize their own image of the feminist dream. They see, as all women may properly see, the women's movement as belonging to them. But if they are like Ms. Allgood, most of them have not sufficiently come to terms with how *they* are oppressed and by whom; they have not identified their own self-interest—that they, too, as women of a certain category have legitimate beefs against the patriarchy; that they, too, and not just minorities, lesbians, and the poor, have grievances. Because of this lack of self-knowledge, they may water down and confuse many issues of profound importance to other women. Leadership which represents everybody usually represents nobody except the leaders themselves.

In Chapter One we also saw an elite, in the correct sense of that term, foisted on us at the Houston conference by the State Department. The fact that a number of those women are respected in the women's movement makes the State Department gesture all the more dangerous to us because it invites us to keep our eyes on the puppets and not on the puppeteers. The precedent this sets is a real step toward state control of its opposition—otherwise known as *fascism*. Had the delegates at Houston (who were not elected by legitimate democratic methods, that is, at the polls) approved of a cabinet-level Department of Women, that would have been a further step toward fascism—and I am using this word with extreme care!

Fascism (in case anyone has forgotten) is a form of government which controls all segments of a society by organizing them into guilds (*fasci* in Italian). The guilds are manipulated through their leaders who are responsible to the rulers—not to the guild members. The role of the guild leaders is to pacify the factions rather than to bargain for them.

The women's commission which set up the conference at Houston was appointed by the State Department. Delegates to the conference were elected at state conventions which did not include more than a minute fraction of the women in those states. For instance, in New York, with a population of around fifteen million, only nine thousand people attended the convention in Albany. These people were not chosen by their communities but came because they had been invited by a federal appointee or because the news somehow reached them and they were able to make the trip to the state capital. The convention was not widely publicized in advance, funds for travel expenses were limited, and in any case there would hardly be room in the capital for half the state's adult population—give or take a million or so children who couldn't be left at home. As a result of similar and probably more stringent limitations in Mississippi, there were no black delegates from that state, and four people chosen as "women's" representatives were white men reputed to belong to the American Nazi party.

Can you imagine a *labor union* allowing the State Department to appoint its leaders? Can you imagine a labor union allowing nonmembers to vote for delegates to its convention — nonmembers opposed to labor unions?

It is astonishing that politically sophisticated women would press for a conference under such circumstances. The fact that many of the women on the commission have the respect of feminists and the reforms proposed at the conference were, for the most part, liberal, serves only to make a dangerous precedent dangerously acceptable.

In this instance, the women's movement gained control of the essentially undemocratic process and manipulated it to its own benefit. But such procedures are inherently fascistic. Feminists should protest conferences sponsored by the government in this way. The International Women's Year conference in Mexico City was vigorously protested and the one quixotically scheduled for Iran in 1980 will be, too.

One of the problems here is that women have a hard time comprehending the immense political significance of our own movement. Because we are voters and do, by and large, vote in patriarchal elections, we tend to think of ourselves as factional only *within* the structure; as Democrats or Republicans or, perhaps, Socialists. We do not yet fully appreciate ourselves as a separate interest bloc, comparable to labor unions. In fact, we are the largest interest bloc in the nation!

QUESTIONS ABOUT NETWORKS

Although government appointment of movement "leaders" presents the most obvious danger of a fascist takeover, the tendency toward structurelessness of many new feminist networks can also present serious problems. As early as 1972, Joreen warned feminists:

Correctly, an elite refers to a small group of people who have power over a larger group of which they are a part, usually without direct responsibility to that larger group, and often without their knowledge or consent. . . .

The inevitably elitist and exclusive nature of informal communication networks of friends is neither a new phenomenon characteristic of the women's movement nor a phenomenon new to women. Such informal networks have excluded women for centuries from participating in integrated groups of which they were a part.[29]

However, Joreen does go on to point out that elites are not usually conspiracies but a few friends who work well together and often innocently come to dominate the group. So what then is so alarming about elites? They are just a bunch of old friends who enjoy working together on political projects.

As long as they function in small, one might call them "amateur," groups, they are just cliques and not very dangerous at all—though perhaps annoying to those who are outside and have trouble circumventing them. But when the groups of which they are a part begin to gain power and have patronage at their disposal, grave problems can arise if one must go to the elite for *approval* of projects in order to assure their success.

The whole network concept deserves intensive reevaluation. For one thing, the term "network" has become a fashionable catchall for any group of women who support each other within the patriarchy. It is so overused that by the time you read this it will probably sound dated, even if the reality it was intended to convey still exists. The network idea was suggested by studies of male bonding: the way men connect with each other to support their collective political power.

Some feminist writers—among them Phyllis Chesler and Lois Gould—have expressed admiration and/or envy of male network strategy. Chesler's admiration appeared in a kind of wistful comment in *About Men*:

> In truth, when I hear of a man forgiving another man for injuring him; when I hear of a man redeeming another man's mistakes for him; when I hear of men putting aside their "differences," even temporarily, to gain a common "good"; when I hear of father surrogates teaching and protecting younger male apprentices; when I hear the lovingly insane roar of male spectators for male athletes or "heroes" of any sort; when I hear men praising other men for their good work or goodwill; when I hear men mourning the misfortune of other men—then, then I burn with shame. I blush with envy. I covet men's sense of their own power, their education, their common sense, their allegiance to self-interest—because it allows them, sometimes, to take those risks and losses that make for solidarity, at whatever price, with others of their own sex.[30]

But in *Women, Money, and Power*, Chesler and her coauthor, Emily Jane Goodman, express a full awareness of how male business and professional networks *exclude* the majority of *men*. While in the paragraph from *About Men*, Chesler sentimentalizes the joining together, the rest of *About Men* is nothing less than an exposé of the negative side of male bonding. Certainly Chesler would have us imitate the positive side of "brotherhood," to use it to unite use against the patriarchy. But she would not advocate the exclusion of the majority of women from important positions, which *could happen* if feminist networks really copied their male counterparts.

Lois Gould does not speak of excluding other women either. On the contrary, she proposes that we set out to attract women of the right to our movement through projects they might support (presumably by deemphasizing those aspects of feminism—sexual preference and reproductive self-determination—which they find an anathema). She writes in *The New York Times*:

The night after that meeting, I saw "Godfather II" on Home Box Office, and also read a book called "The Managerial Woman." Both were filled with the sobering images of determined men getting where they want by doing business with their sworn enemies—or else. Ethnic-slurring U.S. Senators and proud Mafia dons. Pragmatic industrialists and greedy military dictators. Big wheelers and dirty dealers . . . a riveting photograph of the essential amorality that supports the American dream twins, "Family" and "Winning."
Feminists are hardly godfathers (or mothers) in training; nor do we want to be. But we do want power; we do want to win. And we do need to be aware of what it takes. . . .
Something to do with tolerating, putting up with, and using, the people one can't stand.[31]

This observation reflects the desperation of many women in relation to the male power they see exhibited so unapologetically around them. Of course, as Phyllis Chesler was to remark to me in conversation, you can't *act* like the Mafia unless you *are* the Mafia, that is, have guns. And whom are the guns of organized crime directed at? Not the government. They are directed at underlings, to keep them in line—to keep them working as prostitutes, drug pushers, hoods. However indirectly, they are ultimately pointed at women.

Gould neglects to mention that the people we would be "tolerating" would be those who are trying to stop us and who, at the moment, own all the guns. We would be "tolerating" ourselves into submission.

Later in her article, Gould says, "So if a woman who was against the ERA, against abortion, against homosexual rights walked into that roomful of feminists and said, 'I'm with you on rape, child abuse and pornography; what can I do to help?' could we really afford to cut her dead? I don't think so."

One woman? No, there would be no need to cut *her* dead. Unless she came in bringing money from Right to Life and said we couldn't have it without abandoning proabortion policies, or money from Save Our Children with the stipulation that we must stop supporting lesbian rights. Then we might tell her she had entered the wrong door.

Of course we want to attract women of the right to feminism, but involving them in feminist projects by soft-pedaling basic feminist goals can lead to trouble. A better way would be to set up a network of battered wives' shelters. It is hard for me to believe that men who belong to the American Nazi party, the Ku Klux Klan, and/or the National Rifle Association are gentle husbands. When their wives find a way to leave them, those women will gain the courage to struggle for their own rights to control their bodies, their minds, their souls. When they discover that their self-interest as women is not served by right-wing ideology, they will change their political perspective as so many women formerly attached to the male left have. In this way we would not be manipulating women of the right, but simply making it possible for them to join us if they so choose.

Feminism does not have to compromise its basic principles: not to obtain concessions from the government, not to attract new women, not even to collect money. Our principle of complete self-determination for women is understood in the gut of every woman. Every woman will respond when she is able—in her own time. For those of us who are already committed to feminism, our job is clear. We have no right to intimidate women or trick them into joining us; we have only to make such joining possible.

Few nonviolent means which have a good prognosis for early success are available to the powerless. Comprising 53 percent of the population, women feel that power should, by right of numbers alone in a society of majority rule, *belong* to us. We feel it lies just outside our grasp. As in a nightmare, it seems to evaporate each time we reach out for it.

But a close examination of the way networks operate for men should make us wary of using this strategy to overturn male hegemony. Men bribe each other, blackmail each other, exploit each other to get ahead. Those at the top may even kill those below to prevent them from encroaching. The male hierarchy works like a pyramid club, with those on the bottom destined to lose out. To insure the allegiance of men on the bottom, the ruling class supports the privilege of all men, including working-class men, to possess and oppress women. What would women on the top have to do to insure the allegiance of women at the bottom?

Because there are so few women anywhere near the top at the present time, the inerent dangers of networks may seem minimal. But the networking process has already affected women in negative as well as positive ways.

It is fine to make a telephone call to a business for cooperation with some struggling feminist enterprise and hear a woman's voice answering where one had expected a man's. It is even finer when the answer is an enthusiastic "yes." This has begun to happen as women who have risen to executive positions, in part because of the movement, recognize their obligation to help others. In *The Jewish Woman in America*, the authors point out that, starting at the turn of the century, Jews who had established themselves economically in this country were able to help two-thirds of their immigrant brothers and sisters escape poverty within one generation. Additionally, Jewish-American women virtually eliminated prostitution among female coreligionists.[32]

But less than 3 percent of the population is Jewish, and so the entrance of Jewish immigrants into the labor market, especially in the early 1900s, was statistically negligible. Similar strategies attempted more recently by "black capitalists" have been less successful, in part because black people make up more than 20 percent of the population. Women, who comprise a majority, are likely to run into even heavier opposition. The "yeses" some of us receive from female executives with a delicious note of joy and complicity in their voices may, not very far off in the future, turn to "noes" as more and more women demand advancement. We are already beginning to see ugly pressure exerted by some women on the way up, and even uglier patronage behavior among some women who are in a position to help. As women attempt to advance in the economic hierarchy, real trust diminishes. Bonding becomes the antithesis of sisterhood. And as rivalry for the dollar increases, professional and business networks begin to exclude "upstarts." Where money is involved, the temptation of corruption is always present.

THE HEART OF THE MATTER

Problems of structure and leadership reach into the heart of feminist analysis. From the start, radical feminists have been dissatisfied with all the forms men have invented to cross the barriers of self into cooperation. The prototype is the army, and every patriarchal organization is somehow a regiment or a corps in the never-ending warfare of "peaceful" male competition. Even the marital relationship, the family, is a self-protective unit with all the organizational forms. One way or another, whether we are female or male, we are organized to protect ourselves against marauding males. Men ally with each other and subordinate women to them *against* other men. Without people to be seen as "the enemy," male bonding would cease to exist.

But these rigidities are not only the result of xenophobia; they help to produce and reinforce it. We tell ourselves the goal is to win, to survive—and in the end we lose, we die, without much life in between.

Unfortunately, women are at war, too. We are in the early stages of an immense revolution. For many of us, the deepest hope is that unification itself will accomplish the changes we seek—that we will never find it necessary to arm. The means we use are all-important, because we seek not only equality but also an end to the whole competitive nightmare.

And so we look for nonviolent ways to subsume the superstructure and remake it according to a more nurturing, generous, inclusive design. Our horror of the military and its consequences makes some of us shy away from overtly hierarchical forms. We recognize in those forms the visage of man—his ruthless domination over the planet and all the "things" on it, among which women are included. We recognize that man's ends and means are ultimately consistent, even when he chooses nonviolence. He refuses to see that underneath his aims to change the status quo there remains a determination to continue possessing women. This is never more clearly revealed than when men use the First Amendment to the Constitution to protect the institution of pornography, which debases and endangers women, rather than search for a means to reinterpret freedom of expression so that both it and women's civil rights can be secured.

While we realize that the goals of men are not our goals, and that means do determine ends—we know only those revolutionary means that we have learned from men. Often, we have learned their ways by struggling alongside them. We refine this knowledge by adding to it the manipulating and maneuvering tactics we have learned as slaves. Altogether, this seems a self-defeating and morally repugnant way of achieving the decent, peaceful, collective, nurturing goals most feminists desire.

Some of us are ashamed to emulate any known structures. Our "fear of success," derided by proponents of assertiveness at any price, is more than the fear of its known consequences for women in the patriarchy: envy, exploitation, debasement. We also fear *becoming like men*. We have seen so many male revolutions simply replace one set of tyrants with another. We fear ourselves becoming tyrants; even a slight acquaintance with patriarchal history informs us this fear is rational.

But we cannot, we will not, remain slaves.

Perhaps the new forms we seek require a deeper analysis than we have yet been able to attempt. To sophisticated and struggle-weary feminists, the suggestion that we return to consciousness-raising may seem naive—but it appears to this veteran, at least, that we have not yet formulated the right questions. As we experiment with bonding, networks, alternative spaces, we should continue to examine the effects of these trials on ourselves, both individually and collectively. There is no better method than the empirical one of consciousness-raising. Unfortunately, however, the rivalries imposed on us as we elbow our way into the patriarchal structure cause us to trust each other less and to retreat into a new kind of isolation.

There is a reason, we learn, why men shut themselves off emotionally from one another, why they deride the confessional mode: were they to expose their true feelings to one another across their class barriers, the whole hierarchy would disintegrate.

In Part Two of this book, I will analyze further certain problems women face trying to survive and advance within the patriarchy. My hope is to arrive at some different approaches to make the goal of sisterhood more possible and to help bring about the profound changes radical feminists originally set out to achieve.

CHAPTER FOUR

The Lesbian Revolution: Lilith and Eve

"women who love men
stare through glass walls
at the miracle of woman and woman,
the richness of possibility
they long
for that most sensible of longings,
and touch their bodies
only in themselves." — Karen Lindsey[1]

"Being a lesbian means to me that there is an erotic passion and intimacy which comes of touch and taste, a wild, salty tenderness, a wet sweet sweat, our breasts, our mouths, our cunts, our intertangled hairs, our hands. I am speaking here of a sensual passion as deep and mysterious as the sea, as strong and still as the mountain, as insistent and changing as the wind." — Andrea Dworkin[2]

In her foreword to *The Lesbian: A Celebration of Difference* by Bernice Goodman, Adrienne Rich says: "One current and cruel cliché of the homophobe is the statement that, after all, today it's perfectly tolerable, even chic, to be 'bisexual' or 'gay.' It erroneously assumes the lesbian experience to be more or less identical with that of the male homosexual, and it reduces the lesbian, like the male homosexual, to the mere follower of a 'lifestyle,' thus erasing both the pain of her oppression and her political significance in the patriarchy.

"In no profession, least of all the profession of motherhood, is it chic to be 'gay.' "[3]

Rich's statement is tragically true, particularly in terms of motherhood and the archaic laws which allow a man, who may with impunity bed processions of women within earshot of his custodial children, to wrest these children from a mother who lives in a stable, loving relationship with another woman. But this truth, let us hope, is a temporary reality. The care all women are forced, by men's hypocrisy, to use in selecting lovers; the political Sturm und Drang which today attends such choices and makes us view each attachment as a potentially permanent "commitment"—these must eventually become obsolete. In the future we may not need to place so much emphasis on living two-by two; women and men molded by our efforts now may become so trustworthy and love-worthy en masse as to lighten the burden of choosing. A certain frivolity, playfulness—even chic—may then be permissible, even desirable, for women as well as men. But this is Eden I am thinking of, the garden of Lilith and Eve—the postpatriarchal world.

Irreverently, perhaps, my thoughts embrace the illusion of "lesbian chic," because I have been reading about the women artists and writers who lived in Paris in the early part of this century. It is hard to restrain a perhaps frivolous envy of their "chic" (what other word for it?) salons and soirées. To the outsider, distanced by more than time, whose imagination has been fed by Colette and Gertrude Stein and art nouveau, it seems that the very secrecy of their love affairs imparted a glamor to them. It is inconceivable that those dazzling women ever gave a fig for what other people thought, that their dash and snobbery might have covered a desire for openness and respectability, a jejune fear of rejection. And yet, too many went mad or killed themselves or barely survived their private nightmares: we know of the books not published, the manuscripts not risked out of the desk drawer, the words withheld from consciousness. But the works they did publish—they and many who went before, the "spinsters" whose secret loves we know nothing of—are worthy of our admiration and even, perhaps, nostalgia.

But ours is an age of open wounds. In the hope of a new healing, in the indignant demand for it, we all—whatever the source of our pain—expose our stigmata to the world's gaze. Subtlety gives way to the "unvarnished" truth, which in turn makes possible a new complexity. This is no time to look back at the drawing room with its velvet curtains hiding a multitude of imagined sins. This is the time of plate-glass windows and floodlights in the operating room.

Today the cries and the even more daring laughter of lesbians, so long suppressed, have opened a world of suffering and wonder. At once I empathize with the pain of exclusion (not hard: the exclusion of women is so universal, comes in so many forms) and am invited to the pleasures of love, to marry politics and sensuality. "The richness of possibility," as Karen Lindsey put it.

Possible . . . and yet not possible . . . not always.

At what age was the ability to desire a woman snuffed out of my mind? At twelve, when I was told I shouldn't have a crush on a girl in my class who imitated Frank Sinatra (circa 1943)? Some years later when I admitted to my analyst a fascination with breasts, and he said I should concentrate on my problems with men? (*My* problems.) How much more rich my fantasy life might have been had it encompassed those (also devoutly heterosexual) young women who were my dearest friends, to whom I confided everything, to whom I couldn't wait to return after a "romantic" encounter with a man for a night of erotic storytelling.

I suppose it is necessary for me to confess this here after womanning the barricades of heterosexuality so long: I am not immune to the deliciousness, the cuddliness of women — to my own charms. I have, when younger, stood in front of the mirror proud, not only of what men might see and admire (that, too) but of my own beauty to *myself*. My plump little body all smooth and soft down to the modest apron of pubic hair.

The world of possibility opens my imagination. Recently I had an erotic dream about a woman, the first brought to consciousness, far away from home. Not long ago I would have regarded such a dream as a nightmare and rushed to a therapist for salvation. Now I know, and believe, that my monosexuality has been a limitation. But my body ages and the world of possibility shrinks, becomes an abstraction, a fantasy world more useful to my work than to my life.

I have made a good life within the confines of what was expected of me, and have found good people to share it. Since lesbianism is not a matter of chic, as Rich rightly points out, but a profound commitment subjecting those involved to a particular kind of oppression, it is not an alternative at the moment to be played at lightly. Those tentative yearnings, so brutally ruled out in my adolescence, must remain untested since my commitment lies elsewhere. I come to this discussion as a sister, but not as a participant. I come to understand, to empathize — and also to communicate my own struggle in the world where I am vulnerable to many of the same forces that oppress lesbians; and within the women's movement, where I must maintain my own right to be and to make my own choices.

About these choices of whom to love and live with — not

always within our complete control, not always deliberate—there has been serious conflict. I think in the beginning that conflict was unavoidable and even healthy. But now it is time to begin to resolve it if we can.

Adrienne Rich says that it is particularly unchic to be a lesbian mother. For such a woman, the veil which usually cloaks lesbians in invisibility, often against their will since it serves to negate their very existence, suddenly lifts in the compromising glare of the courtroom. She faces having her child stolen from her on the grounds that she is an "unfit" mother, immoral, the carrier of a plague which can infect the young. A heterosexual woman can also face such charges and such consequences—the difference being only that she is called a "whore." Even in this age of liberalized sexuality, having a baby out of wedlock is debasing, at the very least. But the ultimate irony is that married women who have children are also penalized. Woven around this "good" woman is a net of conformity from which she dare not escape and which may strangle her whole human potentiality.

And so we come to understand that in this society all of the choices women make, or are forced to make, are fraught with danger. None of us is a winner. We have more in common than that which divides us.

THE POLITICAL SIGNIFICANCE
OF LESBIANISM

If the mother who is a lesbian is not uniquely oppressed, then let us consider her "political significance in the patriarchy." Here we do indeed find a unique effect.

Far more than a woman who leaves her husband for another man, the lesbian mother poses a threat to male hegemony. The father of the child (or children) feels he has been used as a stud. He cannot accept that he might be used for breeding purposes only, though women have been used that way by men time and time again, when we weren't even less valued.

So the political significance of the lesbian mother in the patriarchy—the political significance of the *lesbian* (mother or not)—is first of all that she undermines the notion that the penis is essential to a woman other than for purposes of reproduction. This tells men that women can be self-sufficient in all ways, including our sexuality. Such knowledge banishes him from his assured place in the world of nurturance, a world he has outwardly despised but which, in truth, supplies him with his very reason for being. The lesbian appropriates to herself and, by implication, to other women, complete jurisdiction over her own life and production.

While fathers are permitted to abandon children at will, mothers cannot do so without putting themselves in legal jeopardy. And yet, when a mother *takes her children with her* to another home she shares with a woman, men—and the courts run by men—are enraged. She has not only declared her own self-sufficiency: she has enunciated a basis for matriarchy. She imparts the message to other women: "Children belong *by nature* to the mother. The role of the father exists by our sufferance alone." The future can, it is implied, belong to women. Boy children as well as girl children can be raised according to the will of the mother. The father image, so beloved by psychologists, in most cases only serves to propagate the artificial differences between the sexes which support the patriarchy. The fear is that both boys and girls might grow up like their mothers!

Such a consequence might mean the end of manhood as we know it now, the end of rape and degradation of women, the end of escalating violence, the end of oppression. For if women can foster the values necessary for a wholesome adaptation to the modern world, the qualities most likely to turn technology to the benefit of people, and the behavior of men toward women which would make us comfortable with one another, we could develop ways of raising children that might, in a few generations, end our fearsome struggle. Removing children from the traditional "father image" could help to bring about that end.

But for a variety of reasons, such a solution on a wide scale would not be possible nor, even, realistically, desirable. The force needed to exclude men entirely from contact with women and children would turn us, who used it, into manlike monsters. (I wanted to say that men totally bereft of women and children would lose complete control of themselves, but it would be hard to imagine them more mismanaged than they already are!) Furthermore, the massiveness of such a solution is fascistic: it fails to take into account those individuals among men who are more highly developed than the rest, and those men we simply love. I do not like the philosophical injunction that what seems morally right for one person must be imaginatively extended to include everyone in order to determine its moral validity. This is patriarchal thinking in its most authoritarian form. If some women remove their children from unwholesome fathers and develop new ways of raising them which can serve as models for other women to learn from, even within the presence of men, that is a valuable beginning of change. It is not necessary to extend this, or any other "trend," to its extreme.

But men *do* think in terms of sweeping revolutions. The idea of a few alterations to the status quo made here and there fills them with terror, because they project their own imperialistic animus onto them: any change may signify total upheaval. The thought of turning boys into "sissies" appalls them. Always, *always* they are dogged with a fear of being "unmanned." Rather than such an eventuality, it is clear from their present behavior that they would destroy the planet. And so, the "unmanning" of boy children is the second threat lesbian mothers present to the patriarchy.

There is a third way in which the existence of women who choose to live with other women exerts a significant political influence. Lesbians, particularly women who have lived with men and *left* them for women, force heterosexual men to reconsider their own sexuality. If women can be inherently bisexual, then might men be as well?

Such a thought turns the world upside down for a heterosexual man, for he has carefully kept it divided into two kinds of people: those who ejaculate semen, and those who ingest it.

A man's first ejaculation takes him by surprise, even if he has been taught to expect it. Often it happens during the night, and he wakes up in a wet bed. It comes, he observes, from the same orifice as urine—a despised waste product. He has been carefully trained as a child, moreover, to control his urine, to feel shamed if he cannot.

In the same drastic way, he learns to control his ejaculations of semen, though here his control is less reliable. By any psychological reasoning it follows that men must identify semen as a waste product. (Their very glorification of it in religion would imply a motive of overcompensation.) The person into whom it is ejaculated, then, must somehow be befouled. Women, we know, are thought to be masochistic: they ingest men's waste products.[4] We know also that men do not consider a man to be homosexual if he only *ejaculates* semen into another man. He must *ingest* it to be given that title.

Therefore, to the heterosexual man, homosexuality means the willingness to ingest another man's waste product—a demeaning position to be in on the heterosexual man's scale of values. The thought that he, himself, might harbor such a potentiality, perhaps even such a *desire*, cannot but be extremely threatening.

And just such a thought must present itself to a man whose female lover leaves him for a woman. In this way, the lesbian unbalances heterosexual men even further.

But the ultimate political significance of lesbianism is not to the patriarchy at all, but to the woman, herself. It is for freedom, for pleasure, for love that she chooses women, as Andrea Dworkin indicates in the quotation at the beginning of this chapter. There is the very greatest political significance in the happiness of a woman.

THE PRESSURE FOR SEPARATISM

Many radical feminists seized onto lesbianism almost by instinct as the ultimate means for self-determination. This was one of the organic changes to come about, for many women, through conciousness-raising. They thought, primarily, of its potential for liberating themselves on an individual basis. In a sense, lesbianism was chosen as a personal solution. But the logic that attends the concept that the personal is political leads inevitably to the conclusion that choosing lesbianism on a massive basis would move all women toward greater freedom.

Without stating this logic, and without even understanding it fully, some feminists began exerting psychological pressure on other feminists to become lesbians. Many of the women who were most zealous as missionaries were newly converted themselves. It is not surprising that they wanted to share their new happiness with other feminists, or that, in their neophyte enthusiasm, they felt they had found the only politically viable way of life.

In January of 1971, Ti-Grace Atkinson drew up a very elaborate game plan for the women's movement[5] which she delivered in a speech to the Daughters of Bilitis, a prefeminist lesbian organization. In it she described lesbians as a "buffer group" between the oppressor (men) and the oppressed (the totality of women). Employing an opaque, quasi-military jargon which seems at times to have proved impenetrable even to *her*, she defines the "buffer" group as a "criminal" element: "Individuals within the 'criminal' element are permitted a certain edge of power above the individuals within its [sic] original class (the Oppressed). This 'edge' takes the form of greater freedom of movement, money, general independence."[6]

How this applies to lesbians is difficult to imagine. Is she suggesting that lesbians have greater freedom and more money than other women? Or is she simply trying to guilt-trip them into taking a more active part in the women's movement?

Guilt-tripping is certainly one of the techniques Atkinson used over the years to enlist support for various schemes. At Catholic University for instance, where she courageously lambasted the Church for its misogyny, she included the laiety, female as well as male, in her attack: "In any society remotely resembling a democracy, every individual is responsible for acts committed in its name. Thus, in any given case, one is an accomplice or a revolutionary. Blood on one's hands or blood on one's head."[7]

Within minutes of this remark, a woman in the audience advanced to the stage and struck her. (A photograph of this occurrence appears in *Amazon Odyssey*.)

The reaction of liberals to guilt-tripping is often to accept the guilt without considering whether or not they are truly culpable. Indictment by a self-annointed "revolutionary" is sufficient condemnation. Men like Stokely Carmichael, H. Rap Brown, and Eldridge Cleaver of the black civil rights movement used guilt-tripping most effectively—particularly on white women. (We should all know by now, white women are virtual sponges for guilt earned by white men. This is one of our primary functions as relations, however poor, of the ruling class.)

When Atkinson spoke to the Daughters of Bilitis, she attacked lesbians as collaborators with the oppressor:

As an early witness in the Women's Movement . . . I now know that the greatest counterrevolutionary force *within* this early women's movement were the lesbians within it. These women didn't identify themselves, then, as lesbians, but they have since. And I can't tell you how astounded I was to find that, instead of being *for* women, they were the most reactionary on feminism. And in inter-movement struggles, they fought—quite literally—*alongside* the men and for their interests.[8]

The point of this speech, it later developed, was to enlist D.O.B. members into the front lines of the revolution she was proposing. As far as I can make out, Atkinson advocated drawing on lesbians for "leadership" of the movement once they became politicized. (Identifying consciousness-raising as the "most virulent expression" of movement cowardice, she did not explain how she hoped to politicize lesbians without it.)

Atkinson used a great many charts to demonstrate her strategy for victory. In them, various elements of society evolve from "anti-rebellion" to "neutral" to "pro-rebel-lion" to "buffer"—all of them confronting the oppressor class until eventually the oppressor is somehow absorbed into the rebellion. It is an extraordinarily confusing document, enough so to make one wonder if its confusion was perhaps intentional; perhaps by it Atkinson hoped to intimidate women into accepting her conclusions as a way of hiding their "ignorance." After all, Atkinson had studied philosophy at Columbia. How many other women could boast such erudition?

At the end of her speech, Atkinson again tried to jog the organization into action with a characteristic attack:

> This center is one of the few respectable contributions to the Women's Movement in the last four years of this fucking movement. And, essentially, only four people made it: Ruth Simpson, Ellen Povill, Eileen Webb and Becky Irons.
>
> *Now*, what are the rest of *you* going to do? I'm not interested in why you *can't* do this or that. All I know is, if you're not carrying your own share of the load, you're adding to mine. And I'm sick of it. And I'm *un*loading. I'm cleaning house.[9]

In a footnote, Atkinson informs us about the fate of one of the women she mentioned above: "Ruth Simpson was forced out as President in May, 1971. . . . After the final meeting, Ruth's opposition left behind 'maps' of their strategy to oust her. Much to my chagrin, I saw the fruits of my 'chart' dedication speech. I was the first, and only, influence I know these charts have had, thus far."[10]

It is doubtful that D.O.B. would have found Atkinson's charts either useful or necessary to vote a woman out of office, but manipulation of lesbians was a clear compo-nent of the plan she had proposed. It is no wonder the D.O.B. were alienated. Their function, after all, was to *support* lesbians, not to exploit them.

At the same time, Atkinson's strategy called for non-lesbian feminists to identify with lesbians:

One minuscule suggestion, as a contribution in this direction, would be if all feminists began wearing buttons reading "I am a lesbian." This could be a way of coopting the enemy's strategy. It's not unlike the tactic of the Danish king against the Germans during World War II. When the king rode out one morning wearing the Star of David, and most Danes followed suit, the effect was to frustrate the Nazi identification of Jews in that area.[11]

Many nonlesbians were willing to undertake this kind of support, both as a gesture of solidarity with lesbians as an oppressed group and as a way of rendering ineffectual the lesbian baiting all feminists are, in any case, subjected to by antifeminists. But right here, with this gesture, confusion began. Lesbians who were not aware that feminists were making a political commitment in this verbal identification suddenly found a whole bunch of "straight" women calling themselves lesbians and continuing to live, and have sexual relations, with men! It may have seemed to many lesbians that this "heroic" gesture was making a mockery of their lives. Very soon they exerted pressure for these feminists to *prove* they were lesbians, not merely to say so.

At the same time lesbians were developing group pride on their own and becoming more and more involved as feminists. Many were beginning to consider themselves the only *real* feminists, because they had early on "seen" through the oppression of men, "almost instinctively." Barbara Deming was to say in her afterword to *Thinking Like a Woman*:

An inner voice has always warned me not to commit my life into any man's hands—warned me to resist the attraction I felt or to be lost to myself, physically overborne . . . A lesbian, I would suggest, is a woman who . . . cannot feel at ease with herself while worshipping The Male. At least at such close quarters. I do think that lesbians have been in a real sense a feminist avant garde, but our refusal to worship The Male has of course been far from complete. We too have placed incense upon that altar. But, as I say, we haven't felt able to at close quarters; have found it disturbing to our deepest sense of ourselves to intimately join our lives with those of "gods." Or let me put it in a positive rather than a negative way: we have been better able to find ourselves by joining our lives with those of other mortals knowing themselves to be mortals — other women.[12]

Deming was by no means one of those who consciously pressured heterosexuals into changing their lives. I quote her only to demonstrate that the Precocious Political Awareness theory was widespread as an adjunct to growing lesbian pride. The effect was to make heterosexual feminists feel stupid by comparison. Women who have been radicals in political movements for many years don't like to be locked out of the "avant-garde." Those who did not, for any number of reasons, opt for lesbianism, on feeling like pariahs in the radical end of their own movement, simply lied or returned to reticence about their personal lives. Lesbians who maintained close nonsexual attachments with men felt pressured to do likewise.

This pressure actually began several years before Atkinson's statement to the Daughters of Bilitis. Anne Koedt delivered a paper at a feminist conference in Chicago in 1968 which might well be called the *feminist* shot heard round the world. It was entitled "The Myth of the Vaginal Orgasm."[13] It drew on the well-known studies made by Kinsey and by Masters and Johnson, and also on a Danish work by Mette Ejlerson called *I Accuse*, in which Ejlerson relates the personal stories of many women who grappled with their "inability" to achieve a "vaginal orgasm" with men. Ejlerson refers to their charades — faked orgasms, trips to psychiatrists to get "cured," and so on—as the "sexual comedy," and certainly these procrustean efforts were, though painful, the stuff of farce. The Victorian woman who wasn't expected to enjoy sex at all could be envied by the "swinging" twentieth-century Scandinavian woman who had to play "alive" in the all-but-paralyzing Missionary Position.

Koedt comments: "Lesbian sexuality could make an excellent case, based upon anatomical data, for the irrelevancy of the male organ."[14]

The conclusion to her paper leaves room for choice, however: "The recognition of clitoral orgasm as fact would threaten the heterosexual *institution*. For it would indicate that sexual pleasure was obtainable from either men *or* women, thus making heterosexuality not an absolute, but an option. It would thus open up the whole question of *human* sexual relationships beyond the confines of the present male-female role system."[15] (Emphasis Koedt's.)

This paper was published in 1970 and it was widely discussed at feminist meetings and in consciousness-raising groups. It had a very liberating effect on feminist attitudes toward sexuality. Supportive to those who already were lesbians, it left the way open for other women to experiment with bisexuality, to demand more varied sexual practices with their male lovers, or to leave men altogether and pursue erotic happiness with women. But there is no indication in her paper that Koedt envisioned massive changes in society to occur through a widespread turn to lesbianism.

We have seen in Chapter Two that The Feminists restricted the number of "married" members of their group and how Radicalesbians forced awareness of the existing lesbian presence at the Congress to Unite Women. Radicalesbians also produced a propaganda paper, "The

Woman-Identified-Woman," which posits lesbians as a kind of natural elite in the movement. It starts out with a definition of the lesbian: "She is the woman who, often beginning at an extremely early age, acts in accordance with her inner compulsion to be a more complete and freer human being than her society—perhaps then, but certainly later—cares to allow her."[16]

This definition could apply to any woman who, as a child, preferred chemistry sets to dolls, came home dirty from climbing trees, or despised "party dresses." It coyly avoids the issue of sexual preference, and sets up an image of the lesbian-as-rebel. Of course, one of the reasons why lesbians have been "invisible" is that so many don't conform to this stereotype at all. There are nurses, ballerinas, and models who are lesbians; doctors, engineers, and mountain climbers who are not.

It goes on to describe the miseries such a young woman faces in society, and then arrives at the following conclusion:

> To the extent that she cannot expel the heavy socialization that goes with being female, she can never truly find peace with herself. For she is caught somewhere between accepting society's view of her—in which case she cannot accept herself—and coming to understand what this sexist society has done to her and why it is functional and necessary for it to do so. Those of us who work that through find ourselves on the other side of a tortuous journey through a night that may have been decades long. The perspective gained from that journey, the liberation of self, the *inner peace*, the real love of self and of all women, is something to be shared with all women—because we are all women.[17] (Emphasis mine.)

There is in this paragraph a true feeling of the pain of being excommunicated from a society which declares only heterosexuals "normal," and which worships nor-

mality. *Of course* in rejecting lesbians the society is re-
pressing its own potential for omnisexuality. Reminding
us of that potential—and not to be afraid of it—is a great
gift to all women.

But then the issues begin to muddy. The paper speaks
of lesbians achieving "inner peace." It is one thing to
come to terms with one's oppression: that is the beginning
of the struggle. Achieving inner peace, however, surrounded by this society as it is, is a conformist rather than
a revolutionary goal. It is impossible, unless one resigns
oneself to all the other horrors of the society.

Americans dearly love the notion of "inner peace,"
and "inner peace" salespeople abound. Young people of
the late sixties and early seventies returned to the land
for it, became vegetarians for it, took up with Jesus and
the Mahara Ji for it. We all want a light to shine in our
eyes, even in the midst of universal desperation. Those
who claim to have found it, though, usually look glassy-
eyed.

Even under the best of circumstances within this society, relationships of all kinds involve struggle. Being acceptable doesn't confer inner peace on heterosexual wom-
en, or even on men, nor does an adjustment to one's
own nonconformist tendencies insure more than a kind of
resignation. Nirvana, except at odd and ephemeral
moments, is a chimera held out to all of us, as much by
cosmetics hucksters as by religious charlatans. It is the
essential teaser in advertising and, as any guru will tell
you, it cannot be found by searching for it! People who
want to bring about change would do well to cherish their
inner *turmoil*, for that is the force that presses us on to
attaining *universal* peace. This is not to say that one
should not court personal happiness. Of course we
should—and will, in any case. It is just that we should not

really *believe* in it, and might do well to value also—and *use*—the other states we find ourselves in.

Suggesting that lesbianism was the only way to inner peace became an important propaganda tactic. Now heterosexual feminists were told they were not only politically incorrect and that they had been dullards as children, but that they had missed out on finding "peace of mind"! All the propaganda techniques were employed—everything but the real radical truth of the matter: that a massive turn to lesbianism *can* undermine the patriarchy and help to achieve the attainment of our rights. To deny that this is a strategy directed at men misleads all women, including lesbians. There is no inner peace in lying about oneself in order to be included in an avantgarde elite, and there is no inner peace in becoming a lesbian and finding that the woman you live with is nearly as impossible as the man you gave up. Furthermore, there is no "inner peace" for a lesbian brought into the women's liberation movement under false pretenses (as a response to Ti-Grace Atkinson's manipulation). Denying that the aim of a mass walkout on men is a strategy to bring the patriarchy to heel won't fool men as much as it will confound us. One wonders in what low esteem women who used such hucksterism held their "sisters' " mental capabilities.

Separatist pressure was to grow even greater: in 1971, a year after "The Woman-Identified-Woman" was published, another polemic, "Realesbians and Politicalesbians," was written by a group calling themselves the Gay Revolutionary Party Women's Caucus. Much of this essay simply parrots the earlier one, but it goes on to spell out separatist dissatisfactions with the "political lesbian" (the woman who calls herself a lesbian to express her support for lesbian freedom):

Other women have not only stopped relating to men in a fairly comprehensive way but consider themselves politicalesbians. This means that their full commitment as they see it is to women and the movement, but most of them do not have sexual relations with their sisters. Within this group are found women who are interested in having a "lesbian experience" or who consider themselves bisexual. Another segment among the politicalesbians are women who quite sincerely want to become gay feminists but feel that only a realesbian can bring them out. . . .

This is the most oppressive of all women's movement routines to the gay feminist, who is personally diminished (to the state of "manhood") and sexually objectified. In the process, the lesbian is required to function in a service role, that of the "butch." Sexual initiative on the part of a woman does not result in direct physical gratification, as it does in a man. The equation, therefore, of "butch" and male is false. In this relation the lesbian is oppressed by the straight-defined woman in the same way that women are oppressed by straight men. Very often after this false lesbian experience, women return to straight men and to privilege without having developed self-definition or gay pride. In the end, to them, women are an *alternative* to men.[18] (Emphasis theirs.)

Here again we hear real pain, if little logic. Included, too, is a generalization about the sexuality of both women and men which betrays a certain ignorance. Seldom do people of either sex achieve "physical gratification" through taking the initiative, but members of both sexes may be *turned on* by the challenge to conquer. Furthermore, to say that the one in the agressive role is "objectified" would indicate that heterosexual women, by accepting the passive role in traditional heterosexual relationships, are "objectifying" men! Such a statement contains the germ of a whole new feminist theory and should be developed!

The pain in the aggressor role comes from the possibility of being rejected, and women, because of our universally passive indoctrination, are perhaps less able to sustain rejection than men, who have built up any number of rationales allowing them to trivialize and even deny the existence of rejection. The heterosexual woman experimenting with lesbianism is in the position of one buying "on approval"—but, after all, she has been sold a "bill of goods." With such a heavy propaganda trip laid on the straight woman, the woman bringing her out has a right to fear that the experimenter will be disappointed—since she has been *oversold*. Had there been fewer testimonials to "inner peace," there would be less likelihood of disappointment. And, after all, in any free relationship, isn't the possibility of rejection always present—on both sides?

But the real mystery is why, after all the evidence to the contrary amassed by Simone de Beauvoir, Betty Friedan, Shulamith Firestone, and others, some lesbians still believed that heterosexual women were "privileged"?

Much hatred of women in the patriarchy comes about by a convenient confusion of women with the men to whom they are attached. We will see, in ensuing chapters, how the left was to identify women married to men in the ruling class with the rulers themselves, against all the evidence that women have no power in the patriarchy at all! Were certain lesbian-separatists at this time doing the same number on heterosexual women by describing them as being "privileged"?

But the attack continues: "the real solution to this difficulty can come only through recognition of the sexual passivity of straight-identified women and their lack of political-emotional-sensual integration. They are still too straight and must become gay by *confronting their passivity* and bringing each other out."[19] (Emphasis mine.)

Now, added to their other "failures" (and remember, straight women at the beginning of the movement were already obsessed with their failures!), heterosexual women were told to confront their passivity, as if it were their *fault* and not a result of patriarchal oppression.

In addition, a particularly vindictive attitude toward heterosexual women who might or might not be in a transitional stage appears earlier in this tract: "[Some women] extoll the pleasures of masturbation but will not take the next step in relating to themselves—to lesbianism. While the ability to relieve tension through autoerotic manipulation is essential to woman's sexual autonomy, the emphasis in masturbation is heavily genital and orgasmic, rather than sensual."[20]

How far we have gone here from the organic, the self-determined, the sisterly. How far, indeed, from "The Myth of the Vaginal Orgasm," which stated every woman's right to a sexual climax.

THE SPLIT BROUGHT HOME

This cutting off of options was not unique to the above papers. Heterosexual women were to meet it in just about every encounter with the "official" lesbian-feminist movement in the early seventies. (Even today I feel nervous about referring to my husband in feminist circles.) I suffered it in a particularly cruel way in the first women's liberation group which came into my neighborhood. Originally a "mixed" group, it was started by two lesbian feminists who claimed to welcome nonlesbians. I was invited to join through my daughter who baby-sat for them. The women who invited me knew that I was married. My daughter attended the first meeting with me, and she could immediately perceive what I could not:

that too much of an issue was being made over sexual preference. "What difference does that make?" she asked, at twelve years of age. But I felt it might be valuable to continue consciousness-raising around it.

We were told that discussing men was irrelevant—even to discuss how those of us who were heterosexual might feel oppressed at home. Naturally, any *satisfactions* we had with men were utterly taboo. (It is one thing, to my mind, to use precious CR time discussing the problems the patriarchy poses to men; quite another to tell about our lives which happen to *include* men.) Those of us who stayed on accepted this inhibition, but it was ironic that one of the founders—who was, incidentally, a recent divorcée—talked frequently about her father, quoting, with not a little reverence, his professional advice for the projects we were working on, and that the other, her lover, confessed at one point it had taken her a whole year to get over her attraction to men. The control these women exerted over the group was apparently an extension of the control they imposed on themselves: separatism did not come easy to them. The proviso that we must not, under any circumstances, talk about men hurt these women as much as it did the nonseparatists. As they urged instant decaffeinated coffee on us at meetings (some of us were sinful caffein addicts, too!), they similarly had no patience to wait for *change* to percolate, to live through their own transitions.

About a year later, I was one of a handful of heterosexuals and nonseparatist lesbians who remained in the group, still struggling for acceptance of differences. I must plead here, against the circumstantial evidence, that I am not a masochist. I had waited a long time for a feminist group to start in my neighborhood and the people in this one were strong, interesting personalities.

Although it had quickly become obvious that non-judgmental consciousness-raising would be impossible, we had begun to organize around two exciting projects: planning a local women's center and publishing a magazine. It seemed a waste of good talent and energy for these efforts to be stymied by the sexual-preference issue. No one in the group was antilesbian. What the non-separatist women envisioned were projects open to all women.

The plan for the women's center was very ambitious. We hoped to solicit large donations and grants so that it could house a crisis shelter, a feminist library, a (decaffeinated?) coffee room, a place for meetings and discussions, and a hall for all sorts of entertainments, including lesbian dances. I considered both projects worthy of serious commitment on my part, and my pacifist background had given me a stubborn streak. But I wasn't clever at political maneuvering, and little by little the nonseparatist majority lost out to the determined separatist few. The interests we all shared were being overshadowed by differences which seemed to me academic in terms of the long-range goals.

For instance, since we were no longer a CR group, we welcomed new members all the time. At one meeting a new woman turned up who spoke disparagingly about lesbians. She expected support for her bigotry, but the mixed group held solid against it. I told her that we were *all* lesbians here, and she soon left. Afterwards I was hounded by questions from the separatists: was I changing? Did I think I would ever change?

I said that "ever" was a long time and anything was possible.

Then I was asked *when* I thought I might change.

I said I didn't anticipate changing but merely understood that life is constantly in flux and all things were theoretically possible. It struck me that never in the civil rights movement had my whiteness been such a disadvantage as my sexual preference was in this movement — which was supposed to represent *me*.

But more serious misunderstandings were to occur. My willingness to give a lot of time to our projects and to work on them in the founders' home was interpreted to mean, I was later told, that I had a "crush" on one of the founders — *which* one I never learned. We put on a fundraising show, organized by one of the founders because she had show business experience. It consisted of songs and films, and I was chosen to emcee. I thought, optimistically, that this meant the barriers might be breaking down. But no: the films and songs were, without exception, about lesbianism and it became clear that my appearance was "tokenism."

In any case, the show was quite professional and the songs sung by the show business founder very moving. I had never seen her perform before and I was touched to learn she was so talented. Afterwards, I joined in the general embracing of the participants. Nothing was said to me about this then, but I'm sure it added to my growing reputation as a closet case, because at the next meeting, which was held to do a post-mortem on the show, I was really put on the carpet.

Apparently, most of the remaining nonseparatists had been put off by the show. Only two or three turned up at the meeting, and there were several new people, all of them lesbians. I suggested that the next fund-raising event be put on by heterosexual women, that we might alternate to give both factions a chance. At this point, the meeting turned into an inquisition, and I was the devil to be exorcised.

Why did I insist on this difference—that we weren't all lesbians? I was asked.

But isn't *everybody* different? I returned.

This was called "ducking the issue."

I cannot now remember all the details of the verbal assault, but I do recall having a vision of the man I had been living with for seventeen years suddenly yanked away from me. It felt as if a vital organ were being torn out of me. My stubborn insistance that change, if it comes at all, must come organically[21] was met by a sudden rush of tears overcoming one of the members I had most admired, a poet. She said to me, "But we *are* all the same. You're making me feel *different* again."

Somehow my insistence on being myself had made her, a recent convert to lesbianism, feel isolated. I still cannot comprehend the emotional logic of this, let alone any objective rationality in it. I am not a cold woman. It felt terrible to see my friend so hurt and to know that in some way I had deserted her. My own tears came. We embraced each other, crying together as I had so often cried with my daughters over some inevitable sadness in life. But this woman and I were both adults. I could not give her the mothering she wanted. In my own family I was gradually relinquishing that role, trying to become a sister to my daughters. Feminism was releasing in me many dormant potentialities. I had begun to take my writing seriously. Decisions I made were taking on a new importance. I was growing out of my identity as a wife-and-mother and into a greater autonomy. I *was* in fact changing—but in my own way, and in my own good time.

I knew that this embrace was my farewell to our group.

Very soon the group divided in two. Some of the non-separatists organized anew, and our first rule was that while nobody *had* to explain her sexual preference, we could all talk quite freely about anything that concerned us. So tired of rigidity were we that we decided not to meet regularly, but only when the spirit moved us. Over the years we have grown apart—without ill feeling. I remember with fondness the evenings we spent bowling or playing basketball or having dinner together or just talking. The pleasure of getting together with a group of women. But we didn't talk anymore of starting ambitious projects.

The separatist half also dwindled. The last I heard of the founders was that they had moved to a commune in New England, and one of them, the singer, was giving concerts around the country to which no nursing mother could bring her male child! Recently I ran into the poet who had cried with me at that last sad meeting. It was in a restaurant. We had both come with our daughters. She was celebrating her daughter's graduation from high school. They both looked proud and happy. I was glad.

THE POLITICAL SIGNIFICANCE OF DIFFERENCE

In 1971, only a year after "The Myth of the Vaginal Orgasm" was published, its author, Anne Koedt, was moved to write:

The often heard complaint from feminists that "we are being defined once again by whom we sleep with" is correct, I think. The lesson to be learned from feminist analysis of sex roles is that there is no behavior implied by our biology beyond, as Wilma Scott Heide has noted, the role of the sperm donor and the wet nurse. A woman has historically been defined, on the basis of biology, as incomplete without a man. Feminists have rejected this notion, and must equally reject any new definition which offers a woman her identity by virtue of the fact that she may love or sleep with other women.[22]

It was a great comfort for me to read this, and a comfort, too, to find these words of Martha Shelley in an essay called "Confessions of a Pseudo-Male Chauvinist":

After I became involved with Women's Liberation, I began to notice something about myself that embarrassed me. I didn't really like women. In bed, yes—but all my friends were men. In rejecting woman's role, from knitting to cooking to wearing mascara, I had also rejected women—except for women jet pilots, executives and astronauts. And since none of my female acquaintances piloted planes or managed General Motors for a living, I snobbishly (and self-destructively) treated women as sex objects and men as intellectual companions. . . .
I was putting myself down by despising my own sex for the roles we have been forced to play—despising the slave for being in chains instead of directing my anger towards the slavemaster who put her there.[23]

In terms of the patriarchy, there is no question in my mind that if all women were at once to leave the beds of men, the effect would be devastating. There is also no question in my mind but that the vengeance men would visit on women would also be devastating. Calculations of massive political consequences, however, whether positive or negative, have not much entered into the thinking of women who have either made or not made this alteration in their lives. Those who became lesbians moved toward what they believed would mean greater happiness for them, and probably, in many cases, it has. Those feminists who remained with men apparently have not felt, in spite of considerable pressure, the need or the impetus to break away. But there is no feminist who has not felt the impact of a great psychological eruption brought on by the decision of lesbians finally to become visible, to live in the open. All of us have been shaken to the very roots of our being—and that, indeed, is the meaning of radical feminism. Great power has been freed in us because we have dared to look deeply within; have dared, as Barbara Deming has put it, "to see ourselves in each other."

Upcoming generations of women are feeling this impact in a wonderful way. As the "sexual revolution" of the sixties freed those who came of age in the seventies to be quite nonchalant about heterosexual "free love," many young women who will come of age in the eighties are already nonchalant about sexual preference—or perhaps more importantly, the refusal to make any permanent choices. Many of them take quite for granted what my daughter observed at age twelve: that sexual preference is barely worth discussing among feminists. Women are moving very rapidly out of that time when "love, sweet love, was thought a crime."

The effect of feminism on the patriarchy may be somewhat more gradual than lesbian separatists desired, but it has a better chance—because the process has been organic—to be lasting and complete. As women acknowledge the many differences among ourselves and begin to meet each other with honesty; as we admit that none of us has cornered the market on virtue and that no rational being can achieve inner peace in a society which still rages with turmoil; we sense the walls of the uterus in which we have so long been confined (cramped as any overdue fetus) stretch.

This image of giving birth to ourselves is already a cliché, but it has become one because it feels like truth to so many women. Unlike those who are "born again" through Jesus—which has to be a head trip—women are being reborn through struggle, through real labor. We do not suddenly see the light, but we stretch the walls and push painfully out into a larger world. It is a labor that has taken many generations and will take many more.

We cannot imagine now what that light will be like, but it is *something* to at last comprehend the darkness. To accept each other as we are must indicate a higher level of consciousness than to try to force each other to be what we are not. To be proud of what one is without delusions of grandeur is a considerable bit of sanity. It is just possible that sanity is as contagious as madness—that some of it might even infect the patriarchy.

There is a good deal of political significance in Lilith and Eve shaking hands.

CHAPTER FIVE

Feminism and the Left

"all History is a history of fascisms, more or less disguised . . . in the Greece of Pericles . . . and in the Rome of the Caesars and the Popes . . . and in the steppes of the Huns . . . and in the Aztec Empire . . . and in the America of the pioneers . . . and in the Italy of the Risorgimento . . . and everywhere, *sèmpar e departút*, free men and slaves . . . rich and poor . . . the buyers and the bought . . . superiors and inferiors . . . leaders and herds. . . . The system never changes . . . it was called religion, divine right, glory, honor, spirit, future . . . all pseudonyms . . . all masks. . . . But with the industrial age, certain masks won't hold up . . . the system bares its teeth, and every day on the flesh of the masses it prints its real name and title . . . and it's no accident that, in its language, mankind is called MASSES, which means *inert matter*. . . . and so, here we are . . . this poor matter, material for work and labor, becomes fodder for extermination and destruction. . . . *Extermination camps* . . . they've already found the earth's new name. . . . *Extermination industry*, this is the system's real name today! And it ought to be written on signs at factory gates . . . and over the doorways of schools, and churches, and ministries, and offices, and in neon on skyscrapers . . . and on the mastheads of newspapers . . . and the title pages of books . . . even the SO-CALLED revolutionary texts. . . . *Quieren carne de hombres*!!"
—from *History: A Novel*, by Elsa Morante[1]

THE WITHERING OF FLOWER POWER

From my view in Central Park's "sheep meadow" almost any Sunday in New York during the sixties, it often seemed as if the pacifists would sweep away the Vietnam

112

War on a wave of sheer good spirits. For—*between* assaults by the police on more threatening antiwar and civil
rights protests; *between* the National Guard massacres at
universities; *between* the right-wing bombings of black
churches and murders of civil rights workers in the
South; *between* the numerous assassinations—masses of
New Yorkers would gather in the park to share their
visions of a better world. Aside from the inevitable
speeches, there would be poetry readings, "guerrilla"
theater, dancing, singing, and the chanting of "Hare
Krishna"—the white pacifists' answer to "We Shall Overcome." (I remember that two real Sikhs in turbans wandered into the sheep meadow when a group of those pal-
lid, head-shaved young men in yellow cotton saris were
doing their thing to this Indian chant. The two bearded
visitors looked at each other, first with astonishment,
then with undisguised amusement. I had always thought
the antics of the Hare Krishna cultists absurd—and now it
appeared they were inauthentic as well! But the exuber-
ance of Allen Ginsberg joining in, jangling what sounded
like a bunch of noisy keys, and smiling beatifically, was
hard to resist.)

After the first shock of seeing America's young men in
long hair (the ones who weren't chanting) and beads, a
large segment of the population found the flower children appealing. America was ready for a loosening of
taboos. Going back to nature, baking bread, and even
living communally are not inconsistent with traditional
American values. The flower children wanted peace and
acted peacefully. The public was growing weary of a war
thousands of miles away which we were clearly losing
and about which we were daily told increasingly indigest-
ible lies. The flower children—or "hippies"—refreshed
American radicalism.

Richard Nixon was elected in 1968 in part because he promised to end the war. As soon as Nixon assumed the presidency, though, he acted as if the only promise he had run on was to restore "law-and-order" (another American fantasy). Vice President Spiro Agnew called for a media blackout on protests and the giant networks obeyed. But the war was to last several more years, with organized nonviolent dissent systematically ignored.

In light of the Watergate revelations, it is hard *not* to suspect that the sudden prevalence of "speed," "downs," and heroin in New York's Lower East Side and San Francisco's Haight-Ashbury in 1969 was somehow one of the early dirty tricks of the Nixon administration. Prior to 1969, the young people who had turned those slums into "alternative communities," decorated with "psychedelic" paintings best seen under "black light" when you were "stoned" or "tripping" on, respectively, "grass" or "acid," had, by and large, accepted the admonishment of the popular slogan "speed kills." Their "good vibes" and occasional "freak-outs" came from essentially soft, nonaddictive drugs. Drinking alcohol, beyond an occasional glass of wine or beer to enhance the effects of marijuana, was frowned upon as a stimulant to violence.

The level of paranoia before that year was similarly low. Or perhaps I should say the level of trust and confidence was high. We knew the police were there; we knew the "Red Squad" existed; we knew the FBI and CIA had planted agents amongst us—but somehow this knowledge failed to produce distrust and fear.

Rather abruptly, in New York and San Francisco, at demonstrations in Washington, one became aware of groups of young people loud and senseless on amphetamines, dizzy on barbiturates, strung out on heroin. No longer joints but pills were passing from hand to hand.

St. Mark's Place, the main street of New York's Lower East Side, stopped being a pleasure to browse in. Emaciated young men waved their arms and screamed staccato curses. Equally emaciated young men drowsed in doorways and smelled of urine. There were deaths.

For *me* the change was sudden. The Lower East Side had been a place to take the children and buy buttons with witty slogans on them. There had been a "free store," where people could bring things they no longer wanted and simply take anything they found that they needed or that delighted them. I came away once with a heavy, huge ceramic bowl and tray, probably the discarded early work of a very talented artisan.

There were daily demonstrations, not only against the war and for civil rights, but to keep traffic off some street, to open the Fillmore East (a rock concert hall) for neighborhood political discussions, to declare that something-or-other belonged to the people. Once there was a demonstration in Washington Square when a man was arrested for trying to climb a tree to rescue his cat! I wanted my children to experience the aliveness of the times, and I learned to move them quickly out of harm's way when the police vans turned up and the men in blue climbed out brandishing nightsticks.

For those of us who merely *visited* the "liberated zones," whose own crises and struggles occurred in other contexts, nostalgia for the sixties in lower Manhattan is inevitable. Friends who *lived* in that neighborhood—women friends—tell a less euphoric story: that their real existence was not a celebration of freedom and joy but a sacrifice of themselves to arrogant and sometimes brutal male sexuality. Their private love-ins were orgies in which, quite traditionally, men took their pleasure indifferent to the needs of women.

The indigenous poor, too, often resented the irreverence of the "voluntary" poor toward God and country and the police—that deadly trinity which at once oppresses the poor and serves as a marker to give their days order and meaning. The *real* poor may rebel against the trinity, but they seldom laugh at it. There were violent clashes between those whose poverty forced them to live on the Lower East Side and those who chose to live there. Still, the image the visitor carried away was of a warm and generous community working with bright colors and music and cheap beads to create the New Jerusalem.

From where I lived it seemed that many of the protests on the Lower East Side were frivolous. Involved at the time in the struggle to end segregation in the schools (a gut issue for any parent who had children in the public schools), *I* thought it was silly to march on the Fillmore East! But after all, who was I to laugh at somebody else's visceral rage at a commercial enterprise which made money off a poor neighborhood and gave nothing back—a neighborhood which "belonged to the people"? The schools were, logically, my turf; for those who lived downtown, the Fillmore was part of theirs.

As a feminist, I now appreciate that struggling on your own turf is not ridiculous, no matter that to others the struggle might seem a tempest in a teapot. We are learning that the small struggle must be waged as well as the large, that there is a vantage point from which a lovers' quarrel and the Equal Rights Amendment carry the same weight, are the same battle. If you live in a teapot, a tempest there is perilous.

In addition to Nixon's dirty tricks, repression, and the continuing escalation of the war, all of which provoked a justifiable despair, there were internal factors also helping to sabotage pacifist tactics and bring on a more violent mood in the New Left around 1969. There were male faces on the left you could look into and know they had never liked "flower power," no matter how effective it had proved itself. There were impatient revolutionaries whose souls screamed for violence, who couldn't abide the pacifists' insistence on rallying mass support with gentleness and reason. The antiwar movement had been split from the beginning, but while the pacifist strategy was working, while the media paid attention to it, while it was obviously changing public opinion, those politicos smiled—at least into the cameras. When it became apparent that Nixon wasn't listening, the hard-line leftists saw their opportunity to do some escalation of their own.

TERRORISM AS AN INSURGENT TACTIC

Terrorism was not invented by the left. Governments determined to hold power at any cost are, by definition (and in action), terrorist. The Ku Klux Klan, the American Nazi party, and organized crime are all *right-wing* terrorist organizations. If they usually get away with murder—and they do—it is because they are terrorizing the weak and not the strong. In fact, even if the ultimate goal is to terrorize the strong, the immediate victim of terrorism—the hostage—must be unprotected and unarmed.

Terrorism is a tactic of warfare, one which erupts logically from sources deep in the patriarchal culture. Rapists, pimps, and wife beaters are terrorists. One way or another, even good parents terrorize their children, and children use terrorism as early as their first temper tantrums. Controlling people through fear is a constant in civilized society. It is written into all laws. It is inherent in the concept of power over others. It is a tactic available to everybody and which, ignorantly, impatiently, or sadistically, we all use.

What we disapprove of or are horrified by in any aspect of society is, more often than not, fundamental to it. The changes we must make go to the root of everything we accept as real and normal. It makes little sense to select one aspect of the terrorism which is a universal way of life for our moral outrage. When terrorism is no longer basic to human behavior, the very plots of our present dramas will no longer seem exciting—will no longer be *imagined*. Our speech patterns and writing and visual arts and music and child raising will have an entirely different style, for it is through style that profound societal changes are revealed.

It is then not the morality of isolated acts of insurgent terrorism that I will be questioning here. Nor, by observing terrorism's pervasiveness in our society, do I wish to urge resignation to such individual acts. Rather, I hope to evaluate these acts in terms of whether or not they were strategically effective—or had any likelihood of being so—and why they were sometimes chosen instead of other possible tactics. (Since there will inevitably be symptoms of such behavior in *this* work, too, I ask the reader not to spare me the enlightenment of her observations.)

We have seen that powerful people get away with terrorist tactics because they are powerful. They control the courts, the military, the police, the media. They can usually make such acts appear to be moral to the majority of the people, and if not moral, then at least necessary; if neither, they can coerce the people to accept them by virtue of greater terrorism. The only way they can be stopped is by another group of people, equally powerful, opposing them, or by a sufficiently large, though less powerful, group creating a nuisance that renders this tactic too wasteful to be worth the effort. The Clamshell Alliance's opposition to the erection of a nuclear reactor in New Hampshire for a while created such a nuisance.

Insurgents, to achieve their ends, must, in the first place, call attention to the immorality of a government action and then enlist popular support for their own *re*action. In a country with the power and the complexity of traditions and temperament of the United States, it is necessary for both the intent and the behavior of people opposed to a government policy to seem absolutely moral—because morality is writ large in our Constitution, if not in all our actions. The policy of the government must also be proved to be, ultimately, impractical—because the people approve of expediency. The reaction must, moreover, be clearly related to the immediate provocation—because the people cannot be expected to ferret out one salient truth from a quagmire of complications. To give a generous concern to the problems of others or even to problems of long-range future interest to themselves is a lot to ask of people who have many troubles of their own, closer to home.

Does isolated terrorism—the bombing of a building, the robbing of a bank, the kidnaping of hostages for ransom, the shooting of a policeman—meet these criteria?

Not, it would seem, in any way: not in this country at this time.

In the first place, all of the above actions seem to be *intrinsically* immoral to the people. Since the media are virtually owned by the oppressor, the acts will be made to appear completely willful. Although the apocryphal burning of brassieres made a graphic statement to many women about their enslavement, the bombing of a military building does little to enlighten people about the immorality of war. The first action has the force of art: it draws women's attention to a constant, almost unnoticed discomfort, and helps them to connect it, probably for the first time, with their oppression. It makes a statement about an experience which has become almost universal among American women. The second draws attention to nothing but the bombers!

The source of provocation, in the latter instance, is a war going on thousands of miles away. The urgency is to make the people care about those who are dying in the war—maybe even to make them care about their own tax dollars. The bombing of a military building diverts their attention from the government's evil to (1) concern for the building, which is theoretically the people's property; (2) fear for their own safety; and (3) the hunt for the criminals. The very sensationalism of the event is distracting, appealing rather to morbid curiosity than to the moral sense. If, as in a kidnaping, there are victims, the public's sympathy turns to them and does not move beyond to an appreciation of unjust conditions (such as the poverty of 3 million people in California, which the Symbionese Liberation Army ostensibly hoped to dramatize by its abduction-for-ransom of Patricia Hearst).

The people will read the headlines, declare the perpetrators insane, and support the immediate victims—as they should. For hostages taken by terrorists or people hurt in bombings are often innocent bystanders, and the public identifies with them self-protectively. In exploiting innocent people for their symbolic value, the terrorist is declaring a lack of concern for human life. This is hardly the way to convince the public of the immorality of the government!

There is another factor also—this one peculiar to the

United States—which distorts the intentions of political terrorists in the public mind. In *other countries* there is a category of crime called political. Class differences are given official recognition and the realities of power and oppression are acknowledged. That groups of people will try to overthrow a regime by violence is an accepted fact of life—and there are laws prescribing the punishments for such activities.

The official line in the United States, however, is that politics means the two-party system. Even a third party is exotic. Marxist abstractions ring "foreign" to Americans who, nevertheless, can be moved to tears by reminders of the nation's own tradition of concern for the underdog. Americans are ill at ease with such terms as "the ruling class." We are supposed to be as classless as any socialist country, all power residing with the people. Any threat to the government that is not merely electoral is officially blamed on the machinations of a "foreign power," and so, except for spying, there is no recognition of political insurrection. The reality of the Civil War in the last century doesn't seem to affect this official complacency. And indeed, in many textbooks that was written off as "The War Between the States," as if the federal government hadn't been involved!

Consequently, here political terrorism is absorbed into the general concept of "crime," or—better still—individual craziness. The American public has been thoroughly sold on mental health: there are only misfits and lunatics—no insurrectionists. Lee Harvey Oswald, to establish a credible motive for his alleged assassination of John F. Kennedy, was called a "loner"; Sirhan Sirhan, who shot Robert Kennedy, a "fanatic." A letter signed by the Weather Underground might as well have been signed by the Boston Strangler! The effectiveness of the American internal propaganda machine which, ostensibly, the government doesn't control at all, is quite possibly the greatest in the world.

Except in rare situations, insurgent terrorism is not a strategically sound tactic in the United States. And since it is seldom spontaneous either, requiring careful planning, the assembling of weapons, all sorts of reconnaissance and intelligence work, terrorists do not have the excuse of acting on a desperate impulse. The chances are their actions will bring retribution not only upon themselves, but upon the whole movement they ostensibly represent.

The notion that terrorist leaders are egomaniacs just out to get headlines is not so far-fetched at all. Certainly that must be part of the motivation. In any case, it is reasonable to ask what the real appeal of terrorism might be for insurgents when other tactics—perhaps requiring greater organization or more imagination—are available.

TERRORISM AND MALE SYMBOLISM

While Sigmund Freud was a dubious authority on the female psyche, his analytical methods are peculiarly well suited for understanding why men act the way they do.

Men *do* live by symbols, identifying their very existence with them. For a man to stand up without weapons before other men who are armed is to, in his own eyes and the eyes of onlookers, *unman* himself. Over the ages, the spear out-thrust has symbolized the erect penis. And the erect penis, as *weapon*, has come to symbolize manhood. The broken sword of surrender is symbolic emasculation. Men are not told, as I was once by a well-meaning gynecologist, "First you are a person, then you are a woman." (He went on to say, "then you are a pregnant woman!")

Person and man are one: to be unmanned—that is, to be unarmed—is, for a man, to cease to be a person. All of his identity hinges on his erection. It takes a very special man to discard the specious but transfixing symbolism his paternal ancestors invented for him and to leap into reality; to decide that thinking, breathing, being may, after all, be better proofs of existence than so unreliable an event as an erection.

There is hardly a man in America who doesn't carry some kind of potential weapon around with him, even if it is only a pocket knife. I know that such a knife is a useful tool, but it is also an emblem. The mystique of weaponry is one we take for granted. The undeclared war is everywhere.

I worked in a tutoring program a few years ago, and one evening a teacher and two children got locked in a room. Nobody who had the key was on the premises at the time. I tried the trick of slipping a card between the door and the molding, but it didn't work. The next building was a police station, so I went there for help.

The policeman smiled and laid his gun on the desk between us. "Here," he said, "take this."

Seeing the gun, I felt myself go suddenly dizzy. I had seen its image a thousand times in the movies, but never before that kind of a weapon "in the flesh." And offered to me, even jokingly, to use!

My reaction amused the policeman. He had terrified me, the "school marm." I recovered, but didn't smile in return.

He put the gun back in its holster and followed me out to see what he could do about the door. When we got outside the locked room, he called in to the teacher: "Stand back. I'm going to shoot the lock."

I saw the grin on his face, but of course the teacher and

the children could not. We heard a scurrying inside, and the policeman laughed. He took out some kind of a file or a ruler (I don't remember which) and accomplished the trick I had attempted. Then he pulled the door open, and we saw the teacher and the children lying on the floor in a far corner of the room.

The policeman had a real belly laugh over that, especially since the teacher was a bearded young man with long hair. The two children were shaking, but being boys, more ashamed at having their fear exposed than anything else. The face of the teacher, a gentle person, worked in silent fury. Afraid to provoke an armed man, I thanked the policeman politely. And my gratitude was indeed profound: he had spared our lives.

The New York City policeman is never without his weapon. That is the Law. And in the neighborhood of that school, the policeman is called The Man.

His little joke was, of course, a terrorist act. The war never ends because it is too much fun to keep it going.

I cannot think that terrorism of any kind is a means to an end. It is an end in itself. (The flush of power.) The "cause" is merely an excuse. The romance of violence is sexual. Before the boy child has reached puberty he has fantasized terrorizing people with an instrument shaped like a penis and which is famous for its ejaculations. He despises lovemaking in stories and films and thrills at the "chase" scenes. We used to laugh tolerantly at this, the charming habit of society in raising boys to be killers.

Men so elevate destruction in their mythology that even women, thinking to become free, are forced to look to the martial arts. And worse—it gets more and more difficult to think any other way. The imagination is blocked by visions of weapons, until those who see no way out kill *themselves*!

Men, then, are moved by at least two motives to terrorism: to prove their existence by brandishing symbolic erections, and for the incomparable pleasure of frightening people. The "cause" is what makes it all acceptable to Mother.

FEMALE DECISION MAKING

Some of the women who participated in terrorist adventures with leftist men in the early seventies—or assented to what they did, or tried to discourage them but stayed on when efforts failed—may resent as condescension my sense that their interests in the events were different from the men's. (If I *am* condescending, it is from hindsight—a position they can join me in.) But until women began controlling our own efforts for freedom in exclusively female groups, we were not even partially in possession of ourselves.

We know, from revelations which have come from consciousness-raising, that women tend to identify with the male heroes in dramas where the heroine is passive. We know, also, that what Freud labeled "penis envy" is the nonbiological envy of traditionally constricted people for the greater latitude of behavior allowed others.

When women strive for freedom, we have no historical image of how free women might behave. What we observe in men is hardly an ideal worthy of our emulation and yet there are elements which tantalize. The freedom of movement, in every sense, which men enjoy is certainly something we mean to have.

But beyond that we are conflicted. If men's confidence and lack of guilt mean complacency and ruthlessness, they are dubious qualities. At our best we want to carry into our freedom the good values—the empathy and concern for, and sensitivity to, others—which may have been in part sloughed off on us by an overcompetitive patriarchy, but which anyone with vision can see must ultimately be the salvation of the world.

However, from childhood on, deprived of all hope of *counting* (knowing that the position most prized by society—that of the male hero—would be forever denied us), many felt a deep frustration. Being noble in silence just didn't look like fun!

Caught in this confusion and ambivalence, we have begun constructing tentative images for ourselves. The images we invent depend not only on our real immediate needs and on our childhood fantasies, but also on an exchange of values and criticism with others. In this way we can check the sources of our aspirations to find out whether they are based merely on the deprivation of some pleasure highly touted by the patriarchy but essentially worthless, or come from a yearning which is maturely just. Without a strong self-image, we are at a disadvantage in any dealings with men.

To be awakened from our long passivity by the kiss of Prince Charming who then sweeps us off to *his* castle (and *his* values) is to be deprived of all possibility of learning to build our own. He will have all sorts of ready-made solutions—but they are not likely to fit those questions we have just begun to formulate. The questions will seem to him bizarre, for they come from a completely different apprehension of things—from dreams that taunted us in the long night he did not share. Walking around his castle, we are likely to pick up and examine things which he takes utterly for granted, and to ask: is this useful? is this good? Even—do *I* want this?

Quickly, he will tire of our questions which challenge too much. And so, unless we simply imitate him, accept his ways as normal and right, and prove how fast we are able to learn, he will either lock us in a cell or throw us out.

The above is analogous to what happens to women, fledgling in our freedom, who join men in political groups. We must, when considering important matters, consult with other women also looking, as it were, at the world for the first time. The questioning we do will seem entirely rational to them: much around us is not useful, is not good, and furthermore, we don't want it.

There is a decided difference between the process of decision making in mixed groups and that process in exclusively female groups. And by process I do not mean only "form": whatever structure the group agrees to, the process is different.

For example, when a group of women come together to plan an action, initially their behavior may be similar to men's: the originator of the scheme may be as wild eyed and enthusiastic as any man embarking on a new adventure. She tells her idea and, generally, in the first round of discussion it meets with an enthusiasm equal to her own. Often others add embellishments to it, and if the sense of humor of the group runs high, embellishments may even run to the absurd, leaving everyone in a state of helpless laughter. If the group is solemn, a mood of deep (and sometimes scarifying) commitment may envelop it. This is round one.

Then, or sometimes later, round two begins. The women start questioning the appropriateness of the plan in relation to their objectives and their resources. Will it make the point in unmistakable language? Will it get wide support and media coverage (if that is desired)? What are the risks? Is everyone realistically prepared to take the risks? Is this the most economical way, in terms of time, energy, and money (three commodities women, with their busy and responsible lives, are generally short of), to reach the objective? Who will it alienate? What retribution is likely? What ambivalence, if any, do some or all of us have in relation to the plan?

In her book *It Changed My Life*, Betty Friedan speaks of an "existential dread" preceding commitment to any new activity—and this sense of dread among women leads to an intense self-questioning. A decision may be overturned or drastically modified because a few women feel it just isn't their "style." Nor is such a reaction regarded by a group of *women* as frivolous: visceral negative feelings which are difficult to define can be deeply valid.

I remember a group of women who had been demonstrating in moderate numbers outside a theater showing *Snuff*, a pornographic film purporting to present the *real* murder of a prostitute. The demonstrations in Times Square had already received nationwide television and newspaper coverage and were, in terms of one of their objectives—to alert women throughout the country about the menace—already highly successful. The immediate upcoming plan was for a much larger demonstration to discourage attendance at one of the busiest hours of the week on a Friday night. Enthusiasm for the demonstration ran very high, and calls went out to people throughout the city to join it.

Then one of the most radical feminists in the planning group got what men would call "cold feet." She pointed out that we had already seen a number of policemen on horseback at the earlier demonstrations. They would surely be out in force on a Friday night in Times Square. At demonstrations there are often agitators who urge a crowd to violence, and if a window were smashed or the crowd decided to mob the theater, there would be danger for all the demonstrators. Many of them would be on a picket line for the first time. The Times Square area, a red-light district and a hotbed of porno shops, may or may not be run by the Mafia with the police in their pockets. Many lesbians, in particular, she reminded us, would be in a vulnerable position if they were arrested.

The woman wanted to call off the demonstration, but that was clearly impossible by this time. Although the appointing of "marshals" among ourselves to police our own demonstrations is generally repugnant to radical feminists, we decided it would be safest if some of us *did* wear armbands and keep the crowd moving. The marshals could also spot agitators and control them.

The woman who raised these questions was a "third world" lesbian with many good reasons for fearing the police and wanting to be in the background of any demonstration. Nevertheless, that Friday night she showed up with an armband, bravely taking her share of the responsibility for keeping order in the face of a brigade of mounted police.

The point of this is that women, in exclusively female groups, are not afraid to express their fears and doubts about a project which may be dangerous. Even the most radical women question bravado for its own sake. Traditionally forced into roles of martyrdom, women with time to plan do not go out of their way to invite it. If women were really masochistic, as we are said to be, we would hardly have such a high survival rate. If we err, it is usually on the side of caution—unlike men, for whom the tortured and dead hero is the most admirable role model (when that position isn't fulfilled, alternately, by the most ruthless conqueror). The image of martyrdom, or what Freud might call extreme masochism, is in fact a male image. Women, as a rule, have as little desire to play the martyr as to play the conqueror. Radical change, to feminists, is deeply considered change which takes into account all the complexities, all the nuances, all the consequences.

Revolutionary men's groups, on the other hand, go to great lengths to prove their "courage." The man who is willing to take the biggest (and often silliest) risks is the hero. As they did when they were little boys, men will vie with each other for the title of "bravest," and any nay-sayers in the group are regarded as cowards, or—a popular epithet of the seventies—"paranoid."

Women in *men's* groups have few choices. If they raise objections to a risky project, the chances are they will be ignored. They can remain on the edge of the group, busy making refreshments and otherwise silent, or they can compete with the men for the hero role—or they can urge the men on to greater and greater risks, challenging them to outdare a "mere" woman.

If a woman should be the initiator of a dubious adventure in a mixed group, she will not be subject to the kinds of cautionary criticism from the men which would be forthcoming from an exclusively women's group. In some cases in a mixed revolutionary group, one woman makes the grade and becomes an accepted hero while the rest of her sisters continue to struggle with the coffee and their squelched doubts. But there is seldom room for more than one authentic female hero in any mixed revolutionary group—although in these days of leftist co-optation of feminism, the glory (and the pain) may be more generously shared with the women.

A woman alone may commit a violent act. A woman in a group of men *and* women may also, even with time to plan, get caught up in a wild and dangerous scheme that holds out little promise of long-range benefits. But women in a group made up *exclusively* of women rarely act without considering the risks, the alternatives, and the consequences.

In what follows, I will be discussing some violent actions engaged in by male and female leftists and pseudoleftists in the United States from 1969 on. I believe that women would not have been involved in these counterproductive adventures had they not been attached to men. The risks were terrible and so were the consequences for everybody: the adventurers, their immediate victims, and the causes they set out to dramatize.

THE MANSON MASSACRE

In August of 1969, Charles Manson and some aides—including several women—tortured and murdered Sharon Tate, a young Hollywood actress, and several of her friends who had been partying with her. Manson's hair was long and he claimed he was motivated by revenge against the rich. The newspapers called him a hippy; the women who helped him they dubbed "Manson's girls,"[2] suggesting he had some hypnotic effect on them. Other than his long hair, Manson had neither hippy nor leftist credentials. But the idea that hippies were murderers and that as such they had great sexual magnetism was established as firmly as the technique of the Big Lie could manage.

The posters of Angela Davis and Che Guevara which decorated the walls of leftist and hippie pads did not, for the most part, come down to make room for pictures of Charles Manson. Most leftists, whether pacifist or not, deplored the massacre.

But Ed Sanders, a pacifist poet famous for promoting the "sexual revolution" with his rock band, The Fugs, did find Manson morbidly fascinating enough to write a book about him—and the Weather Underground identified with Manson's aim: to kill a rich woman. The cult which sprang up around the "hippie killer," promoted in sensationalist tabloids, appealed especially to apolitical and right-wing youths of the Hell's Angels variety, and many anarchists on the left harbored a kind of admiration for these hell-for-leather anarchists on the right. A number of pacifist males sported motorcycles and wore studded leather jackets. That the swastika-adorned Hell's Angels were particularly sadistic toward what the right called the "pinko-faggot" left seemed rather to turn them on!

Whatever the relationship between the male left and Manson, something corrupt and filthy and commercial *was* infiltrating the movement as a whole. *Screw*, the first pornographic newspaper to express the ethics of the early "free speech" movement—with explicit pictures of heterosexual copulation and fellatio—had started selling on newsstands in the beginning of 1969. Though it originated as a movement enterprise, *Screw* went on to become an organ of "free enterprise." Its original intention—to demystify sex—was lost in tawdry, bad-tempered, misogynous journalism which expressed the worst aspects of the revolution against Puritanism, a wallowing in sex as degradation. Imitators followed.

The free be-ins and happenings were co-opted by commercial entrepreneurs and turned into massive marathon rock concerts to which apolitical young people were herded for their money, without adequate concern for their comfort and safety. Accidental death, rapes, and murders occurred. The high point of *Gimme Shelter*, a film about Altamont, the second big concert after

Woodstock, was an actual murder. (The Manson massacre had, reportedly, also been filmed, its prints finding their way to the high-priced porno circuit.)

The machismo of the left, which had been latent in the male-dominated sexual revolution and in the Swiftian irreverence of comedian Lenny Bruce, of anarchist editor Paul Krassner (who originally ran a private "underground" magazine and later would briefly take over, at an enormous salary, the notoriously sadistic magazine *Hustler*), and of leftist politico Abbie Hoffman, began to blend with the previously repressed prurience of the right. Out of disgust, many perceptive women quit the left to become feminists. Maybe they had had experiences and knew something that other women didn't. But some women stayed on in the conviction that, in spite of the misogynous behavior of the male left, Marxism was the *real* revolution and feminism, at best, "cultural."

THE FUGITIVE WOMEN

In the fall of 1969, David Hughey, Sam Melville, and George Demmerle were arrested at the National Guard Armory in New York City "with bombs in hand." The men had been involved in the bombing of several military and war-related corporate offices. They had given prior warning of each bombing. No people were hurt in the explosions.

Demmerle was released as an informer. Melville made a full confession and was held on $100,000 bail, later revoked when the State of New York pressed charges against him. Hughey was released on $25,000 bail. In the roundup of "conspirators," Jane Alpert was picked up at her home and released on $20,000 bail and Patricia Swinton was indicted but not apprehended.[3]

A year before, Jane Alpert, twenty-one years old and an honors graduate in Greek from Swarthmore College, had met and fallen in love with Sam Melville at Columbia University where she had begun part-time graduate work. To support herself as a student, she also held an editorial job. Like so many other promising students at the time, she moved into a "commune" with her lover, dropped out of Columbia, and quit her job. Instead, she went to work for *Rat*, a leftist underground newspaper, which was subsequently taken over by the women on its staff, including Alpert.

Although Alpert probably could have been acquitted of complicity, as Patricia Swinton would be several years later, when she was arrested, she pleaded guilty to "conspiracy" to help reduce Melville's sentence. On May 8, 1970, Jane Alpert left New York as a fugitive. Four days later she was indicted for jumping bail.

Other cases of political violence against property, and sometimes against people, occurred across the country. An explosion at a house on West Eleventh Street, in New York's Greenwich Village, was apparently caused by the stockpiling of homemade bombs. Several people were killed or wounded, and others fled for shelter with the Weather Underground.

For the first time in American history, there were a number of women on the FBI's "ten most wanted" list. Feelings about women earning this dubious "honor" were mixed among feminists. It was hard to resist a strange sense of pride for their "gumption." Radical feminists are fond of neither banks nor government property. In their own way and for their own reasons, most radical feminists are as much against militarism and capitalism as leftists: militarism and capitalism, both blatant exhibitions of machismo, are cruelly oppressive to women.

In addition, implicit in the concept of "sisterhood" is the support of any woman in trouble with the patriarchy. So while these women's alleged involvement in leftist adventurism did not further any feminist aims, radical feminists supported their need for shelter against the patriarchal law.

Women who had not quit the left, however, hailed the fugitives as "heroes" for their actions. Socialist-feminists, many of whom had given up *sexual* relations with men, were still attached to a male dogma. I am not here referring to Marx and Engels's great contributions to economic philosophy, which were certainly as important as Freud's contributions to psychology (and equally inapplicable, with a few exceptions, to women), but to the mindless interpretations of Marxist theory by bourgeois American leftist male postgraduates.

Radical feminism had moved away from blind adherence to a party line. Through the empirical method of consciousness-raising it had gained insight into a complexity of human behavior which defied a simplistic approach. Of course the world was burning—it had always been burning—it would go on burning. If the fires had not been put out in a million years and were only gaining in destructive power, perhaps all the efforts to extinguish them heretofore had been strategically stupid. Radical feminists were working, individually and collectively, to develop an analysis which would cut deeper than Marxism and which could be carried out without the hysteria of the male crisis mentality. They no longer thought that political histrionics could save the world.

A philosophical split began between women who still adhered to the left and women who were searching for answers to more profound, archtypical questions. The left reacted by putting pressure (primarily in the form of guilt) on radical feminists to conform to the Weather Underground's version of Marxist doctrine.

The question leftists kept raising was: were "bourgeois" feminists (the increasingly used pejorative for radical feminists) *sufficiently* against the sins of capitalism? Wherever radical feminists went, they had to state they were indeed against capitalism, as, wearily, many had to reiterate to hard-line lesbian separatists that they were against male domination. The sense of the complexity of life which has been radical feminism's signal contribution to political philosophy—that sense which must so often preface itself with "but . . . "—had a terrible struggle getting expressed. The leftist receiver was off the hook; the party line forever busy.

Originality of thought threatens those who rely on doctrine to avoid the risks of invention. Radical feminists had discovered questions in themselves that Marxism couldn't answer and they saw no reason for blind loyalty to an ideology which no longer served them. If one believed that Marxism had outlived its usefulness, did that mean one must be an adherent of capitalism? If poor women, in their own life experience, had learned that head-on confrontations seldom resulted in anything but bruised skulls, did that suddenly make them bourgeois?

People who had never questioned my "class" when I demonstrated alongside them as a left-pacifist suddenly remembered I was white and a housewife with a passable education—in other words, a "bourgeois parasite"—when I wrote in their journals as a feminist. Although terms like "imperialism" never failed to incite rage in them no matter how many times they were dusted off, the terms "patriarchy" and "sexism" were regarded as archaic almost as soon as they were introduced.

To leftist men I was eventually to become an anomaly.

Since I was neither a passive beauty they could feast their eyes on, nor an earth mother to nurture them, nor a "third world" disembodied symbol they could pay homage to, nor a Rosa Luxemburg to lead their parades—what the hell was I doing drinking wine at their penthouse parties?

"You bore me, woman," was the look they threw me. But I didn't stay to catch it, and I wondered at those women who continued to hang around, darting between insults to find the correct leftist position—for a feminist.

Initially, however, the publications which printed my words didn't seem to notice the extent of my ideological departure. They took my turn to feminism as "cultural": not threatening to what *they* understood as politics. It wasn't until 1974 that they were forced to begin to recognize feminism as *my* politics. More than anything else, the catalyst for my formal break with them that year was the left's harassment of Jane Alpert. Her story is of critical importance to the history of feminism.

But before I resume its telling, let me say that what follows is nothing more than a chronology of events. I realize it cannot satisfactorily describe the woman who is Jane Alpert. Portraying her as an historical figure in some ways robs her of her personhood, although that is not my intention. If this were really a feminist history and not just a chapter in the history of feminism, Jane Alpert would be telling her own story. As feminists see it, all history which is not first hand contains distortions. Hence the diary is regarded as the most reliable historical document.

This caveat is valid for all the lives and thoughts of women that I have presumed to relate in this chapter. I was not a witness to their experiences, and while I am presenting the facts in good faith, only the ways in which these facts affected *me* can be called the truth.

A LETTER FROM THE UNDERGROUND

In September of 1971, there was an uprising at Attica State Prison in New York. Prisoners took guards as hostages and Governor Nelson Rockefeller ordered the National Guard to shoot. Forty-two prisoners and hostages were killed. Among the victims of the massacre was Sam Melville, who had been sent there for the bombings in New York two years before.

Jane Alpert was living in San Diego at the time under an assumed name. She was working as a medical assistant and had joined a consciousness-raising group at the local women's center. Her earlier unhappy experiences in attempting to shelter with the Weather Underground had moved her deeper, in disillusionment, toward a radical feminist analysis. The assassination of Sam Melville, her former lover, at Attica, shocked her brutally. She wrote a moving memoir of their time together, expressing not only her admiration of Melville's irrepressible vitality and revolutionary fervor, but also a balanced awareness of his often irrational overzealousness. It was published as a preface to a collection of Melville's *Letters from Attica*.[4] Her mourning was so profound that it was hard for her to keep it away from her sisters in the CR group; she became afraid of being discovered and somehow implicating these women in her problems with the government. In the spring of 1972, she left San Diego and wandered around before resettling in Denver the following fall, under yet a new identity.

As the healing process continued, Alpert became increasingly convinced of the validity of the radical feminist analysis. There were bitternesses in her relationship with Melville that she couldn't forget—could no longer hide from herself. The amnesia—and amnesty—of mourning was lifting.

This was a time of many feminist speak-outs against rape, for free abortion—about the victimization of women at men's hands. In consciousness-raising groups, women were "telling" about personal atrocities inflicted upon them by male "lovers." The women's liberation movement had been started, in fact, by leftist women needing to assert themselves against the machismo of *their men*.

There should have been nothing surprising about Jane Alpert describing the negative side of her life with Sam Melville a year after his death. Such revelations help to end the conspiracy of privacy which protects men who commit crimes against women. To come out as a woman who has been wronged in ways which society tries to convince women are too "embarrassing" to expose, is to encourage other women to admit being humiliated, raped, and/or beaten by men close to them—by men they were "foolish enough" to *choose*! Pride for a woman exists so much in choosing, and above all, being chosen by, a man who really loves her, who is somehow better than other men—or at least as good. What else but this vicarious pride does the world allow her to enjoy? "A woman is only really beautiful when she is loved," we are told. And the corollary, "A woman is only loved when she is beautiful," is spelled out from Cinderella on. To be cherished by a man is to have one's whole worth corroborated; to be rejected or maltreated is to be declared valueless. And so, confessing mistreatment is a terrible blow to a woman's sense of self-worth, but each confession makes the next more possible, until all women are able to take pride in the *refusal* of mistreatment, as men are.

In her "Letter from the Underground," which was published in *Ms.* and other feminist publications in 1973, Alpert wrote: "I was very much pressured, *against my own sense of tactics and timing*, into playing the role I did in the group of radical bombers Melville half-led, half-dragged along with him." (Emphasis mine.) "The pressure was of the kind peculiar and common to male-female relationships: he threatened to leave me if I backed out."[5]

Her own "sense of tactics and timing": she knew a harebrained scheme when she saw one!

Back to the kitchen with you, Woman: he left a note in black magic marker on the refrigerator saying "wash me." "He wouldn't allow our lease, our telephone, our utilities bill, our bank account, or anything else we shared to be in his name on the ostensible grounds that he was delinquent with his income tax and didn't want to be found through public records. The real reason, it turned out, was that he didn't want his wife to find him and demand the child support he owed her and hadn't paid in years."[6]

Degradation of women was necessary for his sexual self-image: his "love" depended on his hate. "He was sexually impotent unless he could fantasize the woman he was with as a prostitute *and she went along with that fantasy*."[7] (Emphasis mine.)

(Why is it that the idea of making love with a brilliant, accomplished woman so seldom has the effect of enhancing a man's sense of self-worth? Is it really the old Oedipus taboo against making love to one's mother, a woman whom a man presumably respects? Or is it that power-hungry men are so greedy for prestige that they simply can't bear to share it with another person?)

Perhaps the cruelest souvenir in Alpert's possession was the "affectionate" note at the end of the last letter he wrote to her from Attica: "Yes, sweet bitch, I love you. And if they ever let me out and the wind is right, I'll find you."[8]

This particular kind of reduction is, above all, thought

by men to turn women on. If men and women were equally respected in the world for their human accomplishments, to acknowledge the pantheistically mindless nature of sexuality might be a sacrament. But given the constant degradation of women along with the concomitant elevation of men, Melville was naming her, the woman, an animal — the implication being that any other bitch would do as well: women are interchangeable. He could admit the beast, chasing her, in himself, because the world allows that "peccadillo" to heroes.

How many letters, with that identical insult (intended to be interpreted as flattery!) were written to women by prisoners those horny nights at Attica? The locker-room mentality — the fantasized debasement of women which men dignify in themselves as desire — follows them even into the tangible obscenity of prison, while on the outside the women who love them make every sacrifice to obtain their release. Is this trivial — or is it time we looked at this ugliness in men who would lead us out of oppression and saw, finally, that it makes such leadership impossible?

"Letter from the Underground" is bitter — and rational. Alpert says to her "sisters in Weatherman": "I am not asking you to stop loving men, or to break all personal and emotional ties with the men who are important to you. I know that those ties are never broken out of simplistic political decision but only when and if consciousness of oppression makes them so inconsistent with self-respect that they can no longer be borne. Even then it is with enormous pain and grief and in spite of an ever-reluctant part of ourselves that we separate from men we have cared for. I firmly believe that one can be a serious feminist and still live with and relate to a man and to men. The gulf that is between us is not that, but rather that you allow men to rule your politics."[9]

Her own break with the memory of the man she had

loved and who had hurt her so deeply, and with other men who might reasonably be assumed to share his values, contains the disillusionment and finality found in English folk ballads and American "blues"—the bitter anonymous poetry now frequently attributed to women.

"And so, my sisters in Weatherman, *you* fast and organize and demonstrate for Attica. Don't send me news clippings about it, don't tell me how much those deaths moved you.

"I will mourn the loss of 42 male supremacists no longer."[10]

Irreverence toward women in the mouths of Lenny Bruce, of Paul Krassner, of Abbie Hoffman, of Eldridge Cleaver, has received thundering ovations on the left. The cry "Free speech! Free speech!" greets the vilest incitements to violence against women from multitudes of "idealistic" young men and civil liberties lawyers. But a woman's belated recognition and warning to other women that she has been victimized by a leftist "hero" is *heresy*. No civil liberties lawyer will defend her against the slanders of the left.

The risk Alpert took was not the hero's risk of alienating the authorities (*that* risk she had already taken), but the much greater risk of speaking truth to her own people. The risk that kept Moses out of the promised land, that left Jesus without comfort on the cross.

When later I tried to defend Alpert from slander in the pages of a leftist magazine, I was told not to make *her* a hero. So I must not compare, here, a woman whose words helped to lead women into freedom with Moses and Jesus.

God forbid!

THE TRASHING OF A FEMINIST

On November 14, 1974, Jane Alpert turned herself in to

the United States Attorney's Office in New York and was released on a new bail of $20,000 pending sentencing. During November and December, she was interrogated by the government. She gave them an account of her residences, aliases, and employment since becoming a fugitive. She refused to divulge any information about people who had helped her, and when asked about Patricia Swinton, she denied having seen her since Swinton became a fugitive in 1969, and also denied that Swinton was involved in the bombing conspiracy to which Alpert had pleaded guilty. On January 27, 1975, Alpert began serving her twenty-seven-month sentence—eighteen months for the bombing conspiracy and nine months for jumping bail at the State Correctional Institution in Muncy, Pennsylvania.

At this time, I knew nothing of Jane Alpert except what I read in the papers and what mutual friends might say. *Rat* had not been my bailiwick in the late sixties, nor had I been a member of any radical feminist group. Although I knew people who knew people who were fugitives, the Weather Underground itself was remote to me.

Aware of a deepening gap between the orthodox left and feminism, I spoke of the underlying philosophical disagreement at the Community Church in Boston early in 1975. As I do now, I still had friends who considered themselves Marxists. With one Marxist woman (I'll call her Sandra) I had a particularly close friendship, and we often discussed the increasingly competitive analyses of Marxism and feminism. Sandra and I were not always polarized in our talks, and one day when she invited me to meet another friend of hers (call her Millie), I was hardly prepared for that woman's neo-Stalinist approach.

Millie had arrived with a purpose. Alpert had recently gone to jail, and Millie told us she was *sure* Alpert had informed on the Weather Underground, and that members of it would be arrested momentarily. She said a petition must be written against Alpert, just in case.

Apparently Millie wanted me to help write the petition. Every objection I raised—primarily to an attack on a woman without evidence—was twisted into an attack on *my* "bourgeois" way of life. We were, I guess, involved in what leftists call "self-criticism," and I was the self being criticized. Her effect on me was almost mesmerizing. However, I stubbornly insisted I wouldn't sign anything directed specifically against a woman. Ultimately, she agreed I was right—such a position wouldn't be popular. I was left with the idea that the petition would be against "informing" in general.

After Millie left, I had the feeling of having been worked over by a high-pressure salesman; somehow I had managed to avoid buying the vacuum cleaner! I told Sandra I would never sign *anything* offered by Millie.

A few days later, an attack on Alpert as an "informer" was circulated for signatures. It was followed by another document, not accusing Alpert of anything directly, but with a most revealing last paragraph: "Women can no longer afford to be silent on any issue that affects us in the core of our struggle. We are not isolated. We are engaged in a long struggle, a struggle with many battles and many battlefields. We are more than what we are as individuals. We are what we identify with. And our identification must be with all oppressed peoples. We do not 'support' or 'not support' the brothers of Attica. We *are* Attica. We are Attica or we are nothing. Not feminists, not women, not human beings. This is true feminism."[11] It was signed by Ti-Grace Atkinson, Joan Hamilton, Florynce Kennedy, and Susan Sherman.

In the body of this document, these four Marxist-feminists stated: "There are two kinds of justice in this country. The system of justice for people like Jane Alpert, and the system of justice for people like Assata Shakur. Is this what we want the women's movement to represent? The kind of movement Jane Alpert represents. A movement based on class privilege, on white privilege. A racist movement completely cut off from our real needs."

The system of justice for "people like Jane Alpert" had put Jane Alpert in *prison*. Yet she was being accused of class and skin privilege—and of racism—for exposing the emotional cruelty of a *white* man who happened to die at Attica.

A third petition, "A Vindication of the Rights of Feminists," was written in support of Alpert and of feminism. With a sigh—both of relief that this maligned woman and the rest of us who shared her convictions were, at last, being defended; and of sorrow at the depth of the split in the movement—I joined many other feminists in signing it. Its last paragraph read:

We have an organic commitment to all oppressed peoples—but we affirm our own priorities as women. To do otherwise is indeed a betrayal of feminism, one which would send us all back to the ladies' auxiliaries. We will not be divided from one another "by proclamation." The feminist vision is profoundly one of freedom for all creatures on this planet; the feminist reality today is necessarily one of freeing ourselves and each other as women. We are our own people—and no forms of innuendo, guilt-induced conformity, or outright intimidation will ever again make us forget it. This is the root of our unity; that unity the root of our strength.[13]

On March 12, 1975, Patricia Swinton was arrested at a commune in Vermont, one of the most famous communes in the United States. Most of the communards were writers. Several books about it, at least one with pictures of its inhabitants, had been published; outsiders often dropped in for visits. It would be hard to imagine a riskier place to hide out.

On March 21, Patricia Swinton was quoted in the *New York Post*: "I certainly don't think Jane is an informer."

From *Newsweek*, March 24: "Justice Department sources told *Newsweek* that information on Swinton had come from another radical fugitive, Barry P. Stein, 26, the director of a community health clinic in Brattleboro, who turned himself in to Chicago authorities last fall in connection with his role in the 1969 'Days of Rage' violence there."

From a "Government Memorandum in Support of Motion for Pre-Trial Hearing to Determine Whether or Not Witnesses Will Be in Contempt at Trial," submitted by Paul J. Curran, United States Attorney for the Southern District of New York and Attorney for the United States of America:

Alpert denied that Swinton was involved in the conspiracy, and maintained that she had not seen or been in contact with Swinton since Nov. 23, 1969, the date of her arrest following the conspirators' attempted bombing at a National Guard Armory in New York City. The Government doubted Alpert's candor on the subject of Swinton, because of (a) independent evidence of Swinton's guilt, (b) Swinton's close association with Alpert and other self-admitted conspirators, Hughey and Melville, and (c) Alpert's strong motive to lie to protect Swinton from the charges here, and herself from condemnation or reprisal from "movement" groups. These doubts were confirmed in March, 1976 when *Swinton's lawyer* provided the facts which exposed Alpert's bad faith and false statements. (Emphasis mine.)

Patricia Swinton said in an interview in *Off Our Backs*, a left-feminist publication, in July 1975: "I don't think Barry Stein did it at all. . . . It was Jane." (In contrast with her statement of March 21.)

Barry Stein was released after he turned himself in and promptly went to see Patricia Swinton, who welcomed him warmly. (This isn't a whodunit, and I prefer to think that Barry Stein was also innocent of informing.)

While Alpert was in jail, the *Midnight Special*, a leftist publication distributed to prisoners, called her an informer. As a result, she suffered physical injuries inflicted by other prisoners.

There is a sequel to this tale: after Alpert's first prison ordeal was finally over, she was sent back for four and a half months to a halfway house for "contempt of court" *for refusing to testify against Patricia Swinton*. Swinton was acquitted. Since then, several political fugitives have turned themselves in and made deals with the government which allowed them to escape imprisonment altogether, or to reduce their sentences. The left has quietly welcomed their return.

The viciousness of the neo-Marxist attacks on feminists was later explained by Bernardine Dohrn when, as a fugitive with the Weather Underground in 1977, she sent a tape recording to the feminist magazine *Hera*. In it she repudiated the Weather Underground and her part in it. She said:

For seven years I have upheld a politics that is male supremacist and opposed to the struggle of women for liberation. I have attacked the women's movement as bourgeois, separatist, anti-communist, divisive, anti-Third World. . . .

In line and practice, I have given support to the continuing oppression, super-exploitation, violence, brutality, contempt, humiliation and suppression of women. . . .

In 1974, we set out to destroy the women's movement. . . .

By the summer of 1975, the attack on the women's movement and feminist politics was naked and bitter. . . . This attack on women and the women's movement was carried out in a very personal way against women most identified with the women's movement. . . .

Why did we do this? I don't really know. We followed the classic path of white so-called revolutionaries who sold out the revolution. For me to understand this requires much more study and struggle. What I do know is that by standing on my anti-imperialist record in a self-satisfied way and self-justifying way, by assuming that I was beyond white privilege or allying with male privilege because I understood it—I prepared and led the way for a totally opportunist direction which infected all our work and betrayed revolutionary principles.[12]

Dohrn admits to having little insight into her own motivation, although she sees opportunism as the Weather Underground's impetus. Since they applauded both the Manson atrocity and the abduction of Patricia Hearst, it would seem that wanting to destroy feminism was not their only motive in attacking women.

A number of feminist writers—Evelyn Reed, Phyllis Chesler, and Andrea Dworkin among them—have explored the male revolutionary's hatred of his father. Finding the father too dangerous an adversary, does the male revolutionary seek vengeance through the father's possessions—his wife, his daughter? Or does he merely glory in a sadism endemic in the patriarchy? It becomes harder and harder to find any significant moral difference between men on the left and men on the right.

But then there are women involved in or applauding this sadism as well. It is easy enough to understand Dohrn: as a fugitive living with the Weather Underground, she was the captive of dangerous men. She followed one of the roles women can safely play in such circumstances. It is interesting in this connection, to find Ti-Grace Atkinson among the signers of the second statement against Jane Alpert, evidently one of the actions inspired by the Weather Underground's plan.

Atkinson had "divorced" feminism in a speech in 1971—shortly after she outlined her revolutionary strategy to the Daughters of Bilitis. The occasion was a conference on women and violence. Addressing a number of feminist "leaders," she had held up a twenty-foot reproduction of a news photograph showing Joseph Colombo, a member of an Italian-American civil rights organization and an alleged former gangster, after he had been shot by the police. Pointing to the picture, Atkinson accused her colleagues of opportunism and of callousness toward those she now considered the true victims of oppression, working-class men.

In the strategy she had outlined for the D.O.B., Atkinson had fastened on the "criminal element" as a victim class to be enlisted in her hypothetical revolution. Had she been attracted to Colombo as a part of that element? Apart from the fact that any attack on women apparently appealed to the male left, could the Weather Underground have been influenced by Atkinson's strategy when it decided to support white working-class men?

On the other hand, Atkinson's love for Colombo was as real as her incessant search for the ultimate underdog. The victims of the Attica massacre, too, were the "criminal element." Jane Alpert, although imprisoned herself, was an educated young woman from a background Atkinson could identify with. We have seen Atkinson again and again trivializing her own pain, differentiating it quantitatively from that of other members of The Feminists, from women she considered working class, from lesbians.

Feminism means an understanding of and an allegiance to oneself first, and by extension an empathy with all women. But women, and particularly white women who come from families which are not financially destitute; women—especially—who are educated, have been designated by the patriarchy as repositories for ruling-class guilt. Without comprehending fully their own victimization, these women feel severely the guilt assigned to them and cannot understand why other women of their station do not share it to the same degree. For a woman to try to promote her own interests in the world seems to these women an unconscionable opportunism—greater, even, than that shown by men who become gangsters. That a woman might value herself to the point where she refuses to sing the praises of a man who has treated her, by and large, badly; a man who died in *prison*—betrays an unforgivable (unwomanly?) callousness.

The guilt women cannot forgive in themselves inevitably turns to hatred of women who have renounced false guilt. Only men may prosper, they feel. Only the victimization of men, or of women of a different "class" deserves tears. The widow who does not symbolically leap on the funeral pyre is a monster.

Because Atkinson's life has been so public; because she has acted out so many impulses before us, it is easy to follow her odyssey—not as an Amazon but as a modern woman, as a victim. None of us is yet completely free from the curse of self-hatred. The documents Atkinson has given us are a true feminist history. The record of her internal turmoil will help to set other women free.

At the time of Jane Alpert's travail, Bernardine Dohrn's confession had not yet been written, and I had not read *Amazon Odyssey*. I did not know Jane Alpert either. All I knew was that a person is innocent until proved guilty. And I remembered Senator Joseph McCarthy and the House Un-American Activities Committee. I also recalled what I had learned of the Dreyfus affair in history. I wondered how leftists forgot all this as they embarked on their own witch hunts.

The attack on Jane Alpert—the Big Lie of the left which has been repeated over and over again in its publications from 1973 until very recently, and which was so frustrating to feminist writers who were allowed scant space in those "civil libertarian" publications to refute it—was only one of the slanders feminists endured. Other slanders were committed, not the least of which was a concerted attack on Gloria Steinem. Steinem, at least, was not in prison at the time. She was able to defend herself, and her many friends and admirers rushed to her support.

On February 4, 1974, for the sins of her father, Patricia Hearst was kidnaped by a terrorist outfit calling themselves the Symbionese Liberation Army. As her ransom, her father was asked to provide food for 3 million hungry Californians. Patricia Hearst was held captive, raped, beaten, and forced to participate in a bank robbery. The events of her abduction and flights with her captors made headlines for months. She became a "cover girl" on every tabloid in the country—an object of the most hideous male sexual fantasies. Nobody gave a damn about the poor in California!

The country was on a woman-hunt. To "prove" that the rich don't receive special privileges before the bar of justice, Patricia Hearst, the kidnap victim, went to prison with her abductors.

Leftist sentiments went wholly with the abductors—those champions of 3 million hungry Californians!—until it was rumored that some of them may have been working for the CIA. Their sympathy, however, never included the college student who had been kidnaped and whose life was subsequently ruined. One famous civil liberties lawyer was quoted by a New York newspaper as saying he had refused to defend Patricia

Hearst because he "wouldn't work for pigs." He afterwards was heard proclaiming the First Amendment rights of pornographers and Nazis.

There *is* one law for the privileged and another for the oppressed: Richard Nixon and his best-seller-writing henchmen are the privileged; William Randolph Hearst Jr.'s daughter, in accordance with the patriarchal social contract—agreed to by men of many political persuasions—is not: she is a piece of property.

THE HUNT FOR SAXE AND POWER

In September of 1970, four men were arrested in connection with the robbery of the Brighton branch of the State Street Bank and Trust Company in Boston, during which a policeman had been killed. Two were students, Stanley Bond and Robert Valeri, who had been participating in a special tutoring program at Brandeis for ex-convicts. The loot, $26,000, was presumably slated to help the antiwar movement. But making a statement against capitalism by knocking over a bank was certainly more than a side issue.

The report of the capture of the last man in *The New York Times*, September 30, 1970, included the following:

"Still at large were Susan Saxe, 21, of Albany, a June graduate of Brandeis, and Katherine A. Power, 20, of Denver, a Brandeis senior.

"Mr. McNamara [Boston chief of police] said that a radio from the Newburyport National Guard Armory, which was burned and ransacked, had been found in Miss Power's apartment.

"Radical literature was also found in Miss Power's apartment at the foot of Beacon Hill. Miss Power's passport was found and the police indicated she had visited Cuba."[14]

On such "evidence" Sacco and Vanzetti were executed!

In describing Stanley Bond, his lawyer, Robert Mardirosian, was quoted in the September 27, 1970 *Times* as saying he had "an impressive war record—he was a crew member on something like 30 missions when we were bombing North Vietnam—and we are seeing more and more cases like this where we have taken a young man and taught him how to kill and he comes back home and gets into trouble."

The irony here is not to be missed, and Susan Saxe, a poet and a young Marxist, surely had the imagination to see heroic potential in this young man—the disillusioned war veteran turned fighter for the proletariat—and herself, perhaps, as his mentor in revolutionary theory.

Ever since 1970, the FBI had been searching for Susan Saxe and Katharine Power in connection with the Boston bank robbery that year. The two women's pictures were featured on "most wanted" posters across the country and Saxe, in particular, had become a folk hero to left-feminists. After the Watergate revelations, the FBI lost face, and the success of these two women in continuing to elude them for more than four years didn't improve their self-image. During that time, the women's movement had grown to the point where the government apparently considered it a force to contend with.

In January 1975, the FBI began intensive questioning of feminists, and particularly lesbian-feminists, in Connecticut and Kentucky—two states where the government had evidently received reports that Saxe and Power had been seen. Although the FBI could not subpoena people, their technique was to harass women into talking by threatening to order them before a grand jury

if they refused. The information they demanded had little, if anything, to do with the two fugitives they were
seeking. They were apparently trying to build dossiers
on feminists—to get a line on how the women's movement functioned and what its aims were.

Women who knew their rights refused to talk and
were, as promised, brought before grand juries. But there
was no guarantee that women who *did* answer the FBI's
questions wouldn't also be subpoenaed. At the grand
juries those women who stood on the Fifth Amendment
were given "use immunity," under which information
they gave could not be used to prosecute them, and
which compelled them then to answer, under threat of
being imprisoned for contempt as often as they were
subpoenaed and continued to refuse to testify. Knowing
that their testimony could incriminate other women, if
not themselves, quite a number of feminists bravely
withstood questioning and went to jail. This misuse of the
grand jury system, originally designed to protect people
who were accused of crimes, is completely contrary to the
spirit of the Bill of Rights. Several women went to jail
more than once. Alarm and even panic spread through
the radical part of the women's movement, particularly
among lesbians, who were singled out for special harassment by the FBI. In fact, FBI agents took it upon themselves to notify parents, employers, and coworkers of
their sexual preference. A number of lesbians lost their
jobs as a result, and parents whose daughters had not
previously revealed their sexual preference to them—often because they feared such knowledge might *kill* their
parents—were traumatized by being informed by government officials.

The primary concern of feminists was to keep Power
and Saxe safely in hiding. Except for the very real

danger to individuals, the women's movement itself had little to worry about in terms of exposure. Few, if any, strictly feminist activities had been clandestine. But during the course of the investigation, women were terrorized by the FBI through unauthorized searches, mail tampering, and not very subtle snooping.

In its effort to protect the fugitives, the left did some terrorizing of its own. It issued endless warnings in speeches and publications to women not to say *anything* to the FBI. Feminists who were being questioned were in a bind. They knew that, sooner or later, they could be *pressured* into talking, unless they were willing—and *able* (women's responsibilities are such that going to jail for any length of time can pose a double hardship: to them and their children, if they have them)—to sustain lengthy and repeated imprisonment. It was important for women to begin to calculate not *if* they would talk but *what* they might say which would put the FBI and/or the grand jury off the trail without exposing themselves to perjury charges.

Bulletins issued by the left were anything but helpful in this regard. They constantly told women that they couldn't outsmart the officials; that the government could put "two and two together," and that *any* information could be added to other information which would ultimately lead to the capture of the fugitives. They consistently undermined women's faith in their own ability to think under critical conditions. Considering that for more than four years two women had been clever enough to successfully elude capture—or that, conversely, the FBI had been dull-witted enough, although they had scores of informers and infiltrators in the left and the women's movement, not to have caught up with them—the implication that women, using their brains, weren't sufficiently canny to fool the investigators was both insulting and dispiriting.

Women went up against trained inquisitors *terrified* to open their mouths. When, ultimately, they were forced to speak, many of them lacked the cool to be selective. Had they gone to the grand juries with confidence that they were at least as smart as their questioners and that they had a fifty-fifty chance of thinking up suitably evasive answers under fire, there is a strong possibility that Susan Saxe might not, at the present time, be in prison. (Katherine Power has still not been caught.)

Instead, the FBI was able to piece together a picture of the fugitives' habits. Susan Saxe was arrested on a street corner in Philadelphia on March 27, 1975. She pleaded guilty, she said, as part of a deal to prevent the convening of an investigative grand jury in that city. Women in Kentucky and Connecticut who had reluctantly succumbed to their questioners were forgiven by the left and praised as heroines for resisting as long as they had.

THE BROTHERHOOD OF POWER

The only logical explanation of the left's attack on Alpert and other radical feminists is Bernardine Dohrn's. For some reason the left looked upon feminism as a rival movement, rapidly gaining adherents. Were they afraid that women, undirected by men, would upstage their revolution? Or did they really consider feminists bourgeois—more bourgeois than, say, the Columbia University student strike leader Mark Rudd, who was to turn himself in to the government in 1977, about the same time as Bernadine Dohrn? Or did they simply fear, like so many other men and, alas, women, across the political spectrum, the growing independence and power of those who had been carefully programmed, forever and ever, to be the "weaker" sex?

But why do I speak of fear, that word which is used as a hook to catch female compassion? The left is just a group of men out of power who want to replace those men who are currently in power. Their ideology calls for certain economic changes—an end to the inequities most obvious in America's ruthless capitalistic regime. Like Jesus, they see greed for money as the root of all evil. But H. Rap Brown, a black power advocate of the sixties, spoke of a deeper truth. He said that the rulers determine who shall and who shall not have the power that money represents. He remarked in a radio interview that if the people the government wanted to deny money to were able, in spite of it, to amass money in any great quantity, the rulers would simply invalidate the old currency and issue a new one—substituting pink bills for green, is what I remember him saying—to those they wanted to empower. Even under capitalism, money is not a reliable tool for gaining power, and the love of power is a more profound first cause than property greed. Socialist countries manipulate power through other means than access to hard cash (although economic inequities there are readily observable, too). Dissidents are deprived of power everywhere.

By pointing to the inequities of our particular system, the left cloaks itself in the raiments of unchallengeable morality. To be against capitalism is to be against sin. And thus the left makes itself out to be the champion of the poor and disinherited.

Before the world had examples of the results of successful socialist revolutions, that cloak of morality appeared quite spotless. By now the atrocities of established socialist regimes have soiled it so that it will not bear close scrutiny. Hence, the left has tried a new tactic:

to turn Marxism into a religion whose tenets are beyond questioning.

Now along comes feminism to say no, oppression exists everywhere. Its source is in the masculine will to dominate.

Not only are the old "opiates" of God-worshiping religions challenged, but the newer palliative of revolution-worship also is examined. The left is exposed as power hungry. And the means of its exposure is deeply embarrassing. It is, quite literally, denuded.

One by one, women testify to sexual abuses by its apostles. The massive accumulation of personal evidence defies trivialization. The will to dominate in the "best" of men is epitomized by the naked penis fantasized in constant erection, used as a weapon to conquer and humble women. On the other end of the political spectrum, Henry Kissinger declares power to be the greatest of aphrodisiacs.

FEMINIST VULNERABILITY

In 1975, the left attempted to split feminists by forcing us to choose between protecting its heroes (several of whom, conveniently, happened to be women) and exposing ourselves as callous and immoral. Through use of the notorious Big Lie technique, the left convinced many women that prominent feminists were betrayers of fugitives—in the employ of the CIA or simply cowardly turncoats.

Female solidarity is still in an infantile stage. It has not yet built up an immunity to the many insidious viruses of self-doubt and self-hatred congenital to slaves. One of the reasons why women still need so badly to deliberate in exclusively female groups is that most of us are still vulnerable to moral seduction and intimidation of men and their ideologies. Most of us are still in the condition of

Red Riding Hood who, even though her senses told her something was seriously amiss—that "grandma" didn't look like grandma—nevertheless doubted her own perceptions to the point of tarrying in the pretender's company.

Of course radical feminists wanted to protect sisters hunted by the government—however unwise these women might have been in the first place, embroiling themselves in male "revolutionary" histrionics. But the *left's* primary effort was clearly *not* to save, say, Susan Saxe, from martyrdom at the hands of the rulers. It was to hold her up as an *example* of martyrdom with which to flail the growing "bourgeois" (by which it meant "grassroots") women's movement. And Saxe, by joining their attack on radical feminists, accepted that exploitation, allowed herself to be used in the left's attempt to divide her sisters. Perhaps she did this because radical feminists saw her as a victim rather than a hero, whereas the left offered her the status of a legend. But Saxe was not Elizabeth Cady Stanton. Although she had "come out" as a lesbian, her loyalty to male ideology was all too abundantly clear. Radical feminists saw her as a woman rather than a feminist and would extend to her their support in her victimization as they would to all women in trouble, whether or not they accept the feminist analysis of their plight. The battered wife is rescued without respect to her politics.

Feminists eschew false pride. For a slave to be a victim, to *admit* she is a victim, is not ignominious. That she accepted the wolf for her grandmother, when everything in her experience had taught her to doubt her own perceptions and values, was not shameful; it was the most natural of errors.

Neither does the following of false leaders argue naive-

té or stupidity: the truly naive and stupid accept things
as they are, do not experiment for change. Every attempt
to alter conditions is fraught with possibility for error.
Doris Lessing has postulated in her introduction to *The
Golden Notebook* that we will one day find a root cause
deeper than the one feminism currently hypothesizes. To
search, and to stumble, is not reprehensible; the way of
the coward is to stay home in bed.

But Marxist women will argue that they have not
stumbled, that it is condescending of me to suggest they
have. To this I can only say that I invite their arguments
and their proofs, while hoping that false pride will not
take this up as a challenge to debate. I have no taste for
debate which implies a need to defend simplistic and
therefore untenable positions in contrived opposition to
one another. Truth is many-sided, and what I invite is
mutual enlightenment which would alter both positions
and bring them closer, perhaps, to that goal. There is no
doubt in my mind that Susan Saxe and other leftist
women are searchers. It is simply my hope that neither
they nor I will end that search complacently in some bog
along the way.

LEFTIST GUILT-TRIPPING

The destructive effects of the leftists have been felt by
feminists throughout the industrialized world, and even
more extensively in Europe than in the United States,
where the vast majority of women who are rapidly becoming feminists have never had any ties with the left
and know little or nothing of these moral disputes so
hotly argued among *radical* feminists.

Slanders against American radical feminists are widely
believed by European feminists. In London, at the En-

glish National Women's Liberation Conference in 1977, I was to hear radical feminism described as "dead" by an American expatriate delegate. In 1977, both in London and Paris, a feminist challenging Marxist scripture could hardly show her face. The left in Western Europe has been, for many years, an important force. Marxist class consciousness is a way of life for much of the working class there. More so than in the United States, it is heretical for a feminist to contradict this dogma. To be a leftist is the only conceivable way to prove that you make a moral identification with the oppressed, and women are duly classified with men along Marxist lines. There are upper-class, middle-class, and working-class women, according to the men they are attached to. The fact that a number of "upper-class" women have had to seek asylum in battered-wives' shelters is apparently not felt to be contradictory.

Of course there *are* radical feminists in Western Europe who passionately believe that patriarchy, and not only its corrupt offshoot capitalism, is the "enemy." But it drains so much of their energy to have to keep defending the justice of the feminist cause with protestations of virtue that are never finally understood. As a result of this kind of pressure, a radical feminist group in London in 1978 considered adopting the term "revolutionary feminism"—"radical," presumably, not sounding radical enough!

When *Spare Rib*, an English feminist magazine, published an article I wrote about the *American* National Women's Conference, they felt obliged to append a demurral to it, saying that they didn't agree with my version of radical feminism. After some correspondence in which I was accused of that old chestnut—wanting to see a woman chair the board of General Motors(!)—and after a visit in New York by Amanda Sebastian, a member of their editorial collective, it became suddenly clear that the *Spare Rib* radical feminists had *expected* me to be an upholder of capitalism—but that, in fact, our politics were in near-perfect agreement. Apparently, they had internalized the guilt-tripping accusations made by the left against *them* to such a degree that they had automatically assumed the charges must be true for *American* radical feminists! It seems that all their doubts arose from my observation that women are all working class —though this was an observation I had lifted from Friedrich Engels.

The resolution of this misunderstanding occurred in the spring of 1978, just after I had made another trip abroad—this time to Scandinavia. In Stockholm I had a lengthy conversation with Marianne Boye at the women's center (*Kvinnocentrum*) there. She, too, complained of guilt-tripping. Because of Sweden's high standard of living, its many socialistic reforms, and its "liberal" attitude toward sexuality, Swedish women are made to feel obscenely privileged. In reality Swedish sexual liberalism is male oriented, with women treated as receptacles, as usual. Furthermore, women have very little power in the government and their salaries are appreciably lower than those of men. Apparently, having women's meetings from which men are barred is a concept still struggling for acceptance there, and a visit by Shere Hite was poorly received because she emphasized women's need to give primary importance to their own sexual pleasure.

But it goes beyond that, I think. Sweden has become the moral arbiter for the world, and there is (to an American) a smugness about its acceptance of itself in this role.

Demonstrations there are almost invariably against the internal and foreign policies of *other* countries. Before a domestic protest gets properly started in Sweden, the government makes an effort to adjust its behavior to ease the discontent, if not completely to eradicate its cause. Some of the solutions are strangely supportive of capitalism, although they are apparently intended to be perceived as the opposite. Instead of putting a ceiling on outrageously high rents, for instance, the government subsidizes tenants. These subsidies, which augment the profits of landlords, come out of taxes which are also paid by tenants. The lip service which the government gives to socialism is based on some complicated capitalistic manipulations. Socialism is presumably fine for other countries.

Concern about economic oppression in distant lands helps to keep feminist consciousness low in Sweden. Denial of suffering by women is still the rule there: denial of the self, compassion for others. But in spite of the emphasis on female selflessness—while the men grow very rich indeed—women are beginning to create a feminist consciousness there.

Guilt-tripping of women by all factions of the patriarchy is universal. We have been trained, above all, to be good. We close our eyes to the obvious: that the men who insist on goodness in women are often themselves very, very bad—and proud of it! There is no need to reiterate here just how deep into capitalism leftist men are permitted to be and still shout "bourgeois!" at feminists. In fact, nobody looks into the checkbooks of *women* who give their energy to the left, either. Only feminists who do not give priority to Marxism are audited for class purity, and found guilty no matter how many credentials of poverty they have.

"DISARMAMENT": THE ISSUE OF
THE EIGHTIES?

As I pointed out above, leftist guilt-tripping has been less successful in the United States than it has been in the more class-conscious countries of Western Europe. The feminists who came to the movement via Betty Friedan and Billie Jean King are anything but knowledgeable about internecine leftist squabbles or the oppression of women by the left. They feel their oppression coming smack-dab at them on the job, from their husbands, and through the television tube. And so a large part of the women's movement in the United States has grown without reference to the left. The plights of minority-group women, of women on welfare, of the rural poor, and even of crippled women are of considerable concern to these new feminists, as we learned in Houston. They are also intent, with ever-lessening guilt, on personal upward mobility, and furthermore, they are demanding civil rights for lesbians. What guilt they do still feel is most likely to be related to neglect of their families. If radical feminists in large cities help to provide fuel for widespread anger against our common oppressors, grassroots feminists determine their own course. The movement has grown too big to be controlled by any self-appointed avant-garde.

By now the left has seen, and acknowledged, the failure of its efforts to stop or control feminism. But it wants "its" women back!

On May 27, 1978, fifteen thousand people marched for disarmament in front of the United Nations in New York. Many of them were women—and feminists. Most feminists are, of course, for disarmament. That sentiment certainly underlies everything we have been saying. It is unthinkable then, isn't it, for feminists *not* to put ourselves on the line for this most noble cause? Surely this is a common *human* cause, worthy of our most serious efforts.

Yes, feminists are wholeheartedly in favor of disarming men. But should we march in lines that will move for the disarmament of only *some* men? Or should we stay in the ranks of our own movement which would disarm *all* men?

I say that men can fill their own lines around the United Nations, stuff their own envelopes, go limp before the White House, march on the Pentagon again.

I have already been asked several times to join them. And caught unawares by the sweetness of their invitations (I had forgotten the charm men can summon up when they want something!), I have said, well, yes, that's my struggle, too. But then I could not bring myself to go. Something held me back. A recollection of the thinly veiled machismo of Dave Dellinger and David McReynolds, and other men who thought they understood nonviolence and could teach it to us. And other recollections: of Patricia Hearst and Sharon Tate and Assata Shakur and Jane Alpert and Joan Little and Susan Saxe taking the rap. All of the terrible misogynous jokes rush to mind, the terrible ways in which women have been screwed and ignored and driven out of our minds.

No! To end women's slavery is to disarm men—completely. It is to end war and oppression once and for all.

The leftist strategy for the eighties—and very likely for several decades thereafter—will be for disarmament. Into this struggle, on their terms, they will try to draw women back. There will be many women joining the men's lines. And we know that those "nonviolent" men will wield weapons against those of us who don't. We will be called bourgeois a thousandfold and collaborators and traitors and even *witches*. The men who want to disarm other men will be *after our blood*.

Very young women may join them; and women tired of wrestling with the guilt of "selfishness" they have never entirely been able to shake off; and women who have found the internal struggles of feminism too painful; and women who miss the old working contact with men which can be so deceivingly sensual; and women whose compassion is wrung from them; and women who very sensibly fear the end of the world and think those male-directed lines might prevent it.

But I believe that women's energies belong in the struggle to liberate women—no matter what. A poster made in China says that women hold up half the sky. I find this slogan both condescending and untrue. The execution of *all* the real needs of humanity has been our burden. For our efforts, men have blessed us with their useless and destructive military adventures, their romance with cruelty and death. Now they want us to rescue them from the fruits of their aggression.

My guilt—realistic now—turns me away from their United Nations edifices. Women have needs that have awaited attention too long: child care, abortion, rape prevention; shelters for women who must run away; the recognition of our right to reject or pursue men sexually as we see fit; the right to equal pay and advancement up the ladder to success, all the way to economic independence; and probably most important, the right of women to be *heard,* to have our perceptions validated by other women, to give our compassion to ourselves.

All of our efforts spell the disarmament of men. And I'm for that—*verily*, I am!

Women first truly entered the struggle for disarmament when we joined with other women for the liberation of our sex. If we continue and strengthen the work many of us took up when we broke *away from* the left—violent and nonviolent alike—we need apologize to no man or woman or child . . . ever.

POSTSCRIPT

Returning from my trip to Scandinavia in 1978, I picked up a copy of *Atlas*, a digest of news and opinion in the foreign press. There I read the following, by Simone de Beauvoir:

> I thought that a women's victory would be linked to the arrival of socialism. But socialism is a dream; it doesn't exist anywhere. The countries we call socialist are not socialist. Furthermore in these countries the status of women is no better than in the capitalist countries. . . .
>
> I no longer believe that an improvement in the situation of women is connected with the coming of socialism.[15]

PART II   WOMEN AND CLASS

CHAPTER SIX
Slavery, Inequity, Disunity

One of the things feminism is derided for by orthodox Marxists is a lack of economic class analysis. This observation is valid. The movement has grown organically—out of its womb, it often seems (a logical place to begin)—and feminists, as activists first, both in our own lives and in our collective struggles, have had neither the time nor, it appears, a strong inclination to divide women up into economic categories. Time has been the crucial factor, but the break from men who would not look beyond economic causality for fear of facing their own culpability as oppressors probably had much to do with feminists virtually ignoring these differences amongst ourselves. Facing many ugly facts of women's lives which had never been dealt with so thoroughly before, we were leery of confronting directly a subject so potentially divisive as class differences. And at every possible chance, as we have seen, the left *used* it to divide us and to cast blame on the "leaders" whom they accused of being bourgeois, but who, for the most part, are women with little access to money at all. In fact, that has been one of the major problems of the women's movement: a lack of money to carry out its projects. (One of the initial criticisms of feminism by its detractors was that we had no "program," it is ironic to note; later that we had no "analysis." Now it appears we have too much of both to suit them!)

In any case, if ancient women invented language and agriculture, as some authors speculate, I'm willing to go out on a limb and venture the wild guess that they did *not* invent economics. The unpaid labor assigned to women in any system of exchange has been too all-encompassing for women to have been in on the original deal. Classified in the Ten Commandments with oxen and asses, woman's primary position in the economy has been as property—not as proprietor. A useful animal, a status symbol, and a very essential means of production. Also a medium of entertainment! And it talks and, more important, it listens. Does an animal determine its own market value?

There is another reason why it would be illogical to imagine women involved in designing a means of exchange based on money: initial assignments of monetary value were made to commodities rather than for services.

From the beginning, woman's unique contribution to society has been the service of bringing children into the world and caring for them. A quantitative value cannot be placed on such a service since human life is what all other services and products are intended to support. If human life is central, then the nurturer will organize a society which promotes its safe development: a cooperative society. Labor will be seen as *the* criterion of value, and nurturance can only be compensated in kind. Being qualitative, it does not lend itself to barter.

Objects, on the other hand, can be traded since they are expendable. In a society invented by women, however, no object would be of value except as it related to life, and then its value would be inestimable—for how can you put a price on life? Thus, all work would be voluntary, for the purpose of sustaining and enhancing life. (Reason enough, one would think.)

But for men, the miracle was not the sustenance of life but its production. That was the mystery that haunted them, and woman was the center of the mystery. For men, it was not life itself or the business which surrounded it, but the *product* that was sacred. They coveted the marvel of that product—the child—and the woman's ability to produce it.

Man found that with his hands he could create products also, marvelous, lifelike products. With a little imagination they could be made to seem superior to living beings—sacred, magical. Gods! (Many feminist authors have pointed out the irony of male gods portrayed as giving birth to people when it's so obvious in nature that women are the biological creators. Surely, if God were male he would have conferred this power on His sons—created "in his image." Such portrayals are perhaps the strongest proofs available of male womb-envy.)

At first he assigned a religious value to the objects he created; then a monetary value when he found other people desired them and were willing to trade for them. Thus, based on a devaluation of life and labor, an economic system was invented. It could not have been long before women and children were traded for objects, and slavery began. The mystery of woman—a mystery born of man's ignorance—was satisfactorily debased by the values of trade. With property to protect, men competed for dominance. When, much later, men were forced to *pay* workers for their labor, they assigned work on a monetary value, as if time, skill, and care could be judged quantitatively.

All economic societies are based on the notion that the time of a person's life can be equated with objects: so many heartbeats to the dollar. Supply and demand—the number of people available, the number needed for production—determine how much each individual will be paid. This is another way of saying that human life has no intrinsic value, that the purpose of labor is not to sustain human life, that people are valued only for what they can produce. (The ultimate corruption of this product-worship is the preference for an embryo over the woman, the denial of a human being's right *not* to produce.)

When money is introduced, the value of working for one's own survival and that of the community is counterfeited. In this way, people are goaded into doing unnecessary, redundant work for the sake of the most dominant male, for to bypass money is to steal. All the raw materials from which one might fashion one's own livelihood are somebody's property, and the only entrée is money.

Money and trade were developed to give men power and prestige enough to dwarf that of woman's biological accomplishment, an accomplishment which women have undoubtedly always taken for granted as simply natural! I do not want to belabor the question of womb envy in a discussion of economics—but just to point out that competition is counterproductive to nurturance, and a society whose primary interest was in promoting life would have reason enough for laboring without placing arbitrary values on work, without trading it for something as worthless as coins. It had to be an envy of life that brought men to prize its counterfeit.

Be that as it may, the economic systems invented by men have not included women as primary beneficiaries. Every effort—physical, financial, emotional, and intellectual—is made to prevent us from achieving independence, let alone from taking control of society to bring it back into a cooperative mode. Like animals and children, women are instead controlled by chimerical temptations and awesome threats. The specter of our helplessness, which we are taught to look upon as biological rather than enforced, is used to inveigle us into "partnership" with a man who will provide for a woman and her children against incessant (manmade) emergencies. But instead of providing freely, as women have, men demand that their services be paid for by female submission to their will.

The means for a woman to provide for herself, as in agrarian societies, are cut off or greatly curtailed; she is unable to carry her offspring into the fields, so to speak, and forage for an independent livelihood. Even where this is still possible, men manage to share in her harvest and at the same time demand proprietary rights over the woman. Although women are now insisting on the right to economic independence on an equal footing with men, our primary emphasis has been on putting an end to men's physical and psychological acts of domination, because it avails us little to earn an equal paycheck if it is only to be stolen from us on the way home.

It is true that most women in twentieth-century America do work, or have worked, outside the home (albeit for less, as a rule, than a living wage), but the clues we picked up as children, and which are confirmed in adulthood, tell us that all money and power derives, ultimately, from the approval of men. Thus, whether or not we actually marry, and even if we are among those few who earn large sums of money independently, all women exhibit a set of gestures and mannerisms to reassure men that our "inherent" passivity is still intact. To keep her *earned* independence, a woman must present a dependent, almost childlike appearance. The most successful women, financially speaking, are usually those most able to maintain this facade for their iron-willed ambition. A split in the personality develops so that the right hand doesn't know what the left hand is doing: underneath a facade of inept femininity, a style which has become second nature, the mind of a first-class strategist works in its own interests "intuitively"—that is, so rapidly, automatically, and unconsciously that solutions appear as if by magic. The woman, then, cannot be held responsible for her success. She can say truthfully, because she was not conscious of the self-serving process involved, that it was all a matter of luck. In this way she preserves her passive image even to herself.[1]

The class labels men assign to us, and which we generally accept, have little or nothing to do with our own earnings. Our relationship to a particular man—father, husband, even at times a son—is the primary determinant, but evidences of education are counted, too, although these are certainly no guarantee of independent means! (A woman with a doctorate working as a librarian will earn less than a male construction worker who may not have graduated from high school, and who, if he is married to the librarian, will dominate the relationship financially as well as physically—and legally.) In terms of the patriarchy, because of our physical, psychological, and financial subservience, women can be classified only as slaves, or at best, "freed slaves."

Receiving compensation for her work is not a *right* for a woman, but a *privilege*. She must constantly struggle to please men, and to intuit *how* to please them (because they are anything but communicative), in order to be granted some stability of livelihood. It is not enough that the woman do her work efficiently; she must also have a "pleasing" disposition—and this means any way of behaving which might momentarily strike the fancy of the man she is serving. Almost totally unorganized as workers, women in any job, including marriage, have no financial security. Only in the relatively rare instance of inherited wealth can a woman feel she has "something to fall back on."

Even among women who have inherited wealth it is not the rule for them to take an active role in the businesses over which they ostensibly have some control. Indeed such women often seem more frozen into passive roles than "less fortunate" women. The tycoon may be an object of admiration or fear, but the dowager is only an object of scorn. In an article in *The New York Times Magazine* about the revival of a pro-union play of the 1930s called *Pins and Needles*, liberal columnist Heywood Broun is quoted as having said, "The show is too funny. I wish it had less entertainment value and more bite as propaganda. . . . There ought to be one number that would send some dowager screaming into the night."[2]

Dowager—not, mark you, tycoon. Among the many other free services women provide, they act as repositories for male moneymaking guilt. Like Jews, women are not supposed to enjoy any financial advantages they may have, against the odds, attained. Except within a marriage where her decorativeness shows off her *husband's* wealth to *his* advantage, a woman of means is expected to hide her wealth and devote herself to charity—though not too prominently, lest she again become a figure of fun as a "do-gooder." In this way she compensates for not being an *object* of charity herself.

The woman married to a man less wealthy than she is likely to be very self-effacing. On her lips praises for her husband's talents and intrinsic qualities will forever play—and her own accomplishments will gradually diminish beyond discernment: for the woman who has *more* money than a man is unforgivable. She must utterly deny the power money confers on her, or become as Cain, a wanderer among curses. Of all women, she is the chief candidate for the title of "castrater."

These protocols and taboos are still observed in modern society. No matter what changes have apparently taken place, women, especially those who score high in marketability, go on smiling and smiling and smiling.

(I must add here, parenthetically, that recently I visited Susan B. Anthony's home in Rochester, New York. On the walls were many pictures of old feminists, and one thing was immediately noticeable in all of them: their lips were tightly, grimly pressed together above unyielding jaws. Although I know the photographic style of the times called for solemn expressions, sheer unmistakable obstinacy marked these faces, and I thought: so *that's* what it takes!)

For all the real differences in "buying power" among American women (and the differences are of the greatest importance), female slavery has not ended completely for *any* of us. We are not expressing, in our hesitant speech patterns, our mincing walks, residual scars of past servitude. We are responding to the requirements for female survival *today*.

THE WIFE AS TWO-FER

The epitome of female slavery is the First Lady. Although no salary is allocated for her by Congress, it is assumed that the President's wife will both take charge of the household arrangements of the executive mansion and act as the President's chief diplomatic aide. In addition, she will, of course, continue to be responsible for the usual unpaid wifely duties of child care and sex.

When Bess Truman was apparently too shy or awkward to fulfill the roles of hostess and occasional spokesperson to the press, her daughter was drafted into Harry Truman's service. When Eleanor Roosevelt traveled on unpaid diplomatic missions, her daughter was similarly enlisted. Although Woodrow Wilson's remarriage so shortly after his first wife's death scandalized some citizens, it had to be admitted, after all, that the White House needed a hostess!

At this point it would be virtually impossible for a man to be elected to the presidency whose wife was determined to maintain her own career and would not serve in the White House. Even before election, she is a necessity as a campaigner (which may be one reason why women, who usually don't have wives, have such difficulty getting elected). One of Adlai Stevenson's great handicaps was not just the *fact* of his divorce, but that he had no wife on the campaign trail.

While wives are great vote-getters, they exert little or no influence on the government—although the myth of "the power behind the throne" persists. Eleanor Roosevelt garnered radical votes for her husband that his policies clearly didn't rate. And so, while the First Lady might wear, sometimes at great strain (e.g., Mamie Eisenhower, Patricia Nixon, and Betty Ford), the airs of the ruling class, she has less legal accreditation than the President's valet.

Should a President put his wife on the payroll, this would be regarded as heinous nepotism—incomparably worse than John F. Kennedy's appointing his brother attorney general. But the country does not object to *drafting* politician's wives without pay.

In the late fifties and early sixties there were a number of films about executives' wives. While employers are notoriously reluctant to hire married women, particularly of childbearing age, in crucial positions (and older women are too *old*!), they seem most anxious to hire married *men*. Wives, according to these films, are interviewed for top posts with their husbands, although only the husbands are candidates for the jobs. As couples, they are interviewed in appropriate settings: at parties where the wives can show off their charm and taste in clothes, or in the couple's own home, where the boss can see the wife as hostess. The employer knows that when he's got a well married man, he's got a two-fer!

It is clear that these wives, no matter how "favored" by their husbands, are slaves. And yet they are regarded (by those who like to see dowagers run screaming into the night, pursued by rapists, kidnapers, and homicidal maniacs) as having a real position within the patriarchal class system. They are called members of the middle, and even the ruling, classes, according to their husbands' positions.

I have begun with these illustrations of slavery in the upper marital strata because I wanted to demonstrate that slavery can exist in the context of affluence. A slave is a person whose labor, time, and physical presence are subject to the will of another without either stipulated financial compensation or recognition of her own inherent right to self-determination.

In other words, if a person freely contracts to be available on a twenty-four-hour basis for a limited amount of time and for a definite amount of money, she is not, in the full sense, a slave. If the government were to pay the First Lady a salary for the work she performs for it, and if the President himself were to give her an additional salary for the private time she is on call for him, and if these contracts had a time limit, then she would not be a full slave, but only a "freed slave."

But where a contract with specified financial compensation does not exist; when a person's indispensable public work is given no official recognition; when a woman is simply "expected" to weather the vicissitudes of her husband's ambition or fate—"for better or worse"—and can be penalized for looking around for another job . . . ah! parallels become absurd. A man, even a poor man (though perhaps not the most destitute), has but to imagine himself in the role of a First Lady or an executive's wife to realize that such negation of the person is contrary to any idea of freedom or dignity.

ECONOMIC EQUALITY AS A FEMINIST GOAL

Beyond the two-fer concept it is important to look at those real economic divisions among women which are likely, more and more as time goes on, to erupt among us. Since the attempts at a class analysis by the early Class Workshop and by The Feminists, little theorizing in this area has been done, for feminist groups tend to be fairly homogeneous and to concentrate on issues of immediate concern to their members. Large organizations, such as N.O.W., are action oriented.

Most radical feminists who might have addressed the question of economic divisions belong to a class I will call the "educated poor," and both business and government are making powerful efforts to seduce these women away from any effort to collectivize economically. If evidences of discontent in facist and socialist countries are overtly suppressed, in our country the attempt is to maintain an appearance of free expression while the dissidents (and *potential* dissidents) are carefully manipulated to fight amongst themselves. The illusion of abundant and equal opportunity for all is provided by dramatic and well publicized opportunities for a few people among the "out" groups. The rest are thereby made to feel that scrambling (or gambling) for the top is a chance worth taking, and they pour their energies into competing with one another. Thus we see women going to college in their late thirties and even forties, after their children are grown, to develop careers which they hope will make them independent for the second half of their lives, at least. (How many of these women succeed in their reentry trials is doubtful. The attempt, however, does give zest to their lives, and if the results turn out to be massively unsatisfactory, it is possible that these newly aware women will respond with collective action.)

The present emphasis of grassroots feminism is on individual self-advancement. For most women the necessity to earn an immediate survival income precludes their concentrating on anything else. N.O.W. has as its major goal to bring women into the "mainstream." By this it apparently means parity with men on every level of the economy as it is now, without disturbing the hierarchy. It will indeed be difficult, if not impossible, to achieve even that: to raise the incomes of poor women to the level of working-class men, of women in middle-class jobs to that of their peers, and so on. The token advances for which we now wildly compete will not solve this problem, and it is hard to predict how long it will take women to find that out. We are going through a learning process. However long it does take and however painful and discouraging the experience, we must be free to discover for ourselves the limitations of this kind of struggle.

With this new knowledge it is possible women will create new ways to work collectively.

In the meantime, the government and forces on the right are bending heaven (if not earth) to seduce or abduct women back into the family, and the left is making the same kind of effort to trivialize our needs and guilt-trip us into serving the ends of the "working class" —meaning men. We have to be very strong to withstand this double barreled attack and continue to work for our own independence.

But the left is essentially correct in viewing parity with men, within the status quo, as a short-sighted goal for feminists, although not for the reason the left gives: that women should be too "moral" to pursue individual self-interest. And not even for the more practical reason that so few of us are likely to hit the jackpot: it is, damn it, the American way to try, as many heavily achieving male leftists know.

The fact is, the class system among women—in which some women have greater access to money than others; some are "freed slaves"; some act as overseers; and some are apologists for the oppressors—works against achieving feminist unity. Within the women's movement we have already seen considerable rivalry between those who feel they are "more oppressed" than others and those who plead to be allowed to advance as rightful heirs of successful fathers. Feminists have sidestepped this issue by pointing out, truthfully, that women in toto are economically worse off than men. While it is true that a woman can have access to a great deal of money and still have little control over her own life, in fact poor women have even less control over their lives.

One of the objects of feminism is to draw women *away* from being spectators at those quiz shows where a few women, jumping up and down and giggling and kissing the emcee, win a washing machine or a weekend in Las Vegas. The poor woman should not have to stand around applauding, like a good sport, when another woman lands that oft-cited presidency of General Motors. (When *will* that job be open, by the way—and where do I apply?) Pointing to the fact that feminism has, from the beginning, been opposed to political hierarchies, poor women can justly demand that it also oppose the economic hierarchy.

Many poor women see feminism mainly as an opportunity for certain women able to take advantage of token openings, and so they scoff at it, at least in its widely (and often erroneously) publicized manifestations. (Its insights regarding their relationships with men may be privately cherished.) There is nothing arbitrary or stingy about women resenting other women for "getting ahead," even when they don't show an equal resentment of *men* advancing. The hopes feminism has aroused are felt by every individual woman; the political has become very personal. So long as there was virtually no economic opportunity for any woman, or only in terms of catching a rich man, women as a whole didn't feel personally inferior for not succeeding on their own. Now women, instead of feeling guilty for the dirty rings around men's collars, can feel inferior for not having what it takes to get ahead! By stressing parity with men over equality among women, moderate women's groups, and even some radical feminists, have encouraged a new kind of self-blame.

On the other hand, for women who are finding—or, however hopeless the outcome, are looking to find—new economic opportunities leading to independence, it is terrible to hear that we shouldn't try to grab them. The guilt that we have been taught to feel becomes especially painful and seems most unfair when we are just learning to compare ourselves, like men, with the haves instead of the have-nots.

Those of us who do not advance feel a natural resentment—and we should, because the system is patently unfair, advancement having no relation to merit. Women who feel such resentment should not have to put on the smile of the good sport, hoping our turn will come someday. And those who do advance *do,* by and large, feel guilty—so why should we deny it? To compare ourselves with those who are worse off indicates we haven't lost our sensitivity, that at heart we do understand the basic inequity and villainy of the patriarchy, in its economic manifestation as well as in its other modes of oppression. Does it just take hardening of the heart to move up in the hierarchy as the assertiveness-training manuals suggest? I think they are fooling us: the patriarchal club is too tight. It ain't that easy. Keeping our hearts soft enough to join with our peers in collective action will probably get us a good deal further. That is what the patriarchal club is afraid of—and why they feed us such divisive advice.

Without unity there will be no liberation for women. By unity I do not mean total agreement on a party line, but a shared sense that the basic aims of the movement include all women: that our goal is nothing less than equality for all women in every aspect of our lives. As long as any woman can be forced *for any reason*—including financial gain—to give herself sexually to men, no woman's independence is secure. And as long as we accept parity in the male hierarchy, as it is, we will be beset by internal rivalry. Men will extract sexual favors from women as the price of advancement and play all the other games of dominance we are at last admitting are so repugnant. Telling us that we must be ruthlessly competitive like them is one of their games. What they mean is competitive with women—but not with those in power: men. For, after all, *who* will be making that space for us at the top? So whose ass do we continue to lick?

Parity with men *may* be a legitimate and useful goal, but only in conjunction with equality among women. If you think about that sentence a moment, you will realize that I am advocating equality for all—which means the attainment of a cooperative rather than a competitive society, or what women would have had to begin with if we had ordered the economy.

What am I saying, then? Am I just substituting the word "women" for "workers" in the Marxist blueprint?

That, in itself, would be a significant substitution. For the change admits a very different spectrum of means, and means—the steps we take—are truly ends in themselves, as every moment we live is a complete entity. Keeping the end in view, for men, with few exceptions, has meant fighting ruthlessly toward it, whether the end was, ostensibly, an equitable and cooperative society or a competitive one. Marx postulated the "dictatorship of the proletariat" as a means toward a cooperative end. The very sound of that is threatening to women, for we know who the proletariat are: the bully boys. And male pacifists, declaring human life to be sacred, have sacrificed an awful lot of it in martyrdom to achieve ends which also, ultimately, proved all but worthless. (Is India significantly better off now than it was under British rule? How many Indian lives did Gandhi's pacifist effort cost?)

If we examine our goal closely, we will see that it is not exactly as men have defined it. A cooperative society depends on the desire to cooperate. Thus, what is needed is a change of heart.

Like most feminist insights, this one is easy for men to trivialize. "How naive!" we can hear them expostulate. "What about power? Will the president of General Motors give up his power?" (Him, again.) "Will Brezhnev?"

Alas, no. But these men will die eventually. We give too much weight to their power, too little to our own. We have the numbers and the genius—all untried—to work out ways of cooperating amongst ourselves, to develop sisterhood where brotherhood has failed. For all that the preceding chapters of this book, and of our lives, attest to the sturdiness of conflict among feminists, never before has there been such a will exhibited by women to find a way to peace together.

GUILT: LEGITIMATE
AND COUNTERPRODUCTIVE

The steps toward making over society into what it must become for women to be full and equal beings on this planet will reveal themselves as we continue to test our own perceptions and learn to trust them, accepting the inevitable guilt that must attend all achievement, while inequality exists, as one of our true perceptions. For *this* guilt identifies our acknowledgement that we are not, ourselves, yet free. It is our recognition that our own situations, however "privileged," are still precarious and will remain dependent on the arbitrary favors of men until all women have attained full personhood. *This* guilt, then, derives from intelligent self-interest. A slave who has been "freed," whether by her own efforts or through some special dispensation of a master, can never truly be free while female slavery is an accepted fact of society, for there is no badge or sign she can carry—not even a credit card—which will protect her in the world at large. When the single woman with her own income walks down the street or even participates in business or social engagements with men, she takes the same risks as her less independent sisters: sometimes more, because a woman who is owned by a man may be protected by him, declared sacrosanct at least when she is in his company. So to feel guilt for advancement in the patriarchy is, in reality, to establish a sisterly bond of support *for oneself*.

In itself, advancement within the patriarchy does not hurt other women and may, at times, even be helpful to the movement. Right now, we are much too dependent on funds coming directly through men: from the government and from foundation grants. When women earn more money, we can provide some of the funds needed for feminist projects. Advancement of women as doctors, lawyers, scientists, and in representative government positions can, ideally, help all women to get better treatment in these areas. Advancement of women in the arts and in teaching can help to promote and preserve the cultural heritage we are producing. Advancement of women into better-paying jobs throughout the system, even as it is, helps these women, themselves, to survive and become independent of income sources which might bind them to men in a personal way and prevent them from knowing whether these relationships continue to exist through choice or through necessity. Finally, getting above the poverty line makes many pleasures, and the realization of all kinds of potential talents, possible. Health and spirits improve, and there is nothing wrong with that!

It is important for us to be wary of being guilt-tripped by men who would exploit our compassion for their own purposes, and by women who are richer than us and want to pass their heavier load of guilt onto our shoulders by insisting we give lip service to a party line which is essentially useless to feminism. I have observed, for instance, that it is generally my rich friends (either independently so or attached to husbands who are rich) who become upset when I question Marxist orthodoxy or when I use my energy for domestic feminist problems rather than carrying signs in front of foreign embassies to protest some perhaps indisputable evil thousands of miles away, which I neither fully understand nor about which I can accomplish much. A quick way to stop receiving invitations to fashionable leftist parties is to inquire closely how the host earns his money!

The fact is that whatever we do to make a living in this society involves some kind of oppression of others, or assisting those who oppress others. That is an unhappy truth, and there is no reason to deny it. Hence, there *is* reason enough for *some* guilt in most of our lives. So long as this guilt is related directly to our being instrumental in oppressing others, or even if it is based on having had an opportunity not available to others, it is a reality to be reckoned with. The honorable woman will consider her alternatives and will try to limit her complicity in causing suffering insofar as she is able. She will also participate in collective activities tending toward equalizing opportunity and wealth *among women*. To repress an awareness of injustice is to deny a true perception; the best way to relieve the guilt it may inspire is to act on it.

These are, of course, ethical problems, and every decision carries weighty questions with it. We cannot expect, the world being what it is, to walk around completely free of guilt. There is no easy way out of such problems, and I think we should avoid the panaceas offered by the Book-of-the-Month Club. If we want to get ahead in this rotten world, we must be prepared, at least, to sacrifice some sleep! And we might spend those sleepless nights thinking of ways to create a more equitable society. Or how, very simply, to be kinder to one another.

We *have* the right, each of us, in these imperfect times, to draw our own circles around how much guilt we have honestly accumulated in the process of surviving, how much we can stand to bear, and how much we can realistically throw off by acting according to our deepest convictions. Remembering our class differences and feeling the empathy that concern generates, becoming ever more conscious and sensitive to the ways women are divided against ourselves — these are the disciplines through which we will learn what we need to do.

It is worth remembering, too, that our class differences *as women* were not created by us and are not necessary to our intrinsic sense of well-being or self-respect. The underside of things that we experience not even the poorest, most discriminated against man can imagine. He cannot imagine it because, whoever he is, his sexual superiority is written into every legal and moral code.

Now let us consider class differences among women.

CHAPTER SEVEN

Three Classes of Poor Women

Men have talked at great length, particularly over the last two centuries, about the distribution of wealth. Really, they have been talking about money, because to receive goods freely when one does not have money is, in their lexicon, either to accept charity or to steal. There is no dignity without money and so they keep it for themselves. Whether large sums or small, they retain control of it. This is a simplification, but it is also very largely true. (We are forced to generalize in order to undo men's sophistries.)

We live in a time of revolution. Everywhere men talk about and seek ways to end "human" poverty, by which they mean the poverty of men. Everywhere men take up arms to end "human" misery, while the women who fight beside them continue to wear veils, suffer clitorectomies, bear more children than they want or the world needs, makes vows of eternal loyalty to men they hardly know at altars where men are licensed to revile them. Church, state, and custom imprison women in ignorance and fear of men, until we lack the courage to demand our rights or even to know what they might be.

Therefore, it is time to speak of women's poverty, one facet of our misery. It is time again to speak of *human* poverty and to declare that behind our veils, behind our aprons, behind our broods of children, behind our forbidden love of one another, underneath the conjugal sheets we are human — and we are poor.

The social classes into which we are born or marry in the Western world often obscure even to ourselves the fact of our poverty. On top of that, as other feminists have observed, we expect little.[1] An engagement ring or a washing machine may make us feel middle class when we have not one cent to call our own; a college diploma can make us feel privileged in the typing pool.

In this chapter, I avoid the class terminology we learned from Marx. Our class is slavery. Within that category we are treated relatively well or badly. Most of us are poor. Here I describe, then, three classes of poor women, and some of what we are up against.

THE DESTITUTE POOR

The vast majority of women are poor and struggling, not only to provide for themselves and their children, but frequently under the added burden of male brutality. Where there is no man about the premises, the brutality can come from the state acting *in loco viri*. In both cases the authority a woman must try to please is arbitrary and provides little information about its tastes.

Welfare allotments are treated as a special favor—an act of generosity—by the state. While the woman with children who has no means of support is described officially as the "head" of her family, in fact the state plays that role, and stingily. It provides just barely enough money for rent and a meager diet—no money at all for clothing in most cases. Welfare recipients are apparently expected to give up food when new clothes are required, and with growing children such sacrifices are frequently necessary.

Day care centers for children are scarce, in many places nonexistent. The mother cannot, therefore, look for a full-time job, even if she had the clothes to make herself presentable and even if jobs were more readily available than they are. For a woman with older children, in the kinds of neighborhoods where people on welfare are forced to live, there is the worry about children returning home to an empty house—even if the kids are teen-agers. But then, *children* on welfare are also regarded as expendable.

The woman on welfare is not permitted to develop a relationship with a man, since any man she might choose to live with is considered a breadwinner. In fact, it is rare for a woman on welfare to find a man who is not also destitute.

The woman on welfare is not permitted to take a part-time job to supplement her income. If she does, the state will deduct her earnings from her stipend. Out of desperation, many women on welfare take "off-the-books" jobs as baby sitters and house cleaners. If they are found out, they can be removed from welfare and arrested on charges of fraud.

Of course, if a woman goes certifiably mad from trying to live this way—and many do—she can go on Supplementary Security Income, dispensed by Social Security to people who are incapacitated. All she needs is two psychiatrists to state that her mental condition makes it impossible for her to support herself, even if she *could* get a job. SSI in some cases is less than she would receive on welfare, but the Social Security administrators do not demand that recipients report at arbitrary times on their private lives. "Going mad," then, is one of the insane options offered to poor women!

Another alternative to welfare is prostitution. When this was legalized in Nevada some years ago, a number of women were removed from welfare because "legal" work had been opened up to them! Since laws are made for men, the categories of work are divided into "legal" and "illegal," with no room for the gray areas where women's "work" often falls. Thus, women advocating decriminalization of prostitution must be wary of the language they use in framing bills, lest men once against turn an essentially humanitarian effort to their own crooked advantage.

In New York, where prostitution is not legal, I joined a demonstration in front of a "massage parlor" in which a prostitute had been murdered. By simply calling them "massage parlors," pimps in large cities throughout the country are able not only to bypass laws against bordellos, but to advertise them with street leaflets, right under the noses of the police. The flyers show pictures of nude women with siliconed breasts or heterosexual couples or trios cavorting on beds, and promise "complete satisfaction guaranteed." A familiar cry in the Times Square area is the massage parlor hawker's "Check it out!"

I was told by the organizer of the demonstration, Marie Magoo of Scapegoat (the prostitutes' "union" in New York), that at first prostitutes had welcomed the appearance of massage parlors because they thought they would be less dangerous than the streets. (Rolling out of movie houses which feature sadism or pornography shops whose still photographs are equally inciting to violence, the pathological-in-everyday-life head for the nearest available hooker, frequently a "third world" woman no more than sixteen years old; prostitutes receive no protection from the police.) In a massage parlor I suppose a woman hopes to find protection by a pimp *on the premises*. But in the one we were picketing, a prostitute had been repeatedly stabbed in view of the manager, who didn't call the police until her attacker had got away. By the time the ambulance arrived, she had bled to death. (To my knowledge, no arrests were ever made.) On the same day as this murder, another had occurred down the street when a pimp threw a prostitute out of a "hotel" window.

Among some feminists these days, it is chic to praise prostitution as an "alternative." If this is an attempt to make the destitute streetwalker feel better about herself, I think it is gravely misguided. There are other ways to support the self-esteem of women who, with few options available, have chosen this form of slavery. To point out that all women are victims, one way or another, of the chicanery of men might give them a sense of solidarity with sisters in other conditions of slavery, while helping them to understand their own situation in political terms. Almost all feminist efforts are compound: (1) to urge women to struggle, as best we can, out of our various conditions of slavery, and (2) to support our needs and demands where we are. Comprehended this way, unnecessary conflicts between those who want to struggle for workers' rights and those who want to end the existence of exploitative work can be avoided. The two efforts are complementary.

Poverty is poverty, and for most destitute people there is no present way out of it. The one decent hope, education, is largely denied to the poor, particularly in big cities. Using rationales as suspect as legalizing prostitution in Nevada, school officialdom systematically lowers the definition of "literacy" for nonwhite children. Limitations on education serve to keep the poor from rising, either through individual upward mobility or through cogent collective action. Only a few of their number, blessed with some specific marketable virtue—beauty, musical or athletic prowess, an implacable drive for self-education—slip through all the legal and de facto barriers to the place where upward mobility begins to be possible. For most, the poverty they were born into is their destiny. Denied escape through academic achievement and with employment attenuated on the lowest paid, unskilled levels, the other "outs" available to poor people put them in constant jeopardy of criminal charges. Aside from welfare, which some think is no better than imprisonment, the only other options are welfare "cheating," prostitution, drug selling, thievery, and the like. Furthermore, the government, in the name of the most specious and obviously biased "morality," prevents poor women from controlling their own reproductive machinery.

The poor are treated as children, with the government a mean and punitive father. To him, destitute women are factories for the production of cheap labor and cannon fodder. When he wants to limit the number of births, he institutes forced sterilization. In the patriarchy, by whatever means, men (church, state, or spouse) are determined to control reproduction.

There are no advantages, not even spurious ones, to the destitute woman's condition of slavery. For her the shadowy vision of a feminist utopia in which seemingly rich women have broken away from psychologically distressing but otherwise luxurious male-dominated homes is less convincing than the picture of "contented" male-dominated homes which beams at her daily from the television screen. The media's careful selection of feminist "spokeswomen" who look affluent keeps her from identifying with the masses of feminists who are struggling not only for independence but for a *living*. To tell a woman on welfare that The Family is a trap is the equivalent of telling a woman who has finally earned enough money to rent a decent apartment and put some cash away for a vacation that she is guilty of being "bourgeois."

The destitute woman wants the things she sees around her: what the social worker has, what the teacher has, what the lady-of-the-house she works for has. An improved brand of modern female slavery would suit her just fine.

It is this desperation that the patriarchy preys on when it picks out a selected few to bless with upward mobility. And even this blessing is double-edged when it comes to black women: because black women, trained to passivity like other women, usually have more patience with the regimentation and arbitrary insults of the school system, they frequently make more progress there than black men. As a result, they are sometimes better prepared to take advantage of the few higher educational opportunities. Often they get more prestigious jobs even when they are less well paying than the blue-collar jobs occasionally available to black men. The media (read propaganda) then fill these women with guilt for taking opportunities "away from" men. The women are accused of being matriarchs . . . castraters. They are encouraged to wallow in passivity and "catch" husbands who can support them, thus proving their true "femininity."

The fact is, it is a rare woman, married or single, black or white, who can afford to lie around on a chaise lounge drying her pedicure while her husband toils. Nonetheless, to deride that hope without being ready to offer something more realistic in exchange is not visionary but callous. Perhaps the most sensible thing feminists, defined as such more by their concern for women than by their antagonism toward men, can do is to make the option of The Family more realizable for poor women—to demand that the government stop its either-or shilly-shallying and make more and better jobs available for all. Only when the television dream (or, rather, its un-idealized counterpart) is possible will the destitute woman be able to make a rational choice.

THE RESPECTABLE POOR

To feminists destitute women should be the primary reason for change (although *economic* destitution is not the only kind there is), for the depths of exploitation which mark them are held out as a threat to all women. Everything—all the small gains some women have made—can be nullified by the patriarchy on a whim. No true rights exist for women. The *privileges* some women enjoy are simply favors granted by men, compensation for much larger favors extracted from women.

Destitute women are the living example for all women of what our powerlessness, our slavery, means. We do not speak of a "fallen" man. Men's fortunes may change depending upon the fluctuations of the economy, the vicissitudes of power politics, and wars in which they have a hand, but women "fall from grace"—the grace of men.

Women on the lowest levels of "earned" income (their own, their husbands', or both) feel little guilt, conscious or unconscious, toward their truly destitute sisters. Their realistic fear of dropping into that condition themselves may understandably turn into hatred for those who are there. (I am not suggesting that the destitute poor are less respectable in any real sense, but in the patriarchy people with earned income are granted a respect which the destitute are not.)

The respectable poor are those with no more than a

high school diploma who work, or have worked, at clerical jobs, as bank tellers, as beauticians, in factories and hospitals, and the like. If they are married to men in blue-collar jobs, they may have stopped working outside the home temporarily in order to raise children, but they are likely to start again, at least part time, when their children are older, because it is difficult to maintain a family on one salary—even a man's union salary. Their own small wages then go into the family pool, usually to subsidize food and rent, and, if possible, to help at least one of their children attain a higher education.

Whatever their husbands are like, married women in this class are truly stuck with them. If these women are abandoned when their children are young, they go on welfare. Any brutality (not that poor men are necessarily more brutal than rich men) may be felt to be better than that alternative.

It is these women, particularly, who are the targets of such right-wing puppets as Anita Bryant, Phyllis Schlafly, and Marabel Morgan. Because their lives are so circumscribed, because they see "real" poverty as an ever-present threat and have no hope for personal upward mobility (although a glimmer of hope for their children), they can find a kind of comfort in narrow-mindedness. Outcasts—homosexuals, communists, blacks, Jews, women who have traded their ladylike respectability to scream in the streets about rapes and abortions and lesbianism—are to be feared because "there but for the grace of . . ." or "Fools go where angels fear to tread"; but at the same time, the outcast's existence as "other," as less blessed than their own, provides a certain self-esteem by comparison.

The respectable poor are divided from the destitute by clever propagandists who point to welfare as the place where the tax money of the "hard-working" poor goes. It is hard to understand why this obvious fraud is widely believed in a country which blatantly steals from the poor to subsidize the rich. Perhaps the working poor have invested so heavily in the raiments of respectability that they cannot bear to think that respectability itself is a trap: that nobody believes in it except the poor.

From a feminist's point of view, I know how hard it is to admit to oneself that one has been fooled *as a woman*. One feels so stupid and ashamed. To have been taken in by "sweet talk" seems, in the *cock-eyed* lexicon of values we have been subliminally taught, more demeaning than to be the betrayer. It is so hard to say, "I have been had." It is easier to ascribe to one's lover a noble conscience and to believe that he ignores his own happiness for the sake of a cause.

"Charity begins at home," the respectable poor declare, because they have been made to believe they *are* the government's true family. Ponderously, the government points to welfare "cheating." *There* is your rival, it says. The real robbers are too far away, too high and mighty, too *respectable* to be questioned. They are encased in the impenetrable armor of gray suits and clean white shirts, bespectacled, distinguished. They are . . . unimpeachable!

Equal rights for women (meaning independence) threatens particularly working-class men whose self-respect and sense of "privilege" reside almost exclusively in providing for and owning their families. Equal rights might make it possible for their wives to achieve full working-class status, to be rivals for husbands' jobs.

The chances are much less likely that highly skilled women would be admitted en masse to the upper-echelon positions currently occupied by men. Men in such jobs have the power to keep them out of women's hands no matter what laws are passed. Working-class men feel justifiably more threatened by the specter of equal rights than do their bosses, to whom some of the litigation involved and the necessity to appoint "tokens" would just be a nuisance. Powerful men have ways of getting around laws, although they, too, prefer not to be bothered.

Working-class men, on the other hand, may express their fears in the form of anger and bad jokes at home. Women who are totally financially dependent on, and at the physical mercy of, their men generally avoid political arguments with them. They take up their grievances in private conversations with their best friends. For all their "faults," their men *do* bring home the bacon—and beatings, abandonment, "real" poverty, and the rebukes of their best friends await the woman who rebels.

The pressure to be respectable—to appear to be bourgeois—is enormous in America. With very little upward mobility available, people are constrained, one way or another, to appear as if they have "made it." Above all, it is the woman who must uphold that status in her community. A man may engage in working-class roughhouse with his cronies, but when he brings them home, the house must be immaculate, his wife well dressed and demure. A man may refuse to go to church (it is considered manly to refuse), but his wife earns stripes for regular attendance. A man may fuss at his wife for being dull and old-fashioned, but he is furious if she isn't!

One of the areas where this is changing is in sexuality. The notion that it is all right to enjoy heterosexual pleasure (fucking) has been around long enough among the educated classes to have filtered down to the respectable poor. On television quiz shows these days, married women of this class confess, with giggles and blushes, to having slept with their husbands before marriage. In some circles "wife-swapping" and even "swinging" are acceptable. The goals of the "sexual revolution" are established. Hugh Hefner reigns.

Wives are now expected to be "naughty but nice." In direct competition with X-rated movie queens, they want to learn the tricks of the harlot. Marabel Morgan is their guide to the delights of creating a respectable brothel at home. There is no longer even the division of labor between the housewife who cooks and cleans and tends the children, and the prostitute who feeds the man's fantasies. The money he might previously have held out for an hour with a streetwalker, he now presumably gives his wife to dress the part. (This is the right's last desperate attempt to hold The Family together.)

There is no room in such a woman's life for thoughts of herself. She is the "totaled woman." The narcissism her behavior suggests is thoroughly selfless. To maintain a perfect image is a matter of survival. Punishment for rebellion is abandonment by both her husband and the community.

As I write this, I recall the peculiar pain of having given up some few aspects of conformity. One does not do this without some terrible inner necessity. In a society where comfort is virtue, there is no real pride in nonconformity. One needs legions of support, and even then there are fantasies of running away altogether to some magic land where the eccentric is the norm. We try to create our own little islands in our cities; are glad to return to these ghettoes; try to see ourselves as superior, but know the bitter truth that we have failed to make it as "normal women." There was no *will* involved: one just didn't measure up!

And so spending one's life in the endless routines that are expected is a way of stemming this pain. No one, of course, completely measures up: that's the game—to keep us all on a treadmill. The rewards are the husband's pleasure, until he gets bored, and bread on the table. But one ceases to think of that, one ceases to think of anything at all except being the perfect carbon copy of the woman in the television ad—and if imperfect, then at least "cutely" so.

The woman in the television ad is superficially changing, though, as the medium hears complaints from outspoken feminists. The women's movement, in all its diversity, is large and growing, and many women in all classes have got the message that the toilet-paper model is neither a dignified nor a flattering image of womanhood. The updated model is slightly more assertive and proud of a quasi-independence; single women are represented.

Now, in addition to all the other demands on her, the respectable poor woman, whether she is a receptionist or a manicurist, single or married, will be pressured into presenting herself as a cool, self-assertive career woman on her way up. The reality changes very little; only the eye shadow is altered.

What this will mean in terms of the opinions she expresses is hard to tell. Whether Schlafly-Bryant-Morgan wins out or the Upwardly-Mobile-Feminist may depend on whether she is single or married and, if the latter, to whom she is married. The time of her life is also important. In any case, the choices above are the ones the media offer her, with collective feminism played down. So long as women's *isolation* isn't tampered with, the status quo remains unthreatened. The chance at real upward mobility is a virtual pipe dream; hence, it is promised freely to block out the real troublemaker: collective political action.

It is important, too, that whatever happens, the specter

of lesbianism be kept as a threat, so that respectable poor women will avoid gathering for group consciousness-raising. For it is in consciousness-raising that the bonds of feminism are forged, and whatever choices a woman makes afterwards will reflect a new awareness of her relationship to society. The difficulties she meets as she tries to move ahead with her life will be seen no longer as personal failures but as the common lot of women, and particularly of women born into her class. Rather than holding a woman back in despair, this knowledge helps her to turn compliance into anger, and anger into energy to persevere. But the fear of becoming a lesbian or even of being with with lesbians holds "respectable" heterosexual women back from gathering with each other to explore their mutual condition of womanhood. Lesbians among the respectable poor remain largely invisible. To "come out" means an open break with respectability—automatically puts one in another social, and often economic class.

ECONOMIC RIVALRIES

There are three basic fears, then, which keep many respectable poor women from moving openly toward feminism: the fear of threatening, and thus enraging, the males they are attached to; the fear of being abandoned to destitution; and the fear of being identified as a lesbian. For these reasons, one often hears such women begin very insightful tirades against their situations with, "I'm not a women's libber, but. . . ."

The first fear is the father of the other two. While men are likely to become enraged by *any* departure from submissiveness in the women they control, one of *their* deep fears of the women's movement is that it will force them out of their jobs in favor of women. Not only will they then lose control over "their" women, but they will lose their own livelihoods. Thus they would become destitute men, homeless and idle.

To reassure men that women are not after *their* jobs but want equally good jobs of our own would seem a sensible concession from feminists, provided the men will support women's right to equal pay. The effort to secure equal opportunity and equal pay for women should not set up a competition between women and men for jobs, the way such rivalries have been incited between poor blacks and poor whites. The feminist demand should be for more jobs for everyone. There are many ways short of war by which the government can achieve full and well paid employment if that becomes its priority. Public facilities such as hospitals, schools, and so on, have become shockingly inadequate in recent years when the priorities of the rich and greedy have blatantly dominated this country. The rise of women should be seen as a step toward positive economic change for everybody. Women construction workers, for instance, should mean *more* construction workers—not just a change of faces. If men feel that equal rights for women means doubling the family income, they will be less difficult to live with while the struggle is being waged than if they feel they are personally being threatened economically. Women then will be less afraid to say out loud they *are* "women's libbers," with the other implications of that statement perhaps reserved for their sisters' ears.

We cannot reassure men that they will keep their wives, but we *can* reassure them that we do not want to steal their livelihoods, and by so doing, women who are dependent on them will not bear the brunt of guilt for competing, or feel that by increasing their own earning power they will necessarily be losing their husbands'. We have enough physical and psychological problems with men without extending the range of struggle into basic economic warfare with working men.

Economics is only one area in which women are oppressed by the patriarchy, but it is crucial to the achievement of independence. It is also the area in which the gravest dangers of intrafeminist rivalry arise. If the demands for equal opportunities and equal pay for women are attached to a demand for full employment, the appeal to both destitute and respectable poor women will be infinitely greater. The guilt that such women now feel about being "selfish" would fall from their shoulders. Yes, men must learn to get along without "wives"; they must learn to cook for themselves and clean up after themselves and change the babies' diapers; they must learn that sex is a desire, not a demand, and that women deserve full pleasure; they must learn that women alone have the right to control reproduction, although men can *ask* (nicely) for babies; they must learn, above all, not to be bullies: but they have a right to be reassured that *their* incomes will not be taken away. On upper levels of the hierarchy incomes may, eventually, have to be reduced, but on the lowest levels men as well as women are entitled to hope for not only equal earnings but improved prospects.

The right will, of course, deal with such a demand as a "leftist plot," and the male left will try to assert leadership. These are two good reasons why feminists have not yet articulated this demand. How can we keep men from taking over our movement when their own jobs are at stake? Up to the present time, men have handled economic issues so crudely! And as soon as they get in control, they forget all about women! Or, rather, they want to control *us*. As union leaders, they have shown little interest in supporting the special needs of women workers.

This is a conundrum which deserves the most serious consideration among those it most directly concerns: poor women. As we shall see, there are really *three* classes of poor women; these comprise the majority of women in this country. By conferring across the divisions of *social* class which at the moment prevent these women from sharing their resources, the three groups together may develop a new understanding of their similar needs which will create a bloc of female workers to confront the male-dominated unions, employers, and government, all of whom have a vested interest in keeping women disunited and passive.

THE EDUCATED POOR

Even in the case of the destitute poor, poverty in America—particularly in large cities—is not always easy to spot. People take great pains to hide it here, where the denial of class makes it seem something shameful: the result of personal inadequacy. A lot of ingenuity goes into achieving a chic appearance. Fortunes are made by the hucksters of cheap, mass-produced goods with their heartlessly built-in obsolescence.

There is yet another class of poor women, one which often hides its poverty so successfully that not only the destitute and respectable poor are deceived into thinking of them as rich, but those who really are significantly better off financially think of them as in their class. I am speaking of the *educated* poor: women who have managed, in spite of the deficiencies of the public schools, to get a substantial education. Among them are older women who grew up at a time when the school system was far superior to what it is now. Others have been tracked in the public schools through "gifted" classes. Although the tracking system is racist, a few nonwhite children do manage to have their talents recognized rather than squelched. There are high schools for the "gifted" also, and occasionally scholarships are available in the private schools.

I put the term "gifted" in quotes, because it is my observation, from working with children declared to be *anything but*, that talent is much more widespread than educators would have us believe. The "gifted" are generally those who *somebody* — almost *anybody* — took a shine to and pushed ahead, while the "ungifted" are those who have been ignored or deliberately intimidated. For this reason, it is no surprise that educators have noted "gifted" children are often better looking and more physically fit than those who don't make the grade: people tend to make a great fuss over children who are attractive and healthy. For other reasons, however, less attractive *female* children sometimes push ahead of their peers. Parents may compensate for lack of beauty by emphasizing the intelligence of a daughter, and her low status in the sex market may help her to turn inward and develop what gifts she has.

Whatever the reason for their educational success, these women find the job market quite unprepared to provide them with the kinds of work and/or pay their skills warrant. They become teachers, librarians, nurses, social workers — earning less money than that paid to male blue-collar workers. Others may become editors or minor "executives" in banks and other businesses which maintain low wages for jobs predominantly filled by women. Still more become secretaries in firms which build their hopes for advancement but never come across. And then there are the artists, who are dreamers in more ways than one. Not only do they have visions of perfect forms and ideal societies, but also the inevitable images of heroic recognition and financial fortune.

Thinking about this class, I reread *Pygmalion* by George Bernard Shaw, for Eliza Doolittle, after her transformation into a "lady," may be the prototype of the educated woman without means. Grasping at the chanciest of chances, Doolittle found a teacher willing to push her ahead, if only as an experiment. At the end of the play she curses her teacher because there is no place for the educated poor woman in her world.

In a postscript to the play, Shaw hypothesizes several options for her: she can become the wife of a rich man, a teacher of phonetics in competition with her former teacher, a kind of secretary and amanuensis to him, or—with some capital investment—a shopkeeper. Shaw sees Doolittle as too independent for the first option, although he does postulate her marriage to a *weak* young man. On the other hand, he sees her as neither aggressive nor "communist" (Shaw's word) enough to grab the second possibility. Too, she has experienced overly much of Professor Higgins's arrogance to be willing to work as an *assistant* to him. The best bet, according to the author, is that she will accept capital from Colonel Pickering to open a flower shop.

This, however, will not raise her into the middle class, according to Shaw. Indeed, one of the basic points this socialist has made in *Pygmalion* is that women are essentially classless . . . from the *male* point of view. Eliza's father, suddenly risen from a dustman to receiving two thousand pounds per annum as a lecturer in philosophy, *does*, in Shaw's perspective, become bourgeois.

Shaw imagined a woman who barely existed in England in his time, at least not out in the *world* (there were apparently all too many governesses). Only later in the twentieth century was she to come into her own, particularly in the United States. But without a Colonel Pickering to invest for her, the modern educated poor woman's choices may be even more limited than Eliza Doolittle's. Yes, some women of this class do marry men, especially professional men, who have means. In such cases, they can expect to be better off financially, at least while they remain married, than women who struggle independently or marry men of lesser means. But should they (and their children) be abandoned, they face the same problems as the respectable—and sometimes even the destitute—poor. Furthermore, if such a woman takes time off to raise children, she will have lost enough professional status so that returning to work often means starting again from the beginning.

The work of the educated poor frequently depends on city or state payrolls. When budgets are cut, the lowest status professionals are laid off first, particularly if they are women. When New York City cut down on its teachers in the seventies, it made a special effort (not acknowledged) to retain its *male* teachers because of a theory that it is good for children, particularly in the lower grades, to have a "father image." In addition, substitute teachers were laid off, and these were almost all women; the breaks in their careers necessary for them to raise children of their own having prevented them from earning "regular" status. Thus, even in a profession where women predominate, they are discriminated against in employment.

The artists, writers, musicians, and actors of this class either work at part-time menial jobs or, if they are very lucky, live on tiny grants. Sometimes, again if they are fortunate, they may hold down part-time work related in some way to their art. But universities, which pay poorly in any case, discriminate against women as teachers, as do the philanthropic foundations which provide grants. Furthermore, all the purveyors of the arts—publishers, gallery owners, museums, theatrical producers—discriminate against women. Misogyny in our culture is so entrenched that even *women* critics are inclined to view the creative products of women as *a priori* inconsequential in comparison with the works of men. Of course, working for male-dominated publications, they *have* to take this view to some extent, or lose *their* ill-paying and much-coveted jobs.

Men have regaled us through the centuries with their romantic stories of struggling *male* artists, but the travails of the woman in the garret have rarely been recorded. When they are, they tend toward the unremitting grimness of Violette Leduc's *La Bâtarde* and Tillie Olson's short stories, or the self-sacrifice of Anaïs Nin's diaries.

For the artist, marriage—even to a rich man—is not usually advantageous to her work. More than other kinds of work, art is hard to put down for a while and pick up again. Usually forced to do her creative work at home, the woman artist will find marriage a full-time job. Her artistic work gets relegated to "spare time" and begins to lose its professionalism. If she does not achieve instant recognition and money, her family begins to think of it as an avocation, and so, in time, may she. Unless she receives very strong support from her peers, she is likely to sacrifice her art completely for the priorities of her family.

In contrast, marriage to the "right kind" of woman can be a boon to the male artist. In addition to taking care of the household and teaching the children to tiptoe around when their father is working, the male artist's wife may also support him and the family with an outside job—because the male artist can achieve the greatest respect among his family and friends when the world *denies* recognition: then he is certainly avant-garde! He is enthusiastically praised for not "conforming," for forcing his wife (although he may not have conferred that dubious legal status on her, preferring to save himself from any vulgar commitment) and children to share fully in his resplendent poverty. Dependent, he remains the lord and master, and can be (according to romantic literature he, almost without exception, *is*) a "swashbuckling" tyrant.

In later years, if he is successful, he is almost certain to leave the woman who struggled to keep him alive in his early period and seek a young woman—or many—to provide new "inspiration." If the first wife sacrificed her own art for his, she is left with absolutely nothing but memories—and if she's smart, she'll turn them into publishing cash while his name is hot!

THE POLITICS OF THE EDUCATED POOR

By reason of both her education and her poverty, the educated poor woman is likely to be radical in her politics. It is in this group that we find the strongest and most radical adherents of feminism. Social and financial opportunities for such women rest just tantalizingly out of reach. On an overt, intellectual level, frequently she has been raised to believe that she is as good as any man. She has been educated to be unsparingly critical of everything she encounters—of herself in particular. If she does have children, the chances are she will not have many, and so she will retain a modicum of independent mobility. Her education helps her to be resourceful and the social position it, by itself, gives her, allows her the option of not keeping up materialistically with the Joneses. Even if she is a teacher or librarian in a small town, she is not obliged to be *fashionable*: neat and clean will do. A slight eccentricity is permitted, particularly if she is single and not young. Although, when it is possible, she may spend money on books and travel, the "right" neighborhood for her to live in may turn out to be the cheap bohemian one.

The educated woman, in other words, can sometimes indulge in a fashionable *downward* mobility if *upward* mobility isn't feasible. In reality, she will be living up to her means.

Again, the educated poor woman has no vested interest in the status quo, and sometimes she *knows* that. She may start out as a Marxist and then wind up hating Marxist men and the male egocentricity which Marxism fails to dampen in them. She may take an interest in politics in order to change what seems a hopeless situation. In this she is not so different from some of her educated brothers. (The chances are they went to the same universities, read the same books, admired the same artists — mostly male.) But her *personal* hopelessness is more profound than theirs.

Unlike her male counterparts, she has had to struggle to maintain and enlarge her capacities *after* her intellect has been recognized. Because intellectual equality in women is as repugnant to men as any other kind of equality, women are discouraged from demonstrating or even experiencing our full cerebral powers. To insist on flexing those muscles is to reduce one's value in the marriage market. At least from the onset of puberty, women receive increasingly emphatic clues to give greater attention to their "femininity" and less to their evolving genius. For a woman to be the wit at a party is to go home alone. Achievement, we quickly learn, leads to ostracism.

The majority of women who have a sexual interest in men learn early to disguise signs of unusual talent from them, and gradually the talent itself atrophies. The reward for a highly intelligent woman who learns this lesson well is marriage to an exceptional and, sometimes, financially successful man, usually a number of years her senior so that her brilliance can be further disguised by her comparative lack of experience in the world. In films, we have seen brilliant women like Mae West, Gracie Allen, and Judy Holliday playing the fool. In real life, brilliant women play this role with greater subtlety, exhibiting just enough wit to keep passivity from becoming boring.

This complicity against one's own capacities is stifling—and infuriating. The rage of a woman who has performed such acts of self-betrayal is unfathomable. The women's liberation movement was catalyzed by this rage in the hearts of educated poor women as much as by any other single factor.

Liberation for these women, then, means first of all the freedom to develop and display and have recognized their full cerebral potential. But many women have found this goal incompatible with close relationships to any man. In one way or another, it is necessary for us to humble ourselves before men in order to be acceptable as social and sexual "partners." Hence, a woman Nobel laureate in science boasts to the world that she keeps house and cooks for her husband. A woman prime minister is divorced because of her serious involvement in world politics—but she, too, is praised by the press for her "chicken soup" and kissed on the cheek. Another woman prime minister (who may or may not have been a "tyrant"—it was impossible to separate out the sexism in the press evaluations of her administration) is decried by her own nation for being a "widow"—one who has not died on her husband's funeral pyre; and still another widow, aspiring to leadership on her revered husband's platform, is vilified by the most "progressive" nation in the world for being a "tramp."

It is a dangerous thing then for a woman to display her genius. And it is like banging one's head against the wall to expect this genius to be recognized with appreciation by the male hierarchy. It is equally foolish to expect that at present the majority of women in the employ of that hierarchy will risk their jobs to value great talent in other women. And yet women persist in trying to make a dent in such concrete.

The male establishment engages in all-out psychological warfare against the educated woman—knowing that the oppression she had to endure while obtaining her education scarred her with a lack of assurance. Women's books chosen for either praise or attack by the male press are those which have been selected by male publishers. They are usually written on a certain level of technical excellence comparable to most books by men. But a peculiar thing happens to books written by women: they are judged not on their esthetic value, but on their submissiveness. Thus we have *Speedboat* by Renata Adler, extolled in the press, while *Burning Questions* by Alix Kates Shulman is vilified. (I have chosen two books which are roughly equal in charm and lightness.) Except for the fact that Adler's heroine maintains a stiff-upper-lip in the face of male brutalities (which she doesn't identify as such) and exudes a tireless compassion, while Shulman's heroine recognizes these brutalities and struggles against them, there is little to differentiate these two books in terms of quality. Both are considerably above average in literary competence, though neither quite reaches the level of an Elizabeth Gaskell. The same can be said of any book by such highly successful authors as Philip Roth, Norman Mailer, and so on down the very long list of untouchable male writers who will be forgotten within a generation. (In that list I'm afraid I must include such "greats" as Samuel Beckett!)

I confess that I am a member of the educated poor class and a writer as well as a feminist, so it is not surprising, if unforgivable, that I have a special feeling for this group. I am a passionate person and passionately angry at my position in the world. My dignity bristles when I think of my work exposed to the judgment of the patriarchy.

Half of my lineage is male. That means I am a self divided. I have come to learn that in a very profound, unconscious way, my father and my grandfather and all my male antecedents hated me. What a cruel awakening this is! And the half that is left is so powerless in its love. With a quivering mouth I take in the judgment of men who are my intellectual peers, and I am unable to determine to what extent their reactions are prejudiced and to what extent just. And yet, even in saying this, I understand that I am displaying a vulnerability, a submissiveness, a request for more kindness than my more openly belligerent sisters are likely to receive. I remind myself of a puppy who lies on her back, paws up, when she faces an unknown dog. It is at once a defenseless and self-protective position.

The educated poor woman is nothing if she is not competitive, for each one of us thinks of herself as having a special edge over the others. We grew up, even more than our destitute and respectable poor sisters, disliking women—for we hated the stereotype that would submerge our unique talents. We identified with men, tried to make them like us for what we called "ourselves"—that part which isn't flesh. Many of us have died trying. The quest is more quixotic than any test Quixote assayed.

But for all the despair it subjects women to, education is a plus, and unlike money, it cannot, once it has become rooted, be dislodged—except by madness or death. With education, the hierarchy itself may not be inevitable; one can look in other directions than the vertical. There is horizontal: the collective. There is depth: the self. There is, above all, time: the great past, present, and future of knowledge.

With it, if I cannot retrieve the pride of all my ancestors, I can try to elicit it in posterity.

I cannot look at the educated poor objectively, being of that class myself, but I offer such experience and insights as I have for the examination and analysis of my collective peers.

CHAPTER EIGHT

Rich Women

This will be a short chapter, for reasons which must be obvious by now. There just aren't a lot of rich women!

We used to be told that women in the United States *controlled* 80 percent of the wealth. The fact is that women are like bank tellers, with much money passing through our hands but little going into our own pay envelopes. The places where we are encouraged to spend the money allocated to us are clearly illustrated in the home and fashions sections of the newspapers and in the "women's" magazines which make fortunes out of our captivity. We are permitted much fantasy, little reality. Thorstein Veblen, in his *Theory of the Leisure Class*, defined the business of rich *married* women very neatly: to display "vicarious leisure" for rich men. They frequently go crazy or become alcoholics or both, and there are expensive sanitariums devoted to their care.

In their display of "conspicuous consumption" they become prime targets for the hatred and ridicule of both men and women with less money, and they, themselves, often feel like parasites. The men they are married to complain about how hard they have to work to support the luxurious tastes of these women who, without such tastes, would not have been candidates for such marriages in the first place.

Being a rich woman is almost as much a matter of destiny in this country as being a poor one. Most women who marry wealth come from rich families. The Horatio Alger trip, which still exists to a very limited degree, is reserved mainly for men who, when they have "made it," often dump the wives who saw them through the difficult years and remarry women born of the rich. Through this rite, men leave behind traces of their earlier poverty and move into the ruling class, which will become the true class of their sons. Although their daughters may inherit wealth and marry into it too, they are not destined to be among those who rule. If they inherit, they will be rich *freed slaves*. Part of their equipment is financial security (people born rich haven't the fear of poverty, as a rule, which plagues people born poor even after their fortunes are assured) and a certain confidence that they deserve respectful treatment. But there is always a D. H. Lawrence gamekeeper lusting to bring such women down a few pegs.

Even with their expensive educations and paternal business connections, women born rich often end their careers when they marry and have children. While it is not at all unusual to find very rich men working frightfully hard developing careers (often in government, à la Nelson Rockefeller, if their businesses no longer require their full-time presence), when Jacqueline Onassis took a job in publishing, there was something rather touching about her decision: an element of middle-aged-female retirement syndrome. Her children were growing up—had she lost her sense of purpose, like other housewives? Similarly, we were touched when Marilyn Monroe went back to school to study acting after she had made a fortune in Hollywood as a sex symbol: this taking herself seriously as an artist was widely regarded as a bit of (forgivable) vanity—patently unnecessary, if not useless. But aside from her repugnance at being regarded as a "thing," Monroe apparently had real worries about her financial future. While Onassis had no such fears, the constant presence of the paparazzi around her was a ubiquitous reminder that she, also, was looked upon as a "thing." The celebrity of her two husbands had made her an object of sexual wonder.

Thus rich women, whether they are born into wealth or suddenly, dazzlingly acquire it, suffer the same sexual objectification as poor women. Their intrinsic value as human beings and their singular individual talents are lightly considered. They drink, they take pills, they go insane, they commit suicide. The fame of the names they carry, whether through their fathers or their husbands or both, makes their own efforts to find identity through work seem superfluous. What does a woman need with an identity? In this connection I cannot help thinking of Oona O'Neill Chaplin, whose two surnames speak of an unthinkable loss. Where is the woman of genius who inherited the genes of her father (and mother?) and claimed the fascination of a great male clown?

If sons of rich and famous fathers are also intimidated at times by their inborn, as it were, celebrity, it is because of a *high* expectation level directed at them, rather than a *low* one. They are afraid of not measuring up.[1] The only real expectation for a woman born rich is that she marry a rich man. The business opportunities available to her are at best optional—not mandatory by any means. But the son of a rich man is expected to take his place in the dynasty, to make his father's name his own and give it an added luster. If he achieves success, his famous antecedents become portraits on the walls of the great house he is deemed fit to occupy in his own right as the present Lord and Master. Even if he does not achieve success, his title to greatness as the inheritor of the *name* is acknowledged. A male Kennedy remains a luminary, whatever deeds occurred at Chappaquiddick. (Ted Kennedy's opposition to abortion is illuminating in this connection.) A female Kennedy is quite another thing: we hear jokes about Ethel's fertility and front-page stories about Joan's "drying out." The dark side of the males remains as hushed as their flamboyancy will allow. Posthumous reports of John F.'s marital infidelities are but flourishes to his masculinity. Ugly behavior toward women no longer mars presidential timber. Even *women* are supposed to disregard such "peccadilloes" when going to the polls.

Rich women have very little impact on the society as a whole except when seemingly miraculously they step out of their preordained roles to exert some positive or negative influence. But even in such circumstances they are carefully observed by their families and restrained as much as possible from making too much of a splash. Jane Fonda's marriage to Tom Hayden, although he is somewhat to the left, politically, of her father, drew a kind of sigh of relief from Henry Fonda.

The cases of Jane Fonda and of Vanessa Redgrave, too, would seem to argue that women who have money and fame (and beauty) achieve through these advantages a certain political independence. As Phyllis Chesler might say, they have done splendidly, "for women." There is a serious question, however, as to whether the orthodox Marxism Fonda and Redgrave espouse is really a break for themselves and not a manifestation of unthought-out guilt imposed on them. As intelligentsia who travel in a fashionably leftist-artistic international set, they are aware of capitalism's economic inequities. Particularly in Western Europe, very rich film directors, most of whom have made their money primarily by exploiting the sexual degradation of women, are great theoretical support-

ers of Marxist principles. Their romances with tyranni-
cal socialist regimes and with the orgiastic cinematic possibilities of terrorism are all too understandable, given
the cops-and-robbers tradition of the medium with which
they work. Complexity has rarely been the forte of the
movie industry; sensitivity toward women, never. To be a
radical feminist in such circles might cut off one's source
of income; to be a supporter of leftist machismo is to elevate oneself above other women, to win enough male respect, even, to obviate "dumb blond" typecasting.

Although leftist identification may be an asset in the
film capitals of Europe, it is not an unmitigated crowd-
pleaser in the United States. Both Fonda and Redgrave
are probably sincere.

What is it that attracts these women to leftism in spite
of the fact that Marxist males are so incorrigibly misogynous? It is hard to believe that Fonda and Redgrave
are too blind to see the leers lurking behind every leftist
montage, too deaf to hear the catcalls beneath the sound-
tracks, too thick-skinned to sense the hypocrisy of the
picking and choosing among women for adherence to the
"correct line" which goes on among male Marxists ostensibly supporting feminism. These are wonderfully intelligent women of tremendous sensitivity. And they *care*.

Is it perhaps that, like most of us, they do not yet care
enough about *themselves*? Is it that they see themselves
as impossibly, guiltily, privileged? In comparison with
other women they are, it is true. But of what does their
privilege consist, and on what does it depend?

First of all, they are both the daughters of rich and
famous men of the theater. They had not just *money*
from their fathers, but protection as well. Were they to
move away from that base of protection; were they to
speak out against male domination *everywhere in the*

world in as strong a voice as they now use to attack just one form of patriarchal imperialism; were they to dissect in their own minds the total imperialism of men over women—their protection and, with it, their sense of personal privilege might be somewhat diminished.

The feminist struggle cannot be waged in abstract terms. Each participant must feel her own peril. Only then can a rich woman empathize with poor women. Then she might see that even the support of male revolutionaries may not be in the interests of the women attached to them, who, like the Irish women pacifists, might wish us to support instead an end to the hostilities. Where we do not hear significant numbers of women's voices independently urging our aid, it might be wisest for us to stay out of distant male cockfights altogether. Otherwise, particularly in countries far away from which it is hard to obtain objective accounts, we may actually be giving comfort to the *oppressors* of women.

Needless to say, Fonda and Redgrave are exceptional women. There are few rich women as vocal and active in any cause—fewer still on the left. Many "know which side their bread is buttered on" and are careful to maintain the outward docility necessary to *keep* it buttered. Like the men they are usually attached to, they avoid associating with people who would challenge their position and instead work off guilt by contributing money and time to charities.

Andrea Dworkin has pointed out with shockingly vivid detail in *Woman Hating*[2] that in old China the feet of rich women were more completely crippled by ritualistic binding than those of poor women, who were needed to work in the fields. She has left us to speculate whether it was more terrible to be unable to walk or to have to worry about starvation—for that was the major difference between the two conditions of slavery. For all that they were crippled, rich women were envied and hated by poor women for their "privilege" of not being starved and worked to death. No doubt the rich women were also reminded of their "privilege" by the men who fed and raped them.

Rich women in America can walk, and some of them earn or have inherited their own money. The crippling they have undergone as the personal property of the ruling class is a subtle variable. Each has her own story, often hidden away, even from herself, behind many veils. It is rich women, after all, who provide psychoanalysts with steady incomes, year in and year out, in return for hope that "inner peace" is simply a matter of proper emotional adaptation. If life isn't perfect for people with so many comforts, conventional reasoning pleads, the problem must be unique to them as individuals; it must lie in some distortion of point of view brought about by a trauma in childhood and buried in some inaccessible corner of the memory. Psychoanalysis perpetuates the isolation of rich women from one another. Those few who get together in consciousness-raising groups find very different answers from those "nondirected" by the man sitting thoughtfully behind the couch.

In fact, a basic affliction suffered by rich women may be symbolized by the one-to-one psychoanalytic session: too much privacy. A great emotional advantage of consciousness-raising is that it is free and untutored. Because she has access to money, however, the rich woman often believes that everything of value has a price, that what comes cheap or free is worthless, and that every service is improved by the presence of an expert. The private psychoanalytic session is more expensive than group therapy, and group therapy costs more than consciousness-raising. Therefore the private session must be best.

It is here that we discover the special crippling of rich women. In a sense, by going over memories of childhood, the analysand relives a time in her life when irresponsibility was appropriate and pleasurable. As an adult she yearns, like other women, for independence, the right to "name" herself. More than other women she is deprived of this by the constant presence of men, who wield power not just over her but over the world. The psychoanalyst is another highly paid authority figure. The rich woman lives always in the shadow of protectors, and so the hours on the couch recalling her *actual* childhood are a comforting escape from the contradictions of her immature maturity. That is, for several hours a week, with the movie of her childhood rerun on the screen of her memory in a darkened room, her infantile position in society presents no conflict to her.

Consciousness-raising among peers, without an authority figure present, allows women to experience life existentially, to learn to stand by themselves on their own two feet. (What a world of appropriate symbolism there is in that expression!) In fact, their feet were never really bound, they learn, although men would have rich women think they were. The psychoanalyst, although he may believe he is promoting autonomy, perpetuates dependency in women. Freud set out to adjust women to their "destined" role. Some modern psychoanalysts no longer preach anatomy as destiny, but the privacy of the sessions, the vulnerable position of the woman in relation to the "doctor," screams the message. In the last analysis, the psychoanalyst works for The Man.

Feminism belongs as much to the rich woman as to the poor woman. It can help her to understand that her own interests are linked with the advancement of all woman-kind; that comfort in dependency is a trap; that the gilded cage has bars, too; and that, rich and poor, we are all wounded in the service of the patriarchy, although our scars are different. The inner turmoil that sends her to a psychoanalyst can generate energy for the movement which alone may heal her, by setting her free.

CHAPTER NINE

The Middlewomen

The categories considered in this chapter are job descriptions rather than true classes. Women of all classes may fall into these groupings, for they include, on the "overseer" side, mothers as well as office managers, and on the "buffer" side, wives, secretaries, teachers, and government officials. In their relationships to people over whom they exert some power, these women are felt to be a superior class, but in relation to the patriarchy they are merely "trusties" — slaves sufficiently conditioned so they can be relied on to supervise and manipulate other slaves for the benefit of the masters. The television series *Charlie's Angels* again comes to mind in this connection, with its women receiving orders from an invisible boss. Often the boss is invisible in real life, too, having been internalized into the female consciousness.

THE OVERSEERS

The overseer is one who is put in charge of other people by a real boss and who is ultimately accountable to him for their performance. Mothers in charge of rearing children, even those mothers who are titular heads of families, can be so classified. Whether or not there is an adult male on the premises, the mother carries out the dictates of the patriarchy, turning sons into acceptable men and daughters into acceptable girls or ladies. Until the present wave of feminism, fashions in child raising in this century have been dictated solely by men. Whether rigid or permissive, the mother has been indoctrinated into producing aggressive, achieving, misogynous sons, and passive, hypersensitive, male-worshiping daughters. Why, one may ask, do most mothers conform to these imperatives? Are they not responsible for the results?

Some of the most execrable white racists have been reared by black nursemaids. Certainly it has never been to her personal advantage for a black servant to teach racism to white children, and surely the results of her labor must often have horrified her, because black women have ever been conscious of their racial peril (if not always of their sexual peril). But the black nurse-maid's most *immediate* danger lay in *not* conforming to the wishes of the children's father, her master. She raised her own children from infancy to be diffident and ob-sequious toward the master's children, because both her own life and her offspring's depended on this early dif-ferentiation.

Similarly, for a modern woman (of any race or finan-cial position) who raises her own children *not* to differ-entiate from the beginning between "proper" male and female behavior would be to court severe penalties. Children raised in nonconformist families can be ex-pected to resent their mothers who did not prepare them to fit into the prevailing "norms." We have only to look at the psychological literature, which *blames* mothers for producing deviations, to find authoritative support for their children's hatred. For a boy to be a "sissy" tied to his mother's "apron strings" or for a girl to remain a "tomboy" after the age of ten brings the same derision to the mother as that accorded to the "dominant" wife of a "henpecked" husband. (It is probable that the novelist

Philip Roth, internalizing the anti-Semitism underlying
American antiintellectualism, could not forgive his
mother for raising him to be a *Jewish* man.)

Now the fashion is changing, and much of the masculine mode of upbringing will probably, gradually, be
extended to girls — but the rough edges of male aggression
may not be rubbed off boys for a long time to come. From
the pervasive propaganda it would seem that the patriarchy is more intent on preserving aggression than on
promoting passivity. If a sacrifice must be made,
passivity will go. *More* soldiers are better than *no* soldiers.

When mothers insist on producing more balanced children, custody of the children is increasingly given over to
the fathers. Any show of financial or sexual independence on the part of divorced mothers can result in legal
judgments against them. The hand that rocks the cradle,
far from ruling the world, is handcuffed by the rulers.
Although quite a number of mothers manage sabotage, it
is important to remember that the mother is a slave
"overseer," not the person charged with determining, according to her own precepts, the guidance of her children. Just as she is not permitted to control reproduction,
she is also not the true guardian of her offspring.

The mother is the archetype of overseer of women. In
harems, where great numbers of women locked in together presented a threat of unification, a eunuch was
traditionally placed in this role. Similarly, in many wom-
en's prisons in the United States, male as well as female
guards are present. Unfortunately, the male guards are
not eunuchs: the state is not so much interested in protecting women prisoners from male lust as it is in pre-
venting them from joining together with female guards in
overthrowing the prison system.

This fear on the part of the state is not totally un-founded. Although women guards can be as ruthless as men, and sometimes behave so under male supervision, women prisoners occasionally have had success in com-municating with female guards about common interests. During my one overnight stay in a Washington, D.C. jail, I spent most of the long night exchanging "family" ex-periences with the woman on duty. She said she had ac-cepted this night work because usually it was possible, with the prisoners safely locked in their cells, for her to catch some sleep, and she could go home in the morning rested in time to take her children to school. I sym-pathized with her and told her I was deeply worried about my thirteen-year-old daughter who had been ar-rested with me in the demonstration, and who had been sent to a different jail. She allowed me unlimited phone calls until I located my child and made arrangements to meet her the next day. She also fetched my sleeping bag for me because I was cold, and she shared her cigarettes with me.

The next morning, very tired after our long rap, she asked me please not to get arrested again in Washington because I had ruined her one job benefit.

This experience was probably atypical, but I believe there is a reason, nevertheless, why male guards are pre-sent in female prisons and why there were only white guards at Attica during the uprising in that predomi-nantly black male prison. In Kenya there is a saying among the Kikiyu tribe that dogs who are used to hunt jackals bark when they near their targets—not to alert the hunters, but to warn the jackals: for jackals are also canines, and therefore their kin.

Alliances between overseers and those they watch are seldom formed until a revolution is underway, but once

the overseers become aware of their own lack of freedom—that uniting with their "charges" is the only way to
true independence—their loyalty to their employers becomes less reliable.[1] Right now overseer jobs in business
are increasingly being made available to women who are
carefully trained in "assertiveness": that is, in imitating
the male's ruthlessness toward underlings. The woman
who truly identifies with her hierarchical inferiors (not
just in a manipulating way) will be told she is not assertive enough. But a great upsurge from the bottom will
probably be necessary for the majority of women newly
flushed with "success" to become conscious of their long-
term interests.

The current emphasis in the women's movement is to
encourage underlings in offices to give women supervisors the same "respect" they show men. The woman
who has "made it" is supposed to serve as a "role model"
for those on their way up. This sounds to me as if the
movement is saying, "Sit still while *I* put my foot on
your neck." There is no reason, of course, to be disre-
spectful of any sister, but the quality of respect should be
different: the fear one feels toward a male boss should
not be instilled by a sister.

If women workers are too terrified of male bosses to
show anger to them (or even behind their backs, at
times), having a female boss may release some of this
anger. By and large, women cannot bring themselves to
think of other women as any better than themselves. Unconsciously, we recognize the sisterhood of slavery, and
resent "airs" put on by people we consider our peers.
This recognition is essentially a democratic force. The
inclination of women workers sometimes to resent female
supervisors *more* than male supervisors occurs for several reasons: (1) the existence of a female supervisor

suggests that the status quo has in fact been broken, which makes the female underling feel that her own position on a low hierarchical rung can no longer be blamed on discrimination against her sex (that is, she must be *intrinsically* inferior, as a person); (2) the worker, even if she is unaware of feminist analysis, intuits that her supervisor has aligned herself with the male boss and, by doing so, has betrayed her sex; (3) on a deeply unconscious level, the female worker may sense a repetition of the family situation in which the mother pays obeisance to the father and carries out his instructions against the children; (4) the woman worker identifies with the patriarchal injunction that women have no *right* to be in supervisory positions: it offends her sense of the "natural" order of things.

The last reason is the one first perceived by female supervisors, and it arouses a sense of injustice in them. For the supervisor has *also* been taught to believe that her position is against the "natural" order of things. Much of her energy is used to struggle against internalizing this patriarchally engendered belief.

If this last were the only reason for resentment in the worker, however, it would soon pass as she became accustomed to a changed situation. Workers and students often overcome racism when they are placed in daily peer-group contact with members of other races, and women workers would be at least as likely to overcome their sexism with exposure to female supervisors. The first three reasons, however, continue to cause irritation even as the fourth disappears.

There is an initial, if inarticulated, hope among women workers that female superiors will be kinder than their male counterparts, that they will make efforts to push other women ahead. Before the advent of modern feminism, this hope was rarely realized. Women supervisors understood the shakiness of their token positions and tended to promote men. If the newly appointed supervisors now concede that they owe their success in part to the pressure exerted by the women's movement, they may begin to behave in more "sisterly" ways toward their female assistants. After all, if feminist pressure *was* partially responsible, it follows that it will be advantageous in the long run to support feminist precepts, to reserve some loyalty for one's female coworkers.

In any case, it is valuable for the female underling to retain the class consciousness which working for a female supervisor may have imparted to her for the first time in a rudimentary form. If she can get past reason 4 in her causes for resentments, she might replace it with the thought that the hierarchical mode may simply be unjust in itself.

I am not advocating class warfare among women. On the contrary, I am hoping that internecine battles can be averted by women who are on different levels of the male hierarchy through realizing that their sisterhood in slavery supercedes their loyalty to that hierarchy. If women in overseer positions would behave like the dogs in the Kikiyu story, a true underground alliance of women workers might be formed to stymie the real masters—the men in power.

A Misuse of Power

Usually, in my working life outside the home, I have been in some kind of underling position, but several years ago I worked for a tutoring program in a black community. I had been hired by a woman who lived in the community and had put enough trust in me to make me a supervisor over a number of tutors. The people working under me were mixed in several ways: there were both "regular" teachers and college students, men and women, black people and white people.

Two of the male (black) "regular" teachers seemed to me both indifferent toward the children they worked with—*bored* might be the word—and arrogant toward me. They "outranked" me in credentials and, of course, also in sex. We were all technically working for the Board of Education (the *real* patriarchal authority) where rank is of the greatest importance, so my "supervisory" position didn't carry much weight with these teachers. Furthermore, the fact that they were black and I was white made the relationship fraught with possibilities for misinterpretations on both sides.

Several times these two teachers were late or did not turn up at all, which upset their students and forced me to rearrange programs without notice. When they did come, they insisted on working together, with all their students in a room roughly 8 feet by 10 feet, although there were other rooms available. Their students, combined, sometimes numbered as many as a dozen.

After a while, an additional tutor was hired: a young black woman who was a college student. (She, also, frequently turned up late or didn't appear, but she did usually call ahead to notify us.) She had one child to work with and insisted on taking him into the same small room the two teachers used. Her student was on the kindergarten level while the others were in the fifth grade. The small room was wildly noisy, and when the pandemonium became too great, the two male teachers would "solve" the problem by yelling at the students or putting them out of the room. This was precisely the kind of behavior which had helped to cause the kids' failures in their regular schools and which our program had been set up to counteract.

Because the male teachers would not separate from one another, I asked the new tutor to take her student into a less crowded room. She refused. I asked her a number of times, and her refusals became more and more determined and arrogant. The apparent class issues here were so hopelessly mixed with racial issues that I suppose she felt she had every reason to flout my authority; and I really saw my job more as one of organizing logistics than of throwing my weight around anyway.

As facilitator for the program, I assumed that the tutors would be moved by their own sense of dedication to do their very best work—which almost all of them were. They were a wonderful group, and the students made good progress. It was rarely necessary for me to interfere in any way. In fact, the general rule was that the tutors would come to me with ideas about how to make the sessions more convenient and rewarding for the students, and I would sort out the program to make these improvements possible.

One day the new tutor came in late without warning and insisted on taking her student, who had been waiting unhappily for some time (for he really loved her), into the crowded room. I guess I was overworked and a bit frantic. There were many associated political responsibilities that went with my job. We still functioned as the civil rights movement, trying to rescue black kids from the unfair destiny laid on them by the establishment. In any case, I lost my temper and fired the tutor—just like that!

She made no defense and gave me no argument.

Of course, we were all losers—the young woman, her little student, and I.

What I had done, I realized later, was to "assert" myself in a way all too common to women. I had taken my wrath out on the easiest target, another woman. But my fury had been instigated by the *men* who worked for me and who had persisted in baiting me. If the "ranking" situation was such that I couldn't deal with those men ·(the other "regular" teachers in the program—three women—were more than cooperative), and I couldn't, then I should have arranged a conference with the young tutor to discuss our difficulties with each other.

But I didn't, at the time, fully understand the problem. I had gone along, without meaning to, with the hierarchical assumption that mine was a position of *power* which should be *respected*—in the good, old-fashioned way. *The power was there*: I could fire her. But that power was patently absurd and went against everything I believed in. Because I had accepted the role laid on me by the patriarchy—a role totally incompatible with the realities of the situation I found myself in—I resented her unwillingness to recognize my position. If I had rejected that role and refused to be anything but a facilitator, I would have realized that we were both victims of a misunderstanding. With that realization, we could have done a little mutual consciousness-raising and probably arrived at an agreement.

Feminist Overseeing

Among many women class issues raised by hierarchical differences due to the patriarchal setup can be worked out if overseers remember the "power" conferred on them is unjust, that it is a surrogate mandate to oppress. However, the refusal to wield power over others does not mean one must reject every supervisory job. (One has to earn a living, and all jobs in the patriarchy are collaborationist.) It simply means that one can refuse, by one's behavior, to accept the male notion of "status"—otherwise known as the pecking order. Certainly, it is possible for the supervisor to covertly give her first loyalty to her female staff. For them should be reserved the benefit of the doubt in difficulties with other superiors; the alert eye for ways to help them advance. The responsibility of a supervisory position for a woman carries with it the need to make conscious ethical choices; to understand at all times that one's position in the male hierarchy is anomalous and inimical. Only then can one look for support from one's sisters when one's own job is threatened—as it inevitably will be.

It is not just for personal advancement within the hierarchy that we turn to feminism, but to re-create the society altogether. The power structure, whether capitalist or otherwise, is built on the slavery of women. The positions of "authority" we are given are for the purpose of more efficiently enslaving our sisters. Only with the end to all power structures will our slavery end.

Such a sentence has the ring of rhetoric, but like many idealistic concepts, it is demonstrably true. An enormous amount of energy gets wasted on ritualizing power relationships—giving and receiving orders which make little realistic sense. If the ends of the work we do for the patriarchy were good, cooperation with it would be easy to achieve because people would participate with their whole beings. It is because the ends are so unsatisfactory as a rule—preserving power at the top!—that workers have to be coerced. Women are extraordinarily cooperative as *volunteers* when the goals we are working toward are recognizably good. As volunteers, we express our commitment freely from one day to the next without fear of personal loss should we at any time decide that a project no longer deserves that commitment. As wage earners, our cooperation is enforced, the major positive incentive being the hope of earning more money if the work is done well. (Though "well" in the patriarchy often means "shoddily.") Therefore the threat of poverty, a kind of terrorism, must be used to keep us lashed to the machine—or the desk.

In a society which really benefited women, neither force nor external incentives would be necessary to assure good work. But I do not, at this moment, want to outline my own version of the ideal society. I am sure when women consult together about a utopian vision the result will be a design for a world based on personal dedication and cooperation. Our cumulative experience of what we like to do best and how we prefer to do it is bound to lead to some kind of voluntary, egalitarian arrangement.

In the meantime, we are forced to play out roles in this patriarchal system. As our consciousness develops, however, we can more and more mitigate the terrorism we pass on as well as the terrorism we absorb. One way to circumvent it is to evolve a new relationship to our jobs: to redesign them, as it were, excluding the notion of power relationships as much as possible. We might ask ourselves such questions as: (1) what is my function in terms of the real production in this firm? (2) what are my own ideas about how I can accomplish this? (3) what assistance do I truly require? (4) what kind of menial services can I do without? (5) how can I make the work of my assistants more enjoyable and, if possible, more creative and lucrative? (6) how can I show that I do not respect the arbitrary assignments of status to our persons in this firm?

It will be objected that this is the kind of thinking

women "normally" do—and it prevents us from advancing in the hierarchy.

I would argue that it is not our penchant for humanitarian concern which holds us back, but the nature of the hierarchy itself. No matter how much like men we behave, men will notice that we are *not* men. If more women advance than have been let through previously, it will be because of the collective pressure the women's movement has exerted—not because individual women have learned to sacrifice their scruples. When men want to exclude us, our adopted ruthlessness will be as good an excuse as any other. I am not proposing individual moral confrontations with management, but that women in overseer positions use some of the maneuverability at their command to support rather than to crush underlings. It is not necessary to accept the *flattery* implied by advancement. It is not in fact flattering to be advanced in an immoral institution. One accepts advancement for the sake of earning a better living and obtaining better working conditions. In all likelihood, one is moving up less rapidly than a man with similar qualifications; the advancement has been granted *grudgingly*.

As a woman moves up, she will be increasingly isolated from the company of other women. She will need more than ever the support of women who have not advanced, but she cannot expect that support unless she enters into some complicity with them: *real* complicity, not just the manipulative appearance of it. Her sisters will be genuinely glad for her advancement if they feel it gives them an ally in a more powerful position. If the entire clerical and secretarial force will walk out when a woman executive's job is threatened, the executive has done her primary job of loyalty to her true peers well. This presumes, of course, that both the overseer and the women she supervises are equally imbued with intelligent self-interest.

This kind of morality is adaptive: it essentially accepts things as they are. But the solidarity built on such interlocking support can lead gradually to more thorough change. As long as women do not reject the insight, borne out by the so-called need for "assertiveness training" (that is, training for ruthlessness), that power relationships *stink*, other valuable insights are sure to follow. The moral sense which men have hypocritically laid on women to keep us down need not be linked with passivity. We can use it actively to destroy men's power.

The Housewife As Overseer

There is another situation in which women serve as overseers that I would like to consider. Women who are married to men who can afford it sometimes employ domestic help. Without ignoring the fact that single women also hire household workers, I want to concentrate for the moment on the more traditional aspect of this kind of employment.

The household worker is an assistant to the housewife in carrying out her *husband's* domestic demands. As we know, the assumption that the wife will run the conjugal house is implicit in the marriage contract—with the corresponding understanding that the husband will support the establishment financially. Again to go over old ground, the ways in which the husband may carry out his end of the bargain are theoretically innumerable, while the wife is restricted to one occupation. (Others she may take on are to be in addition to, not instead of, the running of the house.)

If we accept the wife's responsibility for the household,

we see that she is actually *employed* ("used," if you prefer) by her husband. When she, in turn, hires help, she is not acting as the primary employer, but as the supervisor—or, in our terminology, the slave overseer.

Because the wife's work is not explicitly salaried, she is technically (and often in actual experience) a slave. Her performance is accepted as a matter of course, and therefore regarded as essentially worthless. She may be complimented if she performs well; she can be beaten if she performs badly—or for any other reason that strikes her husband's fancy.

In his work, her husband may have an array of assistants whom he is forced to pay according to prevailing standards and sometimes beyond those if he considers them particularly valuable. He also wants his home kept in order, his meals cooked, his children cared for, and his entertainments catered to. If he desires it or if his position calls for some elegance, he may expect his wife to require assistance, too. But since he regards his wife's work as trivial in comparison to his own, he holds her assistants in lower esteem than his own. Thus, he doesn't expect to pay domestic servants a great deal, nor does he think they are entitled to the kind of working conditions office and factory employees demand. If his wife is on call twenty-four hours a day, so should his servants be.

The housewife has also been conditioned to take her work as a matter of course. She is *responsible* for keeping the house in good order, and as we know from television commercials, it is easy to make her feel guilty about any imperfections. (Advertising is a very good index of the mores of our society. Although the intent of advertisers is to reinforce and even aggravate the guilt of housewives in order to increase their sales, they do not totally *invent* the guilt. When and if that guilt disappears, advertisers will develop a different marketing approach. At the moment, commercials are saturated with guilt-inducements.) No matter how luxurious the ménage, the staff required to maintain it are accorded an extremely low status. The living quarters for servants in mansions are often shockingly impoverished, as if designed deliberately to demean them.

Aside from saving the Lord and Master money, the traditional low pay and poor working conditions of household help effectively underscore the wife's inferior position. Thus a hierarchy exists not only in business, but in the home (where it all started). At the top is the husband, then comes the wife as chief slave (or slave overseer), and then the household workers as underslaves. As the husband lords it over his wife, so she may lord it over her assistants, from whose existence she derives a certain amount of self-importance: she is an overseer, after all, not a "real" slave.

In the traditionally "well-run" home, the wife is supposed to spare her husband any concern about her problems in keeping things humming. She is loath to press demands from the servants for raises and improved conditions, and will seldom do so except when a decrease in the number of people available for that work makes servants "independent." Although the wife must generally ask the husband for increases in her staff's payroll, *she* is widely, and erroneously, regarded as the primary employer of domestic help. As such, the hatred her assistants feel is directed not at the *real* employer—the husband—but at the wife. The wife, then, plays the role of *buffer* (the one who protects men from the consequences of their actions) as well as overseer. But of that, more later.

At the same time that the household helper accepts, on

a conscious level, the wife's authority, on a deeper level she perceives the phoniness of the wife's position. Somewhere in her psyche she recognizes that the wife, too, is a slave, and that she (the assistant) is acting as the slave of a slave. The office overseer may be able to acknowledge this anomaly to her assistant—if not in so many words, then in her behavior. It is more difficult for the wife to enter into such a conspiratorial understanding with her household helper.

The cant of conjugal love in our "romantic" society precludes the practical truth that marriage has an economic aspect as well as an emotional one. According to the self-serving patriarchal tradition, husband and wife are "one"—an axiom which is trotted out only at the convenience of the husband. Unfortunately, as a by-product of feminism which too frequently confuses a disadvantageous institution with the women caught up in it, many married women have grown more, rather than less, defensive of their "chosen" status. They are embarrassed to admit that their husbands control the purse strings and are the ultimate authority for household decisions.

Even when the wife *does* acknowledge her own subservient position and confronts her husband for a raise for the worker, the worker may still feel resentful. The material comforts of the overseer are everywhere in evidence. The comparison with the helper's own meager existence is unforgivable. When she goes home, the assistant has to repeat the same domestic routine she performed at work. She may face her own husband sitting with his feet up waiting for dinner! The "lady" of the house she works for seems unfairly privileged, for a slave. The difference in their positions is clearly an unjust accident, not a question of merit. The overseer not only lives better but she is allowed to palm off her "natural" duties on another. In contrast, the office assistant does not see how her supervisor lives—and anyway, she doesn't have to rub her nose in it.

The wife, too, feels guilt about having an assistant perform duties which have been, as if by God, assigned to herself. If the wife goes out to work, she will often pay the household worker out of her own relatively slight earnings, to assuage her own guilt for neglecting her household "duties." It is this nonsense—that women have somehow been ordained by the deity to care for the home—which makes what should be a normal working relationship between supervisor and assistant (given the abnormalities of present-day society) so degrading for all the women concerned. For having a person to help in the house is no more intrinsically immoral than having a secretary. The same nonsense also makes sisterly cohesion between the household overseer and her assistant nearly impossible. Housewives who have helpers distance themselves even more than women executives do from *their* assistants. The office overseer can console herself with the thought that *her* assistant is really an apprentice: that they are *both* on the way up! Obviously, this is not possible in a household.

Thus the class differences between women imposed by men triumph in the home. The housewife is a most effective buffer for her husband. When revolutions occur, it is no wonder that the wives of rich men often suffer worse than the oppressors themselves. The only suggestion I can offer in this instance is that wives, insofar as possible, get out of the household-running business altogether. Let the husband negotiate directly with servants. Let the real boss show his face. And where the housewife now does the chores unaided, she must either insist on the man fully sharing in them or demand a salary. She need not demand payment for her sexual favors, as some feminists suggest; for when they are not pleasurable to her, the husband is committing rape. The notion that a man can *buy* rape, as Susan Brownmiller has pointed out, only supports his brutal domination.

When both the housewife and the household worker are paid for their chores by the husband, a class identification between the two can begin to be possible. The household, attractive as it is, will be seen to *belong* to the man, with the wife having duties that ultimately extend beyond those required of the assistant. As the man's employee, the wife's assistant will be able to negotiate directly for a fair wage and working conditions. Efforts have been made to organize household workers, and housewives can aid in these efforts. In these ways we can move closer to the kind of bonding of women which ultimately may end the inequities of class.

THE BUFFERS

The wife, as we have seen, is the archetype of female buffer. This role, however, is given to women throughout the society. In businesses—as secretaries and receptionists—this is the primary occupation of women, and it exists widely in other areas of our economic lives. Social workers act as buffers between welfare recipients and the state. Teachers act as buffers between children, their parents, and the Board of Education. Government officials usually have female public relations people (a growing number since the advent of the women's movement) to protect them from their constituents. Nurses traditionally maintain the aloof dignity of doctors. In the Roman Catholic church, where the hierarchy are bereft of wives to do this service, nuns maintain everyday contact with parishioners; and the Virgin protects God.

All of these women create an aura of sanctity about

men and absorb the hostility which accrues to them in their roles as oppressors. It is a sanctity which women, ourselves, come to believe in. When we begin consciously to strip it away, it is as if we are tearing our own skins. Men, predictably, perceive what we are doing as castrating them. On the one hand they tell us we are masochistic, that we love subservience, we love absorbing their pain. When we refuse to absorb it, they do not accept this as a simple rebuttal, but as hostile aggression.

In suggesting that the housewife give up her buffer role in relation to her husband's servants, I am advocating only a minimal refusal. The wife may also be the intermediary between her husband and her children, and here her protective service to those more helpless than she cannot be underestimated. If she protects the husband from the children's rebellion, she also protects the children from the worst effects of his wrath, which can result in assault and even murder. Logically it would appear that the more outside financial options the wife has, the less she need comply, because she can take herself and her children elsewhere if she finds her husband's behavior overbearing. However, such logic doesn't always prevail.

Everywhere the jobs women find involve some form of buffering. Rare is the work she is given so autonomous that it withdraws her utterly from the requirement to protect men from the anger caused by their avarice. And when the woman is paid openly to perform this work, and only this, she can hardly find a way to rebel without losing her livelihood. It is easier for an overseer to ally herself with her female office assistants than it is for a buffer to refuse to fend off the just complaints of customers and competitors. In the first case, the overseer can be seen by men as merely compassionate, as making suggestions or even "begging"—a position which initially, until her solidarity with the other female workers becomes overt, can appear nonthreatening, even charming. In the second, the buffer is acting as incomprehensibly as Herman Melville's Bartleby—refusing the very reason for her existence in the man's employ.

One cannot ask women to refuse such jobs altogether, as few enough jobs are to be had; but how can women unite when we are constantly in the position of having to lie to one another to protect men?

It seems as if there is no end to the means of enforcing the divisions amongst ourselves and our resignation to oppression. It is as if we assimilate defeat from the very gases around us. As feminism gains an increasing hold over the imaginations of women, men will find increasingly subtle ways to convince us that our oppression *is* a form of liberation. This is the next step, which George Orwell was unable to imagine, in the development of "newspeak."

It is ultimately because women don't control the economy, the means to sustain our lives, that we must continue in our powerless, degrading, and dangerous roles. So long as men believe that they need us in these roles, they will fight to the death to keep all of the power systems in the world out of our hands. For all that they have envisioned cooperative utopias in books, they cannot conceive of the reality: a world in which women are autonomous and men must face themselves alone.

Men believe thoroughly in their own intrinsic and inevitable evil, trying to hide this evil behind the "nobility" of works which they permit only themselves to accomplish.

To stop acting as buffers for men's avarice, we will have to end that avarice and the belief men have in the inevitability of it. Perhaps the patriarchy's inequities and barbarities begin, after all, in the cradle. Perhaps that is where we must find the way to end them.

PART III EPILOGUE

CHAPTER TEN

Deals & Dreams

> Only if one is conscious of the danger connected with
> reform will everything go well in the end. —*I Ching
> or Book of Changes*[1]

This is the traditional place for a summing up and for a
look into the future. It would be logical, having argued
with tradition throughout this book, for me to refuse it a
formal concession here, but I won't give in to that temptation. A summation and a look—of sorts—we shall have.

In the beginning, I outlined some basic concepts of
feminism and drew a distinction between the reforms we
seek as a practical political movement and our utopian
goals. What changes we solicit from day to day and how
we work to bring them about will define the ultimate
aims of feminism more completely than any visionary
statement. Therefore I have detailed our agonies over
structure and leadership, the conflicts between various
interest groups within the movement, the controversies
caused by loyalty to external patriarchal factions.

MS. ALLGOOD TODAY

Many months have passed since I listened to Ms. Allgood
enthuse about her anticipated activism. Right now she is
wheeling and dealing with great abandon for the Equal
Rights Amendment. Her efforts have brought her into
contact with right-wing groups, and she hasn't flinched.

Word has gone out that the amendment will not threaten
The Family or The Church: *Kinder, Kücher, Kirch* remain
intact.

Indeed, in itself, ERA will not. All the polls show that
it is a wonderfully popular reform. One hundred
thousand people gathered in Washington to support it. It
has had the amazing effect of uniting people across the
spectrum of patriarchal politics, and only a few men empowered with money from a few quirky religious sects
have prevented its immediate passage.

Whether or not she succeeds in getting women's full
equality in the patriarchy written into the Constitution,
we all have reason to applaud Ms. Allgood's energy and
devotion. And, after all, I have urged feminist unity
throughout this work. So why the note of skepticism in
my voice? I am surely not against equality. I am surely
not against unity. And I am cynical enough about the in-
substantiality of differences between patriarchal factions;
the deep, abiding fraternity which binds men underneath
their warring factionalism of left and right—even as the
German kaiser was the brother of the English king who
fought against him in World War I and George VI, allied
with Stalin, the nephew of the deposed Russian tsar.

But still a doubt obtrudes: what have we sacrificed for
this effort?

The women's representatives appointed by the President and cursorily accepted *en bloc* at the Houston conference promised to support what Ms. Allgood referred
to as a "utopian" platform. But in the interim, the rights
of poor women to free abortions have been whittled away
and the struggle for lesbian civil rights has been muffled.
Congress has quietly refused funds for shelters and care
for battered women. The issue of child abuse is relegated
to organizations which offer peer-group therapy to

violent *mothers*, largely ignoring the brutality of fathers and their incestuous attacks on their little girls. Welfare has never been more unfair.

What has Ms. Allgood, in her disinterested wisdom, traded away?

Ms. Allgood can afford an abortion. She is not a lesbian. She may, for all I know, be divorced, and her children, if she has any, are grown. She is a very unlikely candidate for welfare. She has a job — in fact, a good one.

But she is paid less well than men in similar jobs. Furthermore, she is old enough to be reasonably concerned for her future. Certainly Ms. Allgood has valid feminist complaints and she is expressing them through her single-minded effort for ERA. Other reforms, she tells herself, will follow. She is not unmindful of the pain of her sisters — but first things *first*. And so, such money and power as she can summon go for an amendment which will allow her to sue her boss for a lot of back pay. A good and important amendment as amendments go.

However another doubt obtrudes: are the objections to ERA's passage all that substantive, or are they raised mainly to keep feminist energy *safely* channeled?

And on another level I ask: is the unity among women which the struggle for the ERA has apparently forged *real*, or does it depend on our ignoring the differences among us and pretending we are all happy housewives, regular church attenders, uncomplaining breeders, who nevertheless want recognition in the Constitution and the titular right to equal pay (litigation to follow)?

Continually, we make those strange American political coalitions which manage to maintain the status quo or move us further to the right in the name of reform and unity. The mind of a feminist reels. What is she to *do*? Ms. Allgood doesn't want to lose — but by winning she may lose more than by losing. Perhaps this isn't our ball game, as the boys might say.

Women whose visceral interests don't lend themselves to coalition politics—lesbians, poor women forced to breed or rely on the coat hanger, women on welfare, wives who earn their bread by serving as punching bags, daughters whose fathers have the sexual discrimination of tomcats—still exist in the movement or have empathizers there, but the money and power (such as it is) and the energies of our wheelers-and-dealers are invested in more popular issues, whatever their cost, and the rest of us are invited to trust and be silent awhile longer. Rather than unifying women, some of our women politicos in the patriarchy may be proving that class *counts*. It may not be long before a lot of slaves sense we have been sold down the river again.

Feminism has emphasized the right of women to relinquish false guilt and act in our own interests. This was a big step for people whose first taste of guilt came out of Goldilocks' bowl and who have regurgitated compassion ever since. It has taken us long to understand our own bitterness, to taste the bile.

It took us even longer to begin to *move* on our own interests. Each demand we raised seemed to come in conflict with the whole history of the world. Women screaming in public about rape. Women commenting on construction workers' legs. Women comparing clitorises and learning to enjoy them—our own, each other's—complaining openly about the limitations of male sexuality. Women admitting to having had illegal abortions. Women confessing to having been forced to prostitute ourselves in office jobs. Women telling, finally, about how we feel ugly and inadequate, how we were taught to lie over and over again as if there were virtue in it. Women afraid of being smelly, afraid of being fat, afraid of being thin, afraid of being tall or short, afraid to go out at night, afraid to stay home, afraid to be smart, afraid to call a man on the telephone, afraid to touch another woman, afraid to go to the doctor, afraid of being pregnant, afraid of being barren, afraid of *being*.

And then, slowly, we began to say, to hell with that. We dried each other's copious tears which, thank God, we had always been allowed (that one small, touching, infantile outlet—which men claim loudly now to envy!), and got into what we really were—*inside*; what we wanted to create—*outside*. We began to do.

It wasn't so much a matter of telling men off. That we did at the start; confrontation is the first overt expression of anger. Later we began to forget men were around. We had ourselves and each other. To be companions with, to go to parties with, to show our work to, to have it count with. We founded clinics and publishing houses, restaurants, art galleries, theaters, literary salons, businesses, law firms, libraries—all on a very small scale, cozily collective. We produced many, many newspapers and magazines. Some of them folded, some stayed around. We worked hard and delighted for the first time in our selfishness—the queerest sort of selfishness that's ever existed, because it consisted mainly of working ourselves until we got burnt out.

Those of us who became famous and even a little bit rich began to complain all over again about *that* world. It was a whole new experience, learning to shove and push in the high-class meat market. Learning to deal with the competition (male) who had made it first and bigger, and with the sisters left behind who felt the old rage of powerlessness return, just *looking* at us! For among feminists there are few buffers to protect the successful from those still struggling to get a foothold, and falling back. It would be immoral to turn one's face away, in any case. Guilt returned and was resisted. A woman who succeeded couldn't help feeling a little like an American tourist in Calcutta. Apparently, one can adjust even to that, in time.

Becoming selfish was necessary—and costly. Work, and occasionally celebrity, isolated some of us again. The old cruelties we had once been taught to reserve for each other returned as we drew away from our small groups and the time-consuming conversations which had helped us know ourselves, bound us together. New peer groups formed along new class lines. A few of us began to feel like pros. The movement was becoming a cliché to us—the old neighborhood we had outgrown. We were into higher things, heavier politics.

Curiously, though only one or two of us advanced very far in terms of money, a new kind of showiness appeared. New lies. We had to pretend as men pretend—to be accustomed to credit cards, chic clothes, summer hideaways at the right beaches. Banks offered us loans and we took them and went into debt. Just like men. Some of us.

Selfishness was not easy to come by, and some of us, I'm afraid, overdid it. But we were out in the business world impressing men with our equality, and we had to work ten times as hard at it. That's what's known as "making a living," for a woman. Some of us, poor as churchmice, abandoned our blue jeans for the old reliable thrift shops where we used to buy our clothes before we "burned our bras."

A little of it was fun, like the art nouveau years in Paris—dressing up for each other at poetry readings, exchanging success stories, exaggerating a bit.

I remember a Tupperware party in a housing project I

once went to years ago. It was very much the same thing. Only women boasted about their *husbands*.

It was inevitable, being in that world, that some of us would try for power. (Well, it's silly to hang around there *powerless*!) Some already knew our way around, and being feminists, showed others. Business and professional organizations formed, occasionally with strict rules for admission. The peer group was moving up. We talked about "old girls' networks." We were pretending to ourselves (some of us) that we could just walk into the system and take it over.

There were supporters, also, on the sidelines. Women who had not made it yet but hoped to; women who weren't trying but could truly enjoy their friends' success. Others, repelled by the system but too individualistic and proud—too "old"—to return to feminist collectives flirted with the idea of rejoining the left. Most of us, uncertain about the swing to the mainstream but willing to try anything, gave our rising stars our support and hoped for the best. After all, *they* weren't the patriarchy! *They* offered us all the encouragement in the world, and real help, to boot. They were—they *are*—generous and sensitive, unforgetful of the system's arbitrariness. We told ourselves nobody refuses success.

Some of the feminists who had "made it" joined Ms. Allgood and suddenly found they had a lot in common with her. Their new style quickly convinced her that feminists weren't *all* scruffy, either. She joined them.

And there they are, together, out in the world trading votes to buy ERA. But what are they trading *away*?

Will those of us who aren't in the club, whose personal priorities *may* lose out at the bargaining table, stick around and trust? The problem with Ms. Allgood's selfishness is that she has some money and influence: not much, but some. Can she trade away others' priorities in the name of feminism? Or must she, if she thinks of herself as a representative, bargain for the rest of us at the same time? Is she acting on a mandate, or just exploiting the movement to the exclusive advantage of her own class? What worries me is that many of us—thrilled with the new feminist move into an issue that is, for a change, popular and seems, eventually, to have a chance of passing; an issue that looks to be beneficial, or at least benign, for all of us (someday)—may have stopped asking these questions. We were always too polite, anyway. We worry: after all, Ms. Allgood *could* take all that energy away! The women's movement has always felt like something which might vanish overnight.

REFORMS IN THE PATRIARCHY

For a number of reasons, although I can appreciate the symbolic importance of ERA, I am sorry it was chosen as the central issue to rally the movement. I think the Constitution is worth less today than the vote was when we finally got it. The government doesn't pay any attention to it. Privacy is invaded electronically. Bills curtailing freedom of speech, of the press, and of assembly are passed every day, and the Supreme Court is in no mood to stop them. The CIA is a legitimized Murder, Inc. But I am not going to propose a new Constitution here. (That would certainly please the right. They can't wait to have a constitutional convention and do away with legal abortion.)

Symbolism is wonderful when it represents accomplished fact. But it was the Emancipation Proclamation, drawn up by the President during the Civil War, and the victory of the Union which officially ended black slavery in the United States—not the amendments later added to the Constitution. The amendments merely confirmed what had already been achieved. It would seem that once women have actually achieved equality, it would be a simple enough matter to write it into the Constitution. The problem is achieving it—and that ERA will not do. Because it is chiefly symbolic, ERA may have acquired the charisma of a fundamental goal, but in fact it is less than a real reform. It is just a tool, and not a very powerful one. Its popularity stems from the fact that it is largely viewed as innocuous. But mostly it is popular because the lioness' share of money and energy from mainstream feminist organizations have made it so.

With limited means available, it is right for us to develop a list of priorities. We need so many things immediately that it is difficult to decide which is the most urgent. Although I am not suggesting we abandon ERA, several possible reforms occur to me which would solve more immediate, visceral problems for great numbers of women. If those of us who are not so strongly drawn to the ERA struggle could unite for these goals, the movement would have a better chance of maintaining its credibility among those whose needs are desperate and immediate. In any case, nothing can be achieved as quickly as it needs to be, but some things may truly be more urgent than others.

There is one reform desperately needed by a vast number of women. It would also help to lay the groundwork for more basic changes in the future. We could demand the immediate establishment of child care centers, under the control of the mothers in each community, throughout the nation. These centers would be staffed by experienced and talented women living in the communities, and for their services the personnel would be paid the equivalent of salaries earned by construction workers or high school teachers, whichever is higher. The ratio of child care workers to children should be no greater than one to four.

This would immediately provide personal incomes for a great many women, making them financially independent of men (or welfare). It would give women who wish to pursue occupations other than child care the freedom to do so. These centers would also provide a place to study children and learn new ways to help them become citizens of a cooperative, nonsexist society.

Money for this reform could come out of taxes levied on religious institutions, particularly those which are so eager to promote reproduction.

The pay being relatively high, men would, of course, demand a right to the new jobs, but *experience* in raising children at home would be a primary criterion for such employment. And personnel could reasonably be chosen only from those who have neither a history as rapists (to be defined in the broadest sense), wife- or child-beaters, child molesters, nor a taste for propaganda advocating such behavior. A few men might squeak through.

Administrators of the program should also be chosen by mothers, and should receive lower salaries than the child care workers. This would eliminate most male applicants and also prevent administrators from feeling overly important. It should be mandatory for administrators not to have any additional personal income, so that they won't be tempted to take on these jobs as "charity work."

One hundred thousand women would certainly come to Washington in support of this. We should be able to reassure the fastidious, furthermore, that separate male and female toilets would be maintained in all child care facilities. (The kids can look at each others' bodies during nude playtimes.)

A second proposal to end the unpaid employment of women would be to provide "veterans' benefits" for unsalaried adults. These would include full scholarships at institutions of adult education, with sufficient stipends to maintain living standards conducive to study. Participation in this program would, of course, be voluntary, and it should be available to people for no less than four years, with extensions for those who show real interest and promise.

Drastically reducing the salaries of all government administrators would help to pay for this program and also lessen the inducement for men in administrative work.

"New Deal" reforms, such as structural improvements in housing, the building and staffing of additional hospitals, maintaining better street sanitation (dog shit should be collected and turned into energy), resuscitating mass transportation, and subsidizing the arts would take up further slack in useful paid employment. Money for these programs should be provided by extraordinary taxing of arms producers and the oil industry. The left can have the job of exerting the pressure needed to extract such taxes.

The socialization of medicine, with reduced income for doctors (and even sharper reductions in salary for medical administrators) would lessen the enticements for men in this critical field and generally improve health care.

So much for immediate reforms. I expect that certain others would naturally follow—particularly, if churches were taxed for secular child care they might be induced to support free abortion on demand, improved birth control, and lesbianism.

Upward mobility, within the restrictions listed above, I would leave alone. The object of this interim program is, after all, to extend it to more women.

Caveat: The above is *my* list of priorities. It should be remembered that I belong to a class, too. The important thing is for the movement to be heard on its preferences.

But whether or not it was the wisest choice, we are now launched on an all-out effort to get ERA ratified. Those who want to give it their full or primary attention should continue to push for it—and harder than ever. This is not a time to remove support from one of the few feminist efforts which seems to have a chance of getting and *staying* passed. I, for one, will dance in the streets when it is ratified.

But there is a tendency among many women to withdraw altogether from struggle when their own personal priorities are slighted. To them I suggest renewed and increased involvement in those projects dearest to them. The movement is wide open: anyone can inspire and organize. I remember a time in the early sixties when the moderates in the peace movement refused to allow banners protesting the war in Vietnam to be raised at their demonstrations against nuclear testing. After a while, however, the radicals in that movement didn't seem so radical anymore—and Vietnam became the central issue. Feminists who continue to be radical must not fear the moderates in the movement. And the moderates must continue to hear radical voices.

The next time around we should try to find a more democratic way of choosing priorities. In the meantime, the voices of dissent within the movement should not be silenced for fear of giving ammunition to the backlash. The kind of unity that comes from squelching dissent is not worth having. We must take back the right of abortion for every woman. We must hold onto every sexual freedom we have, and push for more. No woman's need is negotiable.

It is my hope that all our reforms will lead toward some intermediate changes which are so long range in view that they may seem utopian, but which are really only steps on the way to a feminist society. I have made a list of a few of them:

1. the organization of the vast majority of women all over the world into a firm knot of conviction that the patriarchal mode of domination by some over others is destructive

2. the gradual refusal of all of these women, alternatives permitting, to participate in any of the present institutions

3. the development of a radically new attitude toward child raising

4. the transference of technology into the hands of women

5. the transference of the control of media and education into the hands of women

6. a gloriously free attitude toward all nonviolent and nonexploitative expressions of eroticism

7. the rehabilitation of the vast majority of men, who would learn, first of all, to sit still while we are accomplishing the other changes.

SPREADING THE WORD WITHIN THE WOMEN'S MOVEMENT

Other practical work can be done outside the patriarchal scheme to change the "climate of opinion." In this connection I would press for one more reform: the First Amendment should be extended to make its use more commonly available in the following way. The established media and their advertisers should be taxed to support dissident publications, the allotments to be divided evenly between the sexes, and the only restriction being that no publication or art form should produce propaganda promoting sexism, racism, or genocide. (The latter codicil to the First Amendment should be understood, in any case.) This would provide funds for strong and varied feminist media. (Actually, I would like to see equal time given to women to counteract every slur against us on television. This would surely provide us with almost half the air-time of all television programming—including, of course, half the time commercials consume—because there is rarely a moment when some intentional or unthinking derogatory remark against us is not broadcast.)

And in that feminist media, as well as through our possibly more effective grapevine, I would encourage the lesbian option, particularly in the young. Love between women is wholesome, safe, and pleasurable, and has shown itself to be supportive of women's self-esteem.

At the same time that we extend upward mobility, women should continue to collectivize. All our gains will be dissipated unless we hold together and continue to attract new women. (We have seen what happened—and is happening—to our hard-won abortion rights the minute we looked away.) Toward this end, pressure should be placed on institutions of learning to increase feminist studies—the most potent pressure for it will come from the students and their mothers. (Ms. Allgood might get on this case through her alumnae association.) Feminist writers who enjoy speaking should be hired at lecturer's fees equal to those given men. The patriarchal media goes all out to destroy us or dilute what we have to say;

we are a precious and poorly paid resource for the movement. Students should see to it that we are treated with respect by their universities.

Above all, we should encourage cross-class and cross-cultural discussions among women, in order to develop better understanding which might lead to true unity. The movement is beginning to emerge from its infancy. We have learned to speak of hurts inflicted on us by men; we must respond to those criticisms which would help us prevent inflicting damage on each other, and those which would discourage us, in our zeal for the movement's purity or its quick success, from damaging the movement as a whole.

Those of us who want the trust of many must trust the multitude of women enough to communicate clearly, and without holding back. Not to do so is to communicate contempt, which destroys trust in the sophisticated and dulls the thinking processes of the less well informed. If necessary, it is better for men to overhear what we are saying than for us not to hear each other. The double bind of euphemistic lies and sudden exposure to unpleasant truths which afflicts women must be ended. To undo the work of misleading propaganda, we must not indulge in simplistic tricks ourselves, tempting though that may be in the short run. Our effort must always be to advance each individual woman's ability to make *informed* decisions. This is our primary means of self-defense.

One of the great differences between feminist politics and patriarchal politics is that feminism is a personal discipline rather than a party discipline. But there may be a need, in order to secure reforms, to develop a party attitude as well. If we choose representatives for the women's movement and lay down platforms for them to follow (it would be best if we could find ways to pay them salaries, so that neither we nor they will suffer from volunteerism), we must carefully separate the two disciplines in our own minds. We will, of course, select representatives whose intelligence and good will we believe in, but we must nevertheless keep open channels of accountability. Without thinking, most people give preference to their own class interests, and so we will have to remind them constantly of the diversity of ours. This will require a certain amount of active participation in patriarchal politics from all of us, which can have the positive effect of reinforcing our sense of self-worth in the women's community. At the same time, we shouldn't let our enthusiasm for reforms lead us to forget that feminism is fundamentally in conflict with the patriarchal model we temporarily borrow.

In this regard, the loose network structures should be tightened so that we will know who is doing what and under whose mandate. Too loose a national structure can easily be infiltrated and taken over by adherents of one or another patriarchal faction, including a government moving rapidly toward fascism. Alas, maintaining security from the patriarchy inevitably corrupts as much as participation in it. Though we will need to adopt those structures which best prevent secret elites from forming, nothing is foolproof. And in speaking our minds about our fears, we will want to avoid unnecessary rigidity which could destroy our morale without any effort on the part of external forces.

UTOPIANISM

Throughout this book I have dwelt on topical events, trying to extract from them some picture of feminism as it is, some idea of where it might be going. Many writers have put forward utopian ideas: that women will find freedom when technology has relieved us of the need for pregnancy; that we are moving toward an androgynous society in which gender will have little or no importance; that we might return to models of hypothetical ancient matriarchies or a more aggressive Amazon culture; that we might develop parthenogenesis and dispense with the male function altogether in reproduction; that the female principle with its fecundity and nurturance will overcome the hegemony of male destructiveness and save the planet through a metaphysical transformation. Grace Paley hinted, ironically, that we might depend on "enormous changes at the last minute."

To speak of a far distant future at all takes guts in this time of nuclear accidents. All the predictions of an evil end seem to be coming true: the madness of the shape of things to come in the brave new world of 1984. Nostradamus's hordes are arriving on schedule. It no longer takes a bearded lunatic with a bible to tell us Armageddon is near, and quite possibly we will be poisoned by the very air we breathe—going out with "a whimper."

It does seem as if the world suffers from an overabundance of virility. For women to reorganize society out of the depths of our long experience of nurturance and responsibility suggests hopeful possibilities, but the time is very short and turning the world upside down isn't easy. Still, many wills are bending in that direction, many incantations offered.

Approaching the end of this work and the day when I must turn it over to others, I have taken nervously to dipping into the *I Ching*, which I found around the house among other relics of the sixties: old tarot cards, astrology books, some volumes by Alan Watts. I haven't paid much attention to Oriental philosophy because I felt that the

East is in as bad shape as the West. But of course, like everyone else, I am fascinated with the concept of Yin and Yang, and love the mystique of mysticism. My first thrill of this sort came as a teenager reading Albert Einstein on relativity. The train and the trees both moving . . . how beautiful! The concept of a universe which is at once finite and infinite. . . .

A feminist must read very much between the lines of the *I Ching*, but a woman gets used to reading "him *or* her" when only the masculine pronoun appears on the printed page. And so the hierarchical arrangement of Yin and Yang didn't surprise me, until the awkward contrast of rigidly defined sex roles with the "harmony" of the universe warned me something was amiss. This was no blending of contradictions but a distortion created by interpretation, as the Gideon Society distorts the earthy, and therefore poetic, meaning of the Song of Songs. And so I made up a story to myself which might account for it.

A long time ago in the Orient, in a country where all people and all work were equally respected, a philosopher who was also an artist and a mother considered the process of creation. She said, "It is interesting: when I mold the clay into a bowl, I dominate it, but I do so in submission to the laws of form." And then she noticed that when she tended her children, she influenced them, but they grew anyway in accordance with the laws of their nature: at a certain age, like other children, they learned to walk and to talk. And this seemed to be the truth of all animate beings: that they had wills, but they could exert them only within the bounds of what was possible. To decipher the law of form, then, is the creative mission.

The country prospered in a gentle fashion, until one day some barbarous and hungry men invaded it and imposed their own laws on it. When she saw the brutality of their faces, the philosopher killed herself, because she knew it was useless for her to remain alive in their world.

The people of this country were very devoted to the philosopher, and they fought hard against the invaders in spite of their peaceful training. It soon became apparent that the invaders would never fully conquer unless they pretended to worship the philosopher. And so, searching among her parchments they found one upon which something was drawn in bold calligraphy. They asked an old man what it meant, and he tried to explain to them the concept of Yin and Yang. But the invaders did not understand, for in their world all laws came from men or a very angry old father-god who sat up on a mountain and made thunder.

At last one of the invaders thought of an analogy that fitted in with the customs of his homeland: domination equaled rape equaled man; submission equaled victim equaled woman. This satisfied him so that he now felt happy about including the philosopher among his pantheon of gods. And the people of the country made peace because the invader had, they thought, accepted their ways.

But in a short time, the invaders taught their own interpretation to the children, who learned that Yang meant dominance (man) and Yin meant submission (woman).

Of course that was wrong, but passing down beliefs is like playing the game of telephone.

As time went on, the country again became civilized and it produced many creative people, though they were all men. All of them, doing their work which involved dominating clay in submission to the laws of form, came to understand, as every artist and scientist does, the true meaning of Yin and Yang. By this time, however, they had enslaved the women, which was very convenient for them, because it meant they could work all day at creating things, and never have to prepare the food they ate or the clothes they wore. But the understanding that nothing they did could prosper without submission to natural laws offended their self-esteem as men, which depended on their always being dominant. Understanding that submission was also necessary for men in the "act of love"—for the action of the penis follows unknown laws—they grew angry and decided to keep this knowledge hidden from women, eventually hidden from themselves. The works they performed were now all directed at maintaining their domination, and the instruments of destruction they fashioned, modeled after the penis which embodied the mystery of submission, obeyed the laws of man.

The women also understood, performing their own occupations, the true meaning of Yin and Yang, but they dared not speak it, even to each other. Yet even their silence and smiles threatened the men, who wondered—who *knew*—what knowledge lay behind them. And so, again and again, the women acted out submission to men, and taught it to their daughters, in fear for their lives. Only they taught it this way: "You must *pretend* you are not as smart as men, for they are really grown-up children who cannot face the truth. When they are angered, they have tantrums like children, but they practice at being very strong and they will kill. I will submit to their law, therefore, and bind up your feet, for it is better to suffer pain than to die."

Forever after daughters have heard from their mothers this queer speech, and it angered them against their mothers, but it kept them alive and it also kept a certainty somewhere in their minds that they knew the truth of life and the meaning of creation.

Many times women have awakened and rebelled, but always they have been suppressed. Now Western men seek to learn from the East how to stop their tantrums and stay alive. But the Eastern teachers still spread the gospel of the invaders: the inequality which can never comprehend the truth—the *blending* of the two modes of being in every action in the universe.

No one has every created anything beautiful without submission to the laws of·form. No one has ever created anything beautiful by submitting to man.

That is why I do not seek enduring good from laws granted by men. Where there is no understanding, no laws of men will be honored; where there is understanding, no laws of men are necessary.

Let men carry this teaching that women have brought again into the world if they want to survive.

Notes

Introduction

1. Jane Alpert, "Mother-Right: A New Feminist Theory" (Pittsburgh, Pa.: Know, Inc.), a Know, Inc., pamphlet reprinted from *Ms. Magazine*.

2. Boston Women's Health Book Collective, *Our Bodies, Ourselves*, rev. 2nd ed. (New York: Simon and Schuster, 1976); Susan Brownmiller, *Against Our Will: Men, Women, and Rape* (New York: Simon and Schuster, 1975); Shere Hite, *The Hite Report* (New York: Dell Publishing Co., 1976); Adrienne Rich, *Of Woman Born: Motherhood As Experience and Institution* (New York: W. W. Norton, 1976).

3. Phyllis Chesler and Emily Jane Goodman, *Women, Money, and Power* (New York: William Morrow, 1976).

Chapter One: Ms. Allgood, Me, and Some Basic Concepts of Feminism

1. For a full account of the conference, see my article in *Sojourner* (December 1977), a feminist monthly published in Cambridge, Mass.

2. The crucial nature of the Houston conference is confirmed by Anne Taylor Fleming's remarks: "One sensed that these women knew as they left Houston that with their conference . . . they had hastened their own absorption into the political mainstream. They had not tried to change the rules of the game; they had merely asked to be allowed to play. . . . The significance of the lesbian vote was that it reopened a channel of compassion in women long separated by their sexual allegiances" ("That Week in Houston," *The New York Times Magazine*, December 25, 1977).

3. Evelyn Reed does not urge a return to primitive matriarchy,

nor does she spell out her vision of utopia. But she does say, speaking of matriarchy, "All the same, that fundamental chapter of human evolution must be restored and take an honored place in our history. A correct understanding of the remote past can help us see ahead and move forward surely. . . . This is especially true when we consider the outstanding role played by women in ancient times." ("Introduction," *Woman's Revolution* [New York: Pathfinder Press, 1975].) Throughout this anthropological study, Reed points to the more generous morality of regimes in which women had at least equal power and dignity with men, and in some cases were the arbiters of order. It is clear that she thinks no utopian society can exist based on male domination.

4. The technique called consciousness-raising can be traced back to a number of origins. Most often referred to is the practice, developed by women in China in the 1940s, of "speaking pain," that is, of getting together in groups to bear witness against the oppression by the men who ruled over them, usually their husbands. The Chinese male revolutionaries, assuming the oppression of women was a problem of capitalism, approved of this practice as a good tool for organizing women against the system. Variations on "speaking pain" were later used by Che Guevara to organize peasants, both male and female, in Latin America, and by the Student Nonviolent Coordinating Committee in the United States in the 1960s.

Other precedents for consciousness-raising, as it is practiced by feminists today, might include Quaker meetings, in which every participant takes a turn expressing her/himself fully on whatever question awaits a decision, and group psychotherapy, where the style and desired outcome are different, but the encouragement to speak truthfully and emotionally about personal suffering is certainly related to consciousness-raising. (For a fuller explanation of the Chinese practice of "speaking pain," see "Introduction," in Claudia Dreifus, *Woman's Fate: Raps from a Feminist Consciousness-Raising Group* (New York: Bantam Books, 1973).

5. Gloria Steinem used this sensitive expression in conversation to explain what women are deprived of by pornography.

6. This feminist truism has been given psychological validation in Jean Baker Miller, *Toward a New Psychology of Women* (Boston: Beacon Press, 1976).

7. Fran Winant, *Looking at Women* (New York: Violet Press, 1972), pp. 284-290. Available from Violet Press, P.O. Box 398, New York City 10009.

8. The expression "the personal is political" means that oppression of individual women is a political matter. It means that a woman has the right to call on the women's movement and everyone else,

including the state, to support her when she is raped, assaulted, insulted, discriminated against, and so on. It does *not* give other women the right to define her oppression for her nor to judge the way she chooses to lead her life.

9. See Robin Morgan's poem, "The Network of the Imaginary Mother," in her second collection of poetry, *Lady of the Beasts* (New York: Random House, 1976). She uses the term "transformation" to affirm the changes, whether or not self-determined, a woman goes through in life and politics.

10. Ellen Frankfort is the author of *Vaginal Politics* (New York: Bantam Books, 1973); and *The Voice* (New York: William Morrow, 1976).

11. "Personal solution" is a misnomer for the illusion that a solution can be found in an adjustment to the status quo. Hypothesizing "anatomy is destiny," Freudians hoped to adjust women to an acceptance of our inferior status by portraying it as an unalterable fate. The result frequently was to force women into deep depressions and madness. Everybody needs to make reasonable adjustments to temporal conditions while working for fundamental change, but thinking that an essentially uncomfortable adjustment is a cure, with all the self-deceit that implies, is both politically and psychologically counterproductive.

12. See, among others, Phyllis Chesler, *About Men* (New York: Simon and Schuster, 1978); and Robin Morgan, *Going Too Far* (New York: Random House, 1977).

13. See Jon Snodgrass, ed., *A Book of Readings for Men Against Sexism* (Albion, Calif.: Times Change Press, 1977).

14. For an excellent short history of the "early days" of the women's liberation movement, see Cellestine Ware, *Woman Power: The Movement for Women's Liberation* (New York: Tower Publications, 1970).

Chapter Two: The Early Years of the Women's Liberation Movement and the Start of Some Schisms

1. The Yippies (Youth International Party) were a group of protesters in the late sixties who tried to inject humor, or at least an apt irony, into their actions against the Vietnam War. They invented the "zap," the surprise confrontation, intended to catch the opposition with their hypocrisy showing and to make them look ridiculous. In the early days of the women's liberation movement a group called Women

in Media zapped *Ladies' Home Journal* and won a "special issue" from that publication. Feminists zapped hard-hat construction workers by whistling at *them*, and zapped Wall Street brokers on their lunch hour using the same technique. A group called The Feminists zapped couples at the New York City marriage license bureau with leaflets explaining the contract.

I hope what appears here is not construed as "New York chauvinism." It's true that throughout most of the book I have stayed close to home—mainly because I do not consider my travel and correspondence with people in the rest of the United States and abroad to be definitive enough to constitute a study, and neither funds nor time would allow me to do the research I had originally intended. Since the patriarchy rules everywhere, I am inclined to disregard state and national borders in my thinking about feminism, but for purposes of accuracy here I will generally confine my analysis to the island I inhabit.

2. I am indebted to Cellestine Ware's excellent account in *Woman Power: The Movement for Women's Liberation* (New York: Tower Publications, 1970); and to Shulamith Firestone's modest description in *The Dialectic of Sex: The Case for Feminist Revolution* (New York: William Morrow, 1970) for much of the information about the nascent movement sketched in this chapter.

3. Marcia Friedman, formerly a member of Israel's Knesset, told a group of American feminists she thought the greatest contribution American women had made to world feminism was their literature.

4. Reading this chapter in manuscript, Karla Jay shrewdly commented that "the revolutionary man and the rich man can be one and the same." This is frequently true, as people who have attended fundraising parties in Manhattan penthouses and townhouses and East Hampton villas can attest (another reason why the leftist charge that feminists are bourgeois is absurd!) Bourgeois leftists have a lush, Robin Hood fantasy life. However, most of the terrorists who kidnaped Patricia Hearst (those that were immolated by the FBI and the Los Angeles police) were, indeed, working class. Eldridge Cleaver, who advocated raping women, both black and white, as a revolutionary policy, was also working class—at least until the royalties started coming in from *Soul on Ice*.

Similarly, Marxist women are often from upper middle-class backgrounds, or else have white-collar jobs, but they *do* get dishpan hands supporting the fantasies of revolutionary men.

5. Rita Mae Brown, "Take a Lesbian to Lunch," in *Out of the Closets: Voices of Gay Liberation*, ed. Karla Jay and Allen Young (New York: Douglas, 1972), pp. 185-195.

6. I am indebted to Karla Jay for enlightening me about the early development of the lesbian feminist movement, and to Minda Bik-

man for sharing her memories with me of the early days of the women's liberation movement. Unless attributed to them, however, the
opinions I express about both these subjects are, of course, my own.

7. At the National Women's Conference in Houston (1977), Betty
Friedan supported lesbian civil rights in a memorable speech in which
she explained her earlier fears of lesbianism had been inculcated by
her "middle-class" and "middle-American" upbringing.

8. The right-wing Save Our Children campaign has exerted a
Nazilike backlash against these efforts of men to understand and accept each other across lines of sexual preference. It has also had ad-
verse effects on lesbians; when the latter joined demonstrations
against the campaign they were forced to witness gratuitously *sexist*
attacks on Anita Bryant, titular leader of the backlash—attacks directed toward her as a woman.

Subsequently, revelations in Massachusetts of sexual abuse of male
children by some homosexual men there gave substance to the
backlash. The defense of such child abuse by prominent males like
Allen Ginsberg did little to engage the support of women for the male
homosexual cause. Tellingly, the public furor raised about attacks on
boys was incomparably greater than any concern shown for young girl
prostitutes. If Save Our Children were consistent in worrying about
child abuse in the schools, it would push for the elimination of *all* male
teachers.

I believe, perhaps naively, that the vast majority of male teachers,
whatever their sexual preference, restrict their abuse of children to
intellectual deprivation, and in this they are joined, alas, by too many
incompetent female teachers. I do not advocate at this time the elimination of males from that profession.

Chapter Three: Problems of Structure and Leadership

1. Robin Morgan, *Going Too Far* (New York: Random House,
1977), p. 202.

2. Ti-Grace Atkinson, *Amazon Odyssey* (New York: Links Books,
1974), pp. 9-11.

3. Dave Dellinger, an antiwar activist in the sixties, was one of the
eight men indicted, brought to trial, and eventually acquitted on conspiracy charges in connection with protests against the Democratic
National Convention in Chicago in 1968. *Liberation* did eventually go
collective, and Dellinger left it, though perhaps not for that reason. It
subsequently declined in quality and petered out of existence.

4. In a lecture on the "equality issue" she gave at Juniata College
in 1970, Atkinson said, "Within Women's Liberation, there is no for-

mal hierarchy. But demagoguery is immediately evident. A few women dominate all meetings. While lip service is paid to participatory democracy, it is *no more a reality* than what I observed at S.D.S. meetings." (Atkinson, *Amazon Odyssey*, p. 69; emphasis mine.)

5. Nancy Seifer, ed., *Nobody Speaks for Me!* (New York: Simon and Schuster, 1976), p. 294.

6. Cellestine Ware, *Woman Power: The Movement for Women's Liberation* (New York: Tower Publications, 1970), p. 21.

7. It is possible that differences in patriarchal religious affiliations may account for some of the "class" differences Atkinson and The Feminists intuited. Although many feminists have given up these affiliations, the early training they have imposed on us has become, like our training to assume the "feminine" role, inextricable from our personal styles. As the characteristics of the religions they were brought up with remain noticeable among atheists, so they do with feminists. There are Protestant feminists, Catholic feminists, Jewish feminists, and so forth. We *choose* to be feminists; we were *born* into our religions. Empathy across the lines of religious origin may come easily in a superficial way: we *think* we are agreeing—but we are never quite sure, although the words we use are the same, that we are speaking the same language. We tend to retire into ourselves at certain points in arguments when religious differences are present, unable to account for a sudden blockage to further communication—as if we had stumbled on a fundamental point of disagreement somehow sacred to each other. It is simple to construe the mutual lack of understanding as arising from a class difference when it may really arise from a difference in attitude stemming from religious training, which naturally bears "sacred" associations. Insofar as we are able, it might be a good idea for us to consider openly such a possible cause when we find ourselves clashing.

8. The Feminists, "The Feminists: A Political Organization to Annihilate Sex Roles," in *Radical Feminism*, Anne Koedt, Ellen Levine, and Anita Rapone, eds. (New York: Quadrangle, 1973), pp. 368-378.

9. Atkinson, *Amazon Odyssey*, p. 73.

10. Jean Baker Miller, *Toward a Psychology of Women* (Boston: Beacon Press, 1976), pp. 4-5.

11. Atkinson, *Amazon Odyssey*, pp. 25-37.

12. Atkinson, *Amazon Odyssey*, p. 25.

13. Atkinson, *Amazon Odyssey*, p. 26.

14. Atkinson, *Amazon Odyssey*, p. 27.

15. Atkinson, *Amazon Odyssey*, p. 27.

16. For women, the *private* education system may be almost equally disgraceful. The finishing school mentality is too often still

with us there, turning out women who may have learned Greek and Latin and physics, but have majored in passivity.

17. The Feminists, "The Feminists: A Political Organization to Annihilate Sex Roles," *Radical Feminism*, pp. 371-372.

18. Morgan, *Going Too Far,* pp. 119-120.

19. Joreen, "The Tyranny of Structurelessness," in Koedt et al., *Radical Feminism*, pp. 285-299.

20. Joreen, "The Tyranny of Structurelessness," p. 287.

21. The Feminists, "The Feminists: A Political Organization to Annihilate Sex Roles," p. 374.

22. Pamela Kearon, "Man-Hating," in Koedt et al., *Radical Feminism*, p. 80.

23. Atkinson, *Amazon Odyssey*, p. 73.

24. Atkinson, *Amazon Odyssey*, p. 91.

25. Atkinson, *Amazon Odyssey*, p. 99.

26. Atkinson, *Amazon Odyssey*, p. 132.

27. Anne Koedt, "Lesbianism and Feminism," in Koedt et al., *Radical Feminism,* p. 255.

28. Marabel Morgan is a woman who has gained considerable financial independence by traveling around the country glamorizing for *other* women the idea of total dependence on men. She has written a few books on the subject.

29. Joreen, "The Tyranny of Structurelessness" p. 287-288.

30. Phyllis Chesler, *About Men* (New York: Simon and Schuster, 1978), p. xviii (Preface).

31. Lois Gould, "Hers," *The New York Times,* June 30, 1977.

32. Charlotte Brown and Paula Hyman, *The Jewish Woman in America* (New York: Dial Press, 1966), pp. 163-185.

Chapter Four: The Lesbian Revolution: Lilith and Eve

1. From "women who love men," in Karen Lindsey, *Falling Off the Roof* (Cambridge, Mass.: Alice James Books, 1975), p. 34.

2. Andrea Dworkin, *Our Blood* (New York: Harper & Row, 1976), p. 73.

3. Adrienne Rich, "Foreword," in Bernice Goodman, *The Lesbian: A Celebration of Difference* (New York: Out and Out Books, 1977), pp. 1-2.

4. It should be said that women have no reason to suffer from the same confusion. The pain from the first penetration may cause displeasure, but since the woman has no organ which does double duty like the penis (and which must be similarly cajoled and reprimanded throughout her life, worrying her to death alternately by its refusal to

perform and by its eager projection and ejaculation at inopportune moments), she has no cause to attach heavy significance to what it is, other than the penis itself, that enters her vagina.

5. Ti-Grace Atkinson, *Amazon Odyssey,* (New York: Links Books, 1974), pp. 135-189.

6. Atkinson, *Amazon Odyssey,* p. 138.

7. Atkinson, *Amazon Odyssey,* p. 192.

8. Atkinson, *Amazon Odyssey,* p. 145.

9. Atkinson, *Amazon Odyssey,* p. 189.

10. Atkinson, *Amazon Odyssey,* p. 189.

11. Atkinson, *Amazon Odyssey,* p. 155.

12. Barbara Deming, "Afterword," in Leah Fritz, *Thinking Like a Woman* (Rifton, N.Y.: WINBooks, 1975), p. 154.

13. Anne Koedt, "The Myth of the Vaginal Orgasm," in *Radical Feminism*, ed. Anne Koedt, Ellen Levine, and Anita Rapone (New York: Quadrangle, 1973), pp. 198-207.

14. Koedt, "Vaginal Orgasm," p. 206.

15. Koedt, "Vaginal Orgasm," p. 206.

16. Radicalesbians, "The Woman-Identified-Woman," in Koedt et al., *Radical Feminism*, p. 240.

17. Radicalesbians, "Woman-Identified-Woman," p. 240.

18. Gay Revolutionary Party Women's Caucus, "Realesbians and Politicalesbians," in *Out of the Closets: Voices of Gay Liberation*, ed. Karla Jay and Allen Young (New York: Douglas, 1972), pp. 178-179.

19. Gay Revolutionary Party Women's Caucus, "Realesbians," p. 180.

20. Gay Revolutionary Party Women's Caucus, "Realesbians," p. 178.

21. The term "organic" is used frequently here to mean a kind of change that comes naturally with development of consciousness.

22. Anne Koedt, "Lesbianism and Feminism," in Koedt et al., *Radical Feminism*, p. 254.

23. Martha Shelley, "Confessions of a Pseudo-Male Chauvinist," in *The Lavender Herring: Lesbian Essays from the Ladder*, ed. Barbara Grier and Coletta Reid (Baltimore: Diana Press, 1976), pp. 93-97.

Chapter Five: Feminism and the Left

1. Elsa Morante, *History: A Novel* (New York: Alfred A. Knopf, 1977; translation copyright 1977 Alfred A. Knopf, Inc.), p. 480.

2. The television program "Charlie's Angels" was evidently inspired by the Manson story. In the series, the man directing the wom-

en's acts of derring-do (for law and order) is never fully seen on screen. He issues orders by telephone. Apparently the producers wanted to kill a number of birds with one stone: to cash in on the Manson cult; to please teen-age girls with a cops-and-robbers story in which women participate *physically* and, to all appearances, on their own initiative; to perpetuate the notion, satisfying to men, that a man, after all, must be in charge; to suggest that emancipated women will accept the male punitive status quo; and to show off some pretty legs on TV.

3. For biographical information on Jane Alpert I am indebted to the Circle of Support for Jane Alpert and to Florence Rush, who made the data available to me. Some of the information was also corroborated and expanded in Alpert's own published writings.

4. Samuel Melville, *Letters from Attica* (New York: William Morrow, 1972), foreword by William Kunstler and profiles of the author by Jane Alpert and John Cohen. A fascinating self-portrait of a man historical novelists are wont to call a "charming rogue." Also, it is a passionate and terrifying description of one of the worst—and perhaps most typical—inventions of the patriarchy: the prison.

5. Jane Alpert, "Mother-Right: A New Feminist Theory" (Pittsburg, Pa.: Know, Inc.), a Know, Inc., pamphlet reprinted from *Ms.* magazine.

6. Alpert, "Mother-Right," p. 4.

7. Alpert, 'Mother-Right," p. 4.

8. Alpert, "Mother-Right," p. 4.

9. Alpert, "Mother-Right," p. 4

10. Alpert, "Mother-Right," p. 4.

11. "The Crisis in Feminism," copy of petition printed subsequently in several feminist publications, including *Majority Report*.

12. Bernardine Dohrn, "View from the Underground," *Lesbian Tide*, July-August 1977, p. 14 (tape recording reprinted from *Hera*).

13. "A Vindication of the Rights of Feminists," copy of a handout petition printed subsequently in several feminist publications.

14. For information on Susan Saxe et al., as well as on the grand jury investigations relating to her and Katherine Power, I am indebted largely to Karen Lindsey. She collected the documents and made them available to me.

15. Simone de Beauvoir, "Still the Second Sex," *Atlas*, April 1978, p. 31 (reprinted from *Le Monde*).

Chapter Six: Slavery, Inequity, Disunity

1. Phyllis Chesler and Emily Jane Goodman, *Women, Money, and Power* (New York: William Morrow, 1976), p. 69.

2. Tom Prideaux, "Tailor-Made Hit of the 30's," *The New York Times Magazine,* June 4, 1978, p. 35.

Chapter Seven: Three Classes of Poor Women

1. Phyllis Chesler and Emily Jane Goodman, *Women, Money, and Power* (New York: William Morrow, 1976).

Chapter Eight: Rich Women

1. The term "measure up" has a phallic significance which I leave to Freudians who, indeed, have a manual for deciphering the causes of the ills of men if they would only apply some feminist insight to it.

2. Andrea Dworkin, *Woman Hating* (New York: E. P. Dutton and Company, Inc., 1974), pp. 95-118.

Chapter Nine: The Middlewomen

1. My own experience of working for female supervisors contradicts the folklore, undoubtedly perpetuated by men, that women "bosses" are meaner than men. At the Museum of Modern Art under Alexandra McKenzie; at the Educational Film Library Association under Emily Jones; at the *Aeronautical Engineering Review* under Irene Bogolubsky; at the Harlem Parents Union under E. Babette Edwards; and even at my very first job as a temporary secretary to Wayne List, then managing editor of *Good Housekeeping,* I found a great deal of sisterly support and understanding. In contrast, men I have worked for were (1) after my ass, (2) nauseatingly paternalistic, and/or (3) bullies. If women complain more to, and about, women supervisors, it is not because women are less considerate than men in this role. It may be partially because women in such positions arouse greater hopes than can be immediately realized.

Chapter Ten: Deals & Dreams

1. C. F. Baynes and Richard Wilhelm, trans., *I Ching or Book of Changes* (Princeton, N.J.: Princeton University Press, 1969), p. 77.

INDEX

Prepared by Liz Murray

Abbott, Sidney, 32
Abortion, xiii, 38, 40, 77, 221, 252,
    254, 258, 262-263, 264
About Men (Chesler), 75
Abzug, Bella, 23
Activism, vs. consciousness-raising,
    28-29. *See also*
    Consciousness-raising
Adler, Renata, 215
Advertising
    female role models in, 203
    use of guilt in, 241-242
    See also Media, patriarchal
*Against Our Will: Men, Women, and
    Rape* (Brownmiller), xiii, 28
Aggressive image, of men, 30-31,
    122-125, 129-130, 229. *See also*
    Men
Agnew, Spiro, 114
Alcoholism, and rich women, 218,
    220
Allen, Gracie, 214
Allen, Pamela, 26
Alpert, Jane, xii, 133-142, 165
Altamont, rock concert at, 132-133
Amazon culture, 267
Amazon Odyssey (Atkinson), 39, 93,
    150
American Nazi party, 73, 77, 117
Androgynous society, 267
Anthony, Susan B., 178
Antiwar movement, 112-117, 152,
    262
Artists, women as, 209, 210-212. *See
    also* Working women

"Assertiveness training," 203, 231,
    240
Atkinson, Ti-Grace, 37-49, 51,
    57-58, 61-66, 92-100, 144,
    148-150, 278
    See also Feminists, The
Atlas, 167
Attica State Prison, 138, 142, 144,
    149

Bâtarde, La (Leduc), 211
Battered wives' shelters, 38, 77, 161,
    252
Beauvoir, Simone de, 25, 102, 167
Beckett, Samuel, 216
Bigotry, avoiding feminist, 12-15
Bikman, Minda, 27, 33
Black civil rights, 4-5, 113, 233-236
    and leadership, 16, 41, 66, 68
    use of guilt-tripping, 93
Blacks, 79
    policies on self-expression, 55-56
    and slavery, 258-259
Black women, 197, 228
Bond, Stanley, 152, 153
Boye, Marianne, 162
"Bra-burning," 119-120
Broun, Heywood, 177
Brown, Helen Gurley, 67
Brown, H. Rap, 93, 157
Brown, Rita Mae, 32
Brownmiller, Susan, 28, 33, 245
Bruce, Lenny, 133, 142
Bryant, Anita, 199, 203, 277
Buffers, women, 92, 242, 245-248.

See also Middlewomen
Burning Questions (Shulman), 215

Capitalism, importance of elitism in,
    60-61. See also Patriarchal
    society
Carmichael, Stokely, 93
Carter, Jimmy, 67, 69
Carter, Rosalynn, 4, 67
Castration, 178, 197, 246
Chaplin, Oona O'Neill, 220
Charlie's Angels, 227, 280
Chesler, Phyllis, 75, 76, 148, 221
Chicago N.O.W., 41
Child abuse, 35, 252-253, 277
Child care, 192, 259-261
Children
    "gifted," 207-208
    and sex-roles, 88-90, 227-229
    and welfare system, 192-193
CIA, 25, 114, 151, 158, 258. See also
    Patriarchal society
Civil War, 121, 258
Clamshell Alliance, 119
Class
    Americans' attitudes toward, 121,
        207
    and The Feminists, 45-49
    and guilt for privilege, 187-190
    as patriarchal system, 26, 47, 136,
        171-178, 209, 219
    vs. sisterhood, 4, 50-52, 181-187
    See also Female slavery;
        Middlewomen; Poor women;
        Rich women
Class Workshop, of The Feminists,
    47, 181. See also Feminists, The
Cleaver, Eldridge, 93, 142, 276
Colette, 84
Collectivism
    of feminist organizations, 52-61
    for feminist unity, 22, 181-187,
        189, 239, 264
    vs. hierarchical structure, 39-45,
        66-79
    See also Feminist unity;
        Leadership, in women's
        movement
Colombo, Joseph, 149

Communication, feminist
    equality of, 52-56
    reforms in patriarchy for, 263-266
    universal strength of, 37-38
    See also Feminist literature;
        Media, patriarchal
Competition, vs. cooperation,
    181-187, 236-240, 255. See also
    Collectivism
"Confessions of a Pseudo-Male
    Chauvinist" (Shelley), 109
Congress to Unite Women, 97
Consciousness-raising (CR), 14, 138,
    204
    vs. activism, 28-29
    Atkinson's attitude toward, 93
    and concerns for men, 11, 14-15,
        104, 139
    for deglamorizing leaders, 42
    for developing feminist analysis,
        81-82
    of early feminist groups, 26-28
    in history, 274
    vs. psychoanalysis, 224-226
Cosmopolitan magazine, 67
Costanza, Midge, 69-79
Cross-cultural empathy, 50-52, 265.
    See also Class
Crowthers, Diane, 27
Curran, Paul J., 146

Daly, Mary, 8
Daughters of Bilitis, 32
    Atkinson's attack on, 92-94, 96,
        149
    See also Lesbians
Davis, Angela, 131
Day care, 192, 259-261
"Days of Rage," 146
De Crow, Karen, 34
Decision making, female, 125-131.
    See also Feminist processes
Dellinger, Dave, 40, 165, 277
Deming, Barbara, 95-96, 110
Demmerle, George, 133
Democratic National Convention, in
    Chicago, 277
"Disarmament," as goal of future,
    164-167

Dohrn, Bernardine, 147-148, 150, 156
Doolittle, Eliza, 209-210
Drugs, and antiwar movement, 114-115
Dworkin, Andrea, 8, 30, 83, 91, 148, 223

Economic systems, patriarchal
  and brotherhood of power, 156-158
  development of, 172-175
  feminist goal of equality in, 181-187
  hierarchy of, 60-61, 78, 185-186, 236-240, 242
  and marriage, 177-181
  and working women, 175-177
  See also Patriarchal society; Working women
Education
  and growing illiteracy, 53, 195
  importance of, 217
  of poor women, 195, 199, 207-212
  private, 278-279
Effeminist, The, 15
Einstein, Albert, 268
Eisenhower, Mamie, 179
Ejlerson, Mette, 96-97
Elitism
  defined, 74
  lesbianism and, 98
  of National Women's Conference, 71-73
  of network systems, 74-79
  proficiency and, 60-61
  See also Leadership, in women's movement
Emancipation Proclamation, 258
Employment. See Working women
Engels, Friedrich, 46, 135, 162
England, feminism in, 160-162
English National Women's Liberation Conference, 1977, 160-161
Equality of self-expression policy, of The Feminists, 52, 54-56
Equal rights, for women
  employment, 181-187, 204-207
  intellectual, 213-215

working-class men's attitude toward, 200-201, 204-206
Equal Rights Amendment (ERA), 77, 116
  questioning priority of, 251-253, 257-263
Exxon, 53

Fascism
  in history, 112
  and National Women's Conference, 72-73
FBI, 25, 114, 134
  harassment of feminists, 153-156
  See also Patriarchal society
Female slavery, xiv, 198
  defined, 180-181
  vs. economic equality, 181-187
  and guilt, 187-190
  and marriage, 178-180
  reasons for, 172-176
  and women as buffers, 245-248
  and women overseers, 227-245
  See also Middlewomen; Poor women; Rich women
Feminism
  avoiding bigotry and superficiality in, 12-15
  beginnings of, 24-28
  vs. classism, 50-52, 181-187
  and concerns for men, 9-11, 14-15
  and decision making, 125-131
  and destitute poor women, 196-198
  and economic equality, 181-187
  and educated poor women, 212-217
  government's attack on, 153-156
  and leadership, 15-21, 66-79
  and leftist guilt-tripping, 160-163, 164
  left's attack on, 143-151, 159
  moderate vs. radical, 40-41, 43, 45, 252-254, 262
  and prostitution, 195
  radical vs. Marxist, 29-31, 133, 134-136, 213
  and reforms in patriarchy, 7-8, 258-266

and rejection of Marxist theory,
    135-137
and respectable poor women,
    203-204
and rich women, 221-223, 224-226
and right-wing women, 76-78
and sexism of male left, 25,
    132-133, 137, 139
and vulnerability, 158-160
working-class men's attitude
    toward, 200-201, 204-206
See also Consciousness-raising;
    Leadership, in women's
    movement; Lesbians;
    Patriarchal society; Sexism
Feminist analysis
vs. American Marxist theory,
    135-137, 138
importance of, 6, 12-14, 42
and structure and leadership
    questions, 79-82
See also Consciousness-raising
Feminist literature
effect of, on women's movement,
    xii, 37-38, 44, 276
and importance of feminist
    analysis, 12
patriarchal publishers' control of,
    67-68, 215-216
Feminist processes
cross-cultural empathy, 50-52
equality of class, 45-49
equality of labor, 56-61
equality of self-expression, 52-56
and female decision making,
    125-131
hierarchical structure, 38, 39-45
vs. patriarchal procedures, 8-9
See also Leadership, in women's
    movement
Feminists, The, 37, 149, 181, 276
description of, 46-49
equality of self-expression policy
    of, 52, 54-56
formation of, 45-46
rotating labor policy of, 56-61
separatist membership quota of,
    61-66, 97
See also Atkinson, Ti-Grace

Feminist theory
and concerns for men, 14-15
diversity in, xii-xvi
early, 26
vs. Marxist theory, 29-30, 135-137
universal communication of, 37-38
Feminist unity, 18, 252
and cross-cultural empathy, 50-52,
    265
and economic equality, 181-187
and Marxist-radical split, 29-31,
    133, 134-136, 143-151, 158-160
and present feminist goals,
    252-258
vulnerability of, 158-160
See also Collectivism; Leadership,
    in women's movement
Firestone, Shulamith, 8, 26-27, 102
First Lady, and female slavery,
    178-179. See also Female
    slavery
Fleming, Anne Taylor, 273
Flower children, 112-117
Fonda, Henry, 221
Fonda, Jane, 221-223
Footbinding, of women in China,
    223-224
Ford, Betty, 4, 179
Frankfort, Ellen, 14
Fraternization, of women in war,
    64-65
Freedom of expression
patriarchal media's control over,
    52-53, 258
and sexual exploitation of women,
    132, 133, 142, 201-202
Freud, Sigmund, 122, 125, 129, 135,
    225
Friedan, Betty, 25, 33, 102, 128,
    164, 277
Friedman, Marcia, 276
Fugs, The, 132

Gandhi, Mahatma, 16
Gaskell, Elizabeth, 216
Gay Liberation Front, 32
Gay Revolutionary Party Women's
    Caucus, 100. See also Lesbians
Gimme Shelter, 132-133

Ginsberg, Allen, 113, 277
Going Too Far (Morgan), 38, 59
Golden Notebook, The (Lessing), 160
Goodman, Bernice, 83
Goodman, Emily Jane, 75
Gould, Lois, 75, 76, 77
Guevara, Che, 131, 274
Guilt
    feminist relinquishment of, 150,
        254-256
    left's use of, on feminists, 160-163,
        164, 183, 188-189
    legitimate and counterproductive,
        187-190
    of unsuccessful women, 184
    of rich women, 149-150, 177, 189,
        221, 222, 223, 244
    use of, in advertising, 241-242
    use of, for enlisting support, 92-93,
        135-136

Halascsak, Bonnie, 41, 43, 44, 45
Hamilton, Joan, 144
Hayden, Tom, 221
Hearst, Patricia, 29, 30, 120, 148,
    151, 152, 165, 276
Hefner, Hugh, 202
Heide, Wilma Scott, 108
Hell's Angels, 132
Hero role, in political groups,
    129-130
Heterosexual women
    effects of lesbian propaganda on,
        96, 100, 102, 103
    vs. lesbians, 31-34
    lesbians' attitudes toward sexuality
        of, 101-103
    supporting lesbians, 94-95
    See also Lesbians
Hierarchical structure
    feminist reactions to, 39-45
    male, 60-61, 78, 236-240, 242
    See also Leadership, in women's
        movement; Patriarchal society
"Hippies," 112-117, 131-132
History: A Novel (Morante), 112
Hite Report, The (Hite), xiii
Hoffman, Abbie, 133, 142
Hoffman, March, 32

Holliday, Judy, 214
Homosexuality
    early repression of, 85-86
    growing acceptance of male, 35
    male, 91
    and sexual abuse of children, 277
    See also Lesbians
Household workers, 240-245. *See
    also* Working women
House Un-American Activities
    Committee, 150
Housewife
    buffer role of, 245, 246
    as overseer, 240-245
    See also Middlewomen
Hughey, David, 133, 146
Hustler magazine, 133

I Accuse (Ejlerson), 96
I Ching, feminist interpretation of,
    267, 268-271
Illiteracy, of poor, 53, 195
"Inner peace"
    propaganda of lesbians, 98-100
    propaganda of psychoanalysis,
        224-225
Insanity
    and poor women, 193
    and rich women, 218, 220,
        224-225
International Women's Year
    conference, in Mexico City, 73
Irons, Becky, 94
It Changed My Life (Friedan), 128

Jay, Karla, 32, 34, 276
Jewish Woman in America, The
    (Brown, Hyman), 79
Jews, 30, 79
Johnson, Lady Bird, 4
Johnson, Virginia E., 96
Joreen, 60, 74

Kearon, Pamela, 46, 62
Kennedy, Ethel, 221
Kennedy, Florynce, 144
Kennedy, Joan, 221
Kennedy, John F., 121, 179, 221
Kennedy, Robert, 121

Kennedy, Ted, 221
Kikiyu tribe, of Kenya, 230, 233
King, Billie Jean, 164
King, Coretta, 23
King, Martin Luther, 66, 68
Kinsey, Alfred C., 96
Kissinger, Henry, 158
Koedt, Anne, 27, 64, 96, 97, 108
Krassner, Paul, 133, 142
Ku Klux Klan, 77, 117

"Lavender menace," 33. See also
    Lesbians
Lawrence, D. H., 219
Leadership, in women's movement,
    5-6, 15-21
  avoidance of individual, 16-17,
    66-71
  and class distinction, 46-49
  collective, 52-61
  elitist, 71-73
  feminists' reactions to hierarchical,
    39-45
  and importance of feminist
    analysis, 79-82
  network strategy of, 74-79, 266
  patriarchal society's control of,
    19-21, 67-70
  representative, 265-266
  See also Feminist processes
Leduc, Violette, 211
Left protest groups
  attack on feminism, 143-151, 159,
    171
  feminists' rejection of, 134-142
  sexist attitudes of, 25, 132-133,
    137, 139
  terrorist tactics of, 133-134
  use of guilt-tripping on feminists,
    160-163, 164
  See also Marxism
Lenin, Vladimir Ilyich, 25
Lesbian: A Celebration of
    Difference, The (Goodman), 83
Lesbians, xiii, 83-87
  Atkinson's attack on, 92-94
  FBI's harassment of, 153-154
  vs. heterosexual feminists, 31-34,
    95-103

  heterosexual feminists supporting,
    94-95
  as mothers, 84, 87, 88
  at National Women's Conference,
    273, 277
  N.O.W.'s attitude toward, 32, 34,
    40
  and personal liberation, 91-92
  political significance of, 108-111
  realesbians and politicalesbians,
    100-103
  and respectable poor women,
    203-204
  separatist attitudes of, 95-103,
    104-108
  as threatening to male hegemony,
    87-91
  See also Feminism; Heterosexual
    women; Homosexuality
Lessing, Doris, 160
"Letter from the Underground"
    (Alpert), 139, 141
Letters from Attica (Melville), 138
Levertov, Denise, 23
Liberation magazine, 40, 277
Lindsey, Karen, 83, 85
Literature. See Feminist literature
Little, Joan, 29, 165
"Looking at Women" (Winant), 12
Love, Barbara, 32

McCarthy, Joseph, 150
McNamara (Boston chief of police),
    152
McReynolds, David, 165
Magoo, Marie, 194
Mailer, Norman, 216
Male bonding, 75, 80. See also Men
"Man-Hating" (Kearon), 62
Manson, Charles, 29, 131-133, 148,
    280-281
Mao Tse-tung, 25
Mardirosian, Robert, 153
Marriage
  and educated poor women, 210,
    211-212
  The Feminists' attitudes toward,
    61-62, 63
  and household duties, 240-245

vs. intellectual equality, 213-214
and respectable poor women, 199,
200-203
and rich women, 218-220
women's role in, 177-181
Marx, Karl, 25, 135, 186
Marxism, 121
of American New Left, 24-25,
135-136, 157-158
and classification of women, 161
vs. feminist theory, 7-8, 26, 29-31,
133, 134-136, 186, 213
theory on lesbianism, 32
See also Left protest groups
Marxist feminists
attack on radical feminists,
143-151, 159
vs. radical feminist theory, 29-31,
133, 134-136
rich women as, 189, 221-223, 276
and vulnerability, 158-160
See also Feminism
Masochism, 129-130, 246
"Massage parlors," 194
Masters, William H., 96
Matriarchy, in history, 273-274
Media, patriarchal
and antiwar protests, 114, 119
controlling feminist leadership,
67-69, 196
effect of, on women's movement,
xi-xii, 9, 34-35, 37, 203
feminist reforms for, 263-265
and freedom of expression, 52-53,
258
See also Patriarchal society
Mehrhof, Barbara, 46
Melville, Herman, 247
Melville, Sam, 133, 134, 138-142,
146
Men
aggressive image of, 30-31,
122-125, 129-130, 229
attitudes toward women's groups,
3, 23-24
and brotherhood of power,
156-158
and development of economic
systems, 172-175

feminism and working-class,
200-201, 204-206
feminists deferring and referring
to, 9-11, 14-15
and hero role, 129-130
and Horatio Alger trip, 219
nature of revolutionary, 30-31, 148
network strategy of, 75
profeminist, 15
ruling class, 78, 219, 220-221
sexual self-image of, 140-141
and symbolism of weaponry,
122-125
threat of female genius to, 213-215
threat of lesbianism to, 87-91, 97
See also Patriarchal society
Middlewomen
as buffers, 245-248
feminist attitudes for, 236-240
housewife as, 240-245
and misuse of power, 233-236
as overseers, 227-233
See also Poor women; Rich women
Midnight Special, 147
Miller, Jean Baker, 48, 274
Millett, Kate, 8
Miss America contest, protest
against, 23
Monroe, Marilyn, 219-220
Morante, Elsa, 112
Morgan, Marabel, 67, 199, 202, 203,
279
Morgan, Robin, 14, 38, 59, 275
Mothers, 227-229
lesbian, 84-90
See also Lesbians
Ms. magazine, 67, 139
"Myth of the Vaginal Orgasm, The,"
96, 103, 108

NAACP, 41. See also Black civil
rights
National Organization for Women
(N.O.W.), 16, 25, 66, 181
and Atkinson, 39, 40, 44, 45
bureaucratic red tape of, 40-41
goals of, 42, 182
importance of, 43
reaction to lesbianism, 32, 34

National Women's Conference,
        Houston, Texas, 3-6, 7, 161,
        252, 273, 277
    patriarchal procedures vs. feminist
        processes at, 8-9
    patriarchy's control over, 72-73,
        252
Network strategy, of leadership,
        74-79, 266. *See also* Leadership,
        in women's movement
Newsweek magazine, 146
New York marriage bureau, The
        Feminists' demonstration at, 62
New York Post, 146
New York Radical Feminists, 27-28,
        33, 46
New York Radical Women, 23, 26
New York Times, The, 76, 152, 153
New York Times Magazine, The, 177
Nin, Anaïs, 65, 211
Nixon, Patricia, 179
Nixon, Richard, 114, 116, 117, 152
Nobody Speaks for Me! (Seifer), 41
N.O.W. *See* National Organization
        for Women

October 17th Movement, 45. *See
        also* Feminists, The
Off Our Backs, 146
Of Woman Born (Rich), xiii
Olsen, Tillie, 211
Onassis, Jacqueline, 219
Orgasm
    clitoral, 33, 97
    myth of vaginal, 96-97
Orwell, George, 247
Oswald, Lee Harvey, 121
Our Bodies, Ourselves, xiii
Overseers, women
    and feminism, 236-240
    housewife as, 240-245
    and misuse of power, 233-236
    mothers as, 227-229
    supervisors in business as,
        231-233, 282
    See also Middlewomen

Paley, Grace, 267
"Participatory democracy",

    of American New Left, 24-25, 40,
        41-42
    of feminist movement, 39, 43, 278
Passive image, of women
    changing, 229
    in economic system, 175-177, 197
    intellectual, 213-215, 279
    in literature, 215
    sexually, 101-103
    See also Self-image, of women
Patriarchal society
    attack on feminists, 143-151,
        153-156, 183
    and brotherhood of power,
        156-158
    control of media, xi, 9, 35, 37,
        52-53
    control over National Women's
        Conference, 72-73, 252
    co-optation of feminist leadership,
        19-21, 67-70
    development of, 172-175
    vs. feminist collectivism, 181-187
    feminist processes in, 8-9
    feminist reforms for, 7-8, 258-266
    hierarchy of, 60-61, 78, 79,
        185-186, 236-240, 242
    marriage in, 177-181
    respectable poor's attitude toward,
        199-200
    use of terrorism, 117
    See also Left protest groups;
        Media, patriarchal; Men
"Penis envy," 125
Pins and Needles, 177
Pitchford, Kenneth, 15
Politicalesbians, 100-103
Poor women
    destitute, 192-198
    educated, 207-212
    equal employment for, 204-207
    politics of educated, 212-217
    respectable, 198-204
    See also Middlewomen; Rich
        women
Pornography, 81, 128-129, 132, 133,
        194
Povill, Ellen, 94
Power, Katherine A., 152-156

Power
   brotherhood of, 156-158
   feminist attitude toward, 236-240
   hierarchy of, 60-61, 78, 79,
      236-240, 242
   women's misuse of, 60, 227,
      231-236, 256-258
   See also Patriarchal society
Prisons, women's, male guards at,
   229-230
Prostitution, and poor women,
   193-195, 196
Protest demonstrations, males'
   reactions to feminist, 23-24
Psychoanalysis, and rich women,
   224-225
Pygmalion (Shaw), 209-210

Quaker meetings, 274

Racism, xv, 228, 232
Radicalesbians, 32-33
   separatist attitudes of, 97-99
   See also Lesbians
Radical feminists
   vs. Marxist feminists, 29-31,
      134-136
   vs. moderate feminism, 40-41, 43,
      45, 252-254, 262
   See also Feminism; Marxist
      feminists
Rape, 30, 31, 224, 245, 254, 276
Rape prevention, xiii, 28
Rat, 59, 134, 143
"Realesbians and Politicalesbians,"
   100-103
Redgrave, Vanessa, 221-223
"Red Squad," 114
Redstockings
   early attitude toward lesbianism,
      32
   formation of, 26-27
Reed, Evelyn, 8, 148, 273-274
Reforms, feminist, 7-8, 258-266
Religious origin, and feminism, 278
Respectability, and poor women,
   200, 201, 204
Rich, Adrienne, 83-84, 86, 87
Rich women, 218-226. See also

   Middlewomen; Poor women
Right to Life, 77
Robert's Rules of Order, 43, 56
Rockefeller, Nelson, 138, 219
Roosevelt, Eleanor, 179
Roth, Philip, 229
Rudd, Mark, 156

Sacco, Nicola, 153
Sanders, Ed, 132
SANE (Committee for a Sane
   Nuclear Policy), 41
Save Our Children, 77, 277
Saxe, Susan, 152-156, 159, 160, 165
Scapegoat, 194
Schlafly, Phyllis, 199, 203
Screw, 132
S.D.S. See Students for a Democratic
   Society
Sebastian, Amanda, 162
Second Congress to Unite Women, 33
Seifer, Nancy, 41
Self-expression, feminist policy on,
   54-56
Self-image, of women, 125-127, 139,
   150, 163. See also Passive
   image, of women
Separatism
   effects of massive female, 89, 100,
      109
   of lesbian feminists, 13, 34,
      95-103, 104-108
   of The Feminists, 61-66
Sexism
   against female supervisors,
      231-232
   of male-dominated leftist groups,
      25, 132-133, 137, 139, 142
   of movie industry, 221-222
   of psychoanalysis, 224-225
   See also Sex-roles
"Sex objects," women as, 23-24,
   219-220
Sex-roles
   changing heterosexual, 201-202
   children's, 88-90, 227-229
   effect of recognition of clitoral
      orgasm on, 96-97
   effects of lesbianism on male, 88,

90-91, 97
lesbians' attack on straight
    women's, 101-103
in Sweden, 162
weaponry as symbol of male,
    122-125
Sexual exploitation
of film industry, 221-222
and male sexual self-image,
    140-141
and universal feminist goals, xiii,
    26
See also Sexism
Sexual revolution, 96-97, 110,
    132-133, 142, 162, 201-202
Shakur, Assata, 145, 165
Shaw, George Bernard, 209-210
Shelley, Martha, 109
Sherman, Susan, 144
Shulman, Alix Kates, 215
Simpson, Ruth, 94
Sirhan, Sirhan, 121
"Slave mentality," xiv-xv, 65. *See
    also* Female slavery
Snuff (film), 128
Socialism, and feminist goals,
    161-163, 167. *See also*
    Patriarchal society
"Sorority mentality," and feminists,
    14
Spare Rib magazine, 161, 162
"Speaking pain" technique, of
    self-expression, 55-56, 274. *See
    also* Consciousness-raising
"Speak-out" assemblies, feminist, 28,
    42, 139
Speedboat (Adler), 215
Spock, Dr. Benjamin, 38
Stanton, Elizabeth Cady, 159
Steelworkers N.O.W., 41
Stein, Barry P., 146, 147
Stein, Gertrude, 84
Steinem, Gloria, 11, 67, 151, 274
Sterilization, of poor women, 196
Stevenson, Adlai, 179
Stoltenberg, John, 15
Student Nonviolent Coordinating
    Committee, use of "speaking
    pain," 274

Students for a Democratic Society
    (S.D.S.)
politics of, 24-25, 40
sexist attitudes in, 25-26
See also Left protest groups
Study groups, feminist, 27
Supervisors, female
and feminist attitudes, 236-240
and misuse of power, 233-236
supporting women assistants,
    232-233
women workers' resentment of,
    231-232
See also Middlewomen
Supplementary Security Income
    (SSI), 193
Sweden, feminism in, 162-163
Swinton, Patricia, 133, 134, 143,
    145, 146, 147
Symbionese Liberation Army, 120,
    151

Tate, Sharon, 29, 131, 165
Teamsters Union, 11
Terrorism
of American New Left, 133-134
as insurgent tactic, 117-122
and male symbolism, 122-125
Theory of the Leisure Class (Veblen),
    218
Thinking Like a Woman (Fritz), 95
Tokenism, and upward mobility, 182,
    184, 197, 233. *See also* Upward
    mobility
Truman, Bess, 179
"Tyranny of Structurelessness, The"
    (Joreen), 60

Upward Mobility
and corruption, 60, 78-79
and educated poor women,
    208-212
of female supervisors, 231-233
feminist approach to, xi, 236-240
vs. feminist unity, 182-186,
    255-257
and guilt, 187-190
and poor women, 195-196, 197,
    199, 203

U. S. Steel, 41
Utopianism, and feminist goals, 7-8,
    238, 268-271

Valeri, Robert, 152
Vanzetti, Bartolomeo, 153
Veblen, Thorstein, 218
Vietnam War, 22, 41, 112-113, 153,
    262, 275
"Vindication of the Rights of
    Feminists, A," 145

Ware, Cellestine, 27
Watergate, 114, 153
Watts, Alan, 267
Weaponry, as symbol of manhood,
    122-125
Weather Underground, 121, 134-143
    attack on feminism, 143-144,
        147-148, 149
    identification of, with Manson, 132
    See also Left protest groups
Webb, Eileen, 94
Welfare system, and poor women,
    192-193, 196, 199
West, Mae, 214
Wilson, Dagmar, 23
Wilson, Woodrow, 179
Winant, Fran, 12, 13
Woman Hating (Dworkin), 223
"Woman-Identified-Woman, The,"
    33, 97-99, 100

Womb envy, 173-174
Women in Media, 275-276
Women, Money, and Power (Chesler,
    Goodman), 75
Women's bodies, exploitation of,
    xiii-xiv. See also Sexual
    exploitation
Women's liberation movement. See
    Feminism
Women Strike for Peace, 16, 41-42
Woodstock, 133
Woolf, Virginia, 8
Working women
    artists, 209, 210-212
    in buffering roles, 245-248
    and changing system, 78-79, 188,
        236-240
    educated poor, 208-209, 210-212
    equal rights for, 181-187, 204-207
    female supervisors, 231-233, 282
    and feminist attitudes, 236-240
    household helpers, 240-245
    and misuse of power, 60, 79,
        233-236
    poor, 196, 199
    rich, 219, 220
    See also Equal Rights Amendment
        (ERA)

Yippies (Youth International Party),
    22, 275
Young, Allen, 34